The Dialogue
of
Solomon and Marcolphus

Publications of the Barnabe Riche Society

Volume 4

The Dialogue of
Solomon and Marcolphus

Edited with

Introduction and Notes

by

Donald Beecher

With the Assistance of Mary Wallis

Dovehouse Editions Inc.
Ottawa, Canada
1995

Acknowledgments

This book has been published with the help of a grant from the Canadian Federation for the Humanities, using funds provided by the Social Sciences and Humanities Research Council of Canada.

Canadian Cataloguing in Publication Data
Main entry under title:
(Salomon et Marcolphus)
    The dialogue of Solomon and Marcolphus : (1492)

(Publications of the Barnabe Riche Society ; 4)
Critical, annotated edition of the English
    translation published Antwerp : G. Leeu, 1492.
Includes bibliographical references.

ISBN 1-895537-44-4 (bound)
ISBN 1-895537-26-6 (pbk.)

I. Beecher, Donald.   II. Wallis, Mary.   III. Title.   IV. Series.

PR2199.S3 1995   878'.0402   C95-900440-8

Typeset in Canada by Carleton Production Centre, Nepean.
Printed in Canada.

For distribution write to:

Dovehouse Editions
1890 Fairmeadow Cres.
Ottawa, Canada, K1H 7B9

Cover design: Carleton University Graphics.

For information on the series write to:

The Barnabe Riche Society
Dept. of English
1125 Colonel By Drive
Carleton University
Ottawa, Canada K1S 5B6

This book is dedicated to:

Sophie and François

Whose judgment . . . Solomon's(?)

Whose joie de vivre . . . Marcolphus's(?)

Table of Contents

Preface

The publication series of The Barnabe Riche Society has been established to provide scholarly, modern-spelling editions of works of imaginative literature in prose written in English between 1485 and 1660, with special emphasis on Elizabethan prose fiction. The program allows for works ranging from late medieval fabliaux and Tudor translations of Spanish picaresque tales or ancient Greek romances to seventeenth-century prose pastorals. But the principal goal is to supply much-needed editions of many of the most critically acclaimed works of the period by such authors as Lodge, Greene, Chettle, Riche, and Dekker, and to make them available in formats suitable to libraries, scholars, and students. Editorial policy for the series calls for texts carefully researched in terms of variant sources, and presented in conservatively modernized and repunctuated form in order make these texts as widely accessible as possible, while respecting the substantive integrity of the originals. Each edition will provide the editor with an opportunity to write a full essay dealing with the author and the historical circumstances surrounding the creation of the work, as well as with its style, themes, conventions, and critical challenges. Each text will also be accompanied by annotations.

The Barnabe Riche Society is based in the English Department of Carleton University in Ottawa, and forms a component of the Carleton Centre for Renaissance Studies and Research. Its activities include colloquia, the awarding of an annual prize for the best new book-length study dealing with English Renaissance prose fiction, and the editorial management of the series, backed by an eleven-member international editorial board. The society invites the informal association of all scholars interested in its goals and activities.

Acknowledgments

The preparation of a book inevitably produces debts of many kinds, not the least being the one I owe to those most near and dear who tolerated my hours of preoccupied presence. Two of them are acknowledged in the dedication. It remains for me here to thank my wife Marie-Andrée for her patience. Among many supportive colleagues there are two in particular — Faith Gildenhuys and Douglas Wurtele — who pondered early versions of my introduction and offered valuable insights regarding shape and sense. A research grant from the Social Sciences and Humanities Research Council of Canada made it possible for me to engage the help of Mary Wallis, whose contribution, when all was done, merited title page recognition. She helped me initially with the transcription, modernizing, glossing, and keyboarding of the text, and when the project was at last complete, she generously offered to review my work, toning up many a sentence, and checking many a reference, for which we are all in her debt. I owe special thanks, as well, to my colleague Randall Listerman, who has been waiting for a very long time to see his engaging translation of the Hans Folz play, appearing in the Appendix, at last come to print. Given the close affinities between the play and the *Dialogue*, I was keen to have it available. Moreover, I must insert a line or two here about a Latin translating evening with John Butler: great was the hilarity, and mad our inventions, yet together we managed to settle some troublesome passages. In a more sober vein, I am also much indebted to the unnamed readers for the Aid to Scholarly Publications Programme who offered many useful suggestions pertaining both to organization and to critical issues. Finally, an honorable mention is in order to those tireless ecclesiastics who kept this medieval comic tradition alive, and into whose chuckling space each reader is invited to enter.

Introduction

In 1492 the Antwerp printer Gerard Leeu (or Leew) produced a
little book entitled *This is the dyalogus or communyng betw[i]xt the
wyse King Solomon and Marcolphus*. It was the first, and remains
the only, translation into English of a Latin work dealing with
the encounter between the wise king of biblical fame and a wily
peasant. The Latin work survived in Leeu's time in many variant
versions; even the several printed editions reveal groupings that
suggest loyalties to divergent sources. But the immediate source
of the English translation was, by all indications, the Latin edition produced by Leeu himself some four years earlier, bearing
the title *Collationes quas dicuntur fecisse mutuo rex Solomon . . . et
Marcolphus*. Circumstantial evidence suggests that the translation was carried out under Leeu's auspices — it may have been
the work of a member of his own shop. The identity of the translator, however, will likely never be known. Leeu was no doubt
alert to the fact that the Latin editions of this centuries-old work
were more popular than ever, and that several other printers
were producing editions on a regular basis, not only in Latin but
in German versions as well. As a printer who had already supplied reprints of Caxton's titles to the English book-buyers, he
was in a position to choose further titles that he believed would
appeal to their tastes. His choice fell upon the comic dialogue
between Solomon and Marcolphus, the work that is presented
here in a modernized edition.

Although the Latin and German editions of this work went through printing after printing, some of them adorned with handsome woodcuts of the various scenes, the simple English edition called for only a single printing. That fact is perhaps an indicator that English readers did not share the same enthusiasm for Marcolphus's vulgar exploits as did their continental contemporaries. Still, Leeu left no sales record, and there is no sure explanation as to why, of the unspecified number of copies in that single press run, only one is known to survive. It is to be found today in the Bodleian Library, Oxford, having arrived there initially as part of the bequest made by Thomas Tanner, Bishop of St. Asaph, at the time of his death in 1734. Since that first edition appeared, just over 500 years ago, there has been but one further edition of the English text. It was prepared by E. Gordon Duff and was published in 1892 in the form of a facsimile of the original with diplomatic transcription.[1] The fact that only 350 numbered copies were produced in this limited edition has meant that the story of Solomon and Marcolphus remains relatively unknown and inaccessible to modern English readers. It was from the copy numbered 210 in my own library that this present edition has been prepared.

Deserving mention at the outset is the matter of titles, for in dealing with earlier versions of this work we cannot, with accuracy, use either the English or the Latin title cited above, for they apply only to their specific editions. We may, however, speak of a body of works that can broadly be referred to as the Latin *Solomon and Marcolphus*, of which there were literally dozens of variant printed editions. Even more numerous are the manuscripts of the work whose *terminus a quo* was the late fourteenth century, and which were in turn based on a complex stemma of lost documents possibly going back as far as the year 1000, and certainly to the late twelfth century. The English *Solomon and Marcolphus*, then, represents one inflection of a textual tradition rather than a fixed text, a tradition that underwent revisions, experimentations, and accretions that can be reconstructed only in hypothetical ways.

---

[1] G. Duff, ed., *The Dialogue . . . Between . . . Salomon and Marcolphus*.

Equally problematic is the designation "dialogue," for only in the first part of the work as we have it are Solomon and Marcolphus engaged in a dialogic exchange in the form of a proverbs match, while the second and longer part features a series of miniature plots formed around the tricks that Marcolphus plays on the king. This lack of a familiar structural unity and thematic consistency characterizes the work as an expression of the medieval mind, despite the fact that the text itself is a product of the late fifteenth century. While we may describe the reception of this work in pre- and post-Reformation northern Europe, Renaissance values had no influence in its composition. Moreover, it is not the work of an identifiable author; its heterogeneous nature as a text is, in fact, certain proof that it grew from the composite efforts of the many clerics active in its transmission. For these reasons, the critical criteria we normally apply to unified works of fiction fail to make complete sense of the ethos and conventions of this essentially medieval product.

As an example, social probability is replaced in this work by the logic of the practical joke and the procedures of parody whereby quotations from the Solomonic proverb tradition are matched by pragmatic, often obscene, sayings of the *rustici*. The result is an open-endedness which allows for an infinite mutation of content within a very basic structural framework. In effect, this textual tradition that we are calling *Solomon and Marcolphus* was at no point finalized; it remained subject to minor evolutionary changes even in its last stages of production.

Nevertheless, we can speak of a coherent tradition because those who transmitted this work during a three-centuries-long period always preserved its essential defining features: the dialogic game structures, the identities of the protagonists, the sequence of jests, and the victory of the peasant over the king. To have altered significantly any of these elements would have led to the erosion of the tradition. In fact, however, the kind of gradual evolution involving the addition and subtraction of proverbs and episodes that was a by-product of the manuscript culture was largely brought to a halt by the printing press. It is a moot point whether that finalizing process did not also force the work to remain in a fixed state that aged quickly in relation to the changing circumstances of the early northern Renaissance.

What is clear is that after that time, no subsequent author saw fit to take up the Solomon versus Marcolphus formula as the basis for a new jest book tradition. Those who borrowed from it — in particular, Croce, who built up his comic court fool Bertoldo using several of Marcolphus's tricks[2] — did so in order to launch new jest book traditions of their own. This is a sure sign that the formula based on the opposition between a biblical king and a German peasant had come to a natural end as a progressive or inspirational literary idea.

Something should be said about the composition of the text itself. The two parts of which it is composed were, without doubt, conceived by different authors working according to different literary conventions. These parts were wed at some unspecified point, perhaps as early as the twelfth or as late as the fourteenth century. There is little evidence as to which of them came first. A striking feature of even the latest recensions of the grouping is the absence of any attempt to eliminate the conflicting details of fact and characterization that distinguish the two parts. In the English *Solomon and Marcolphus*, the first section consists of a brief introduction of the characters, the respective genealogies of the antagonists, and a sequence of ninety-one proverbs arranged in antithetical pairs. This section comes to an arbitrary close when Solomon tires of the match and cedes victory to Marcolphus. Nevertheless, Solomon is unwilling to pay the promised reward, and Marcolphus is compelled to leave, annoyed and empty-handed. In this section Marcolphus's implicit mockery of the king's traditional wisdom through his irreverent counterproverbs creates a rich field of ironic innuendo and nuance. The second half contains some twelve jests or tricks, several of them

---

[2]Giulio Cesare della Croce created the character of Bertoldo in his *La sottilissime astuzie di Bertoldo* around 1600 using materials from the second part of *Solomon and Marcolphus*. This peasant hero has a madcap career at the court of Alboin, king of the Lombards, together with his wife Marcolpha. Teofilo Folengo in turn based his burlesque poem "Orlandino" on Croce's work. Croce may have used for his source either the Latin text or the Italian translation of it published in Venice in 1502 and 1550: *El Dyalogo di Salomon e Marcolpho*, edited by Ernesto Lamma in 1886.

based on riddles. Certain of these are derived from classical sources, while others are variations on folkloric motifs possibly already associated with Solomonic literature. As a literary structure the second part is based on the principle of the jest cycle, just as the first is based on the Solomonic proverb contest of Old Testament origin.

On many levels, *Solomon and Marcolphus* clearly bears relationships to other texts. The Solomonic proverbs are biblical, while Marcolphus's proverbs belong to the folk. The latter may have been collected prior to their inclusion in the text, enabling the authors to draw from existing literary sources. Marcolphus's tricks all appear to have had literary sources, whether in anecdotes of classical provenance, or in folk tales of eastern origin. What is less certain, however, is whether this text presents a parodic treatment of another textual tradition in which Solomon and Marcolphus (or another character in the same role) confronted one another, possibly as serious contestants in a wisdom match, possibly as opponents in a debate over religious matters. As will be shown, there are grounds for thinking that both such traditions existed, and would have supplied forms, motifs, and materials for parodic treatment.

Clerics in the eleventh century had plenty of contemporary material at hand that could have contributed to the composition of *Solomon and Marcolphus*. Yet it is difficult to determine how and when it might have been appropriated. The *Fecunda ratis* (Loaded Raft), a collection of proverbs compiled for pedagogical purposes by Egbert of Liège before 1024, is a key document because it contains several of Marcolphus's proverbs, but we can never be certain who borrowed from whom and how much time separated them. Likewise, insofar as Solomon and Marcolphus are to be associated with the tradition of scholastic debate, there are a number of early school texts that might have served for pillage and parody, such as those appearing in the school of Alcuin: the *Disputatio regalis et nobilissimi juvenis Pippini cum Albino Scholastico*, the *Altercatio Hadrini et Epicteti*, or the *Altercatio Hadrini et Plinii Secundi.*[3] These early dialogues are related in

---

[3]Gustav Ehrismann, *Geschichte der Deutschen Literatur bis zum Ausgang des Mittelalters*, Vol. I, p. 385.

turn to the wise child genre in which *l'enfant sage* replies to all the questions of a king. The matter employed in this textual tradition was biblical, and the format was question-and-answer, representing a form of *joca monachorum* that remained popular from the tenth to the fifteenth centuries, and that has come down to us in manuscript versions in Latin, Middle English, French, Portuguese, Castilian, Catalonian, and Provençal.[4] This parallel tradition of clerical recreation involving biblical materials and a dialogic format supports a reading of *Solomon and Marcolphus* as a form of clerical play based on passages borrowed from popular school texts and rearranged to fit, but also to parody, the formula of the Solomonic wisdom or riddle contest. In an age of church schools that gave rise to lords of misrule, parodic liturgies, the feast of fools, and the boy bishops, this kind of recreation does not go beyond expectations.

Different questions arise when we think of the two protagonists, their medieval identities, and the means whereby their stories were transmitted and transformed. If one theory of origins takes us to contemporary collections of proverbs and classical anecdotes, another takes us to the biblical foundations of Solomon the king, judge, magus, and sage whose typological representations in medieval Europe are an inevitable part of any literary depiction of him. That is to say, even if our text is something invented, it is full of elements remembered from different pasts. It may recall a Solomonic riddle contest tradition in which Marcolphus was a serious opponent of the caliber of the biblical Hiram, King of Tyre, or it may echo a serious debating tradition in which Solomon was spokesman for Christian doctrine against the misguided beliefs of the pagans. There are indications that Solomon, for his wisdom, was employed throughout the age of missionary expansion in Europe in this capacity, and that simultaneously, Solomon was known to early Christians through collections of proverbs read from the pulpits.[5]

---

[4]Walter Suchier, *L'Enfant Sage*, p. 10; see also Paul Lehmann in *Die Parodie im Mittelalter*, who discusses *The Dialogue between the Emperor Hadrian and the Wise Child Epitus*, pp. 22–23.

[5]James G. Williams, "Proverbs and Ecclesiastes," in *The Literary Guide to the Bible*, pp. 268–69.

In effect, then, several Solomons were inherited by the Middle Ages, all of them in one way or another creations of the ancient world. The *Talmud* contributed a mythologized Solomon who became the protagonist of heroic poems. Josephus left a quasi-historical account that was widely known and annotated, and that furnished a number of legendary details.[6] There was an orientalized Solomon with his magic powers, his affiliation with demons, and his magic ring. Stories of his life, his remarkable rise to power and grandeur, and his fall into luxuriousness and apostasy circulated widely. There was the Solomon of an eastern epic tradition, versions of which found their way into Europe through Byzantine sources.[7] Finally, there was the Solomon who

---

[6]Flavius Josephus wrote the *Jewish Antiquities* in Rome around 93 to 94 AD. In his account of the life of Solomon, he not only elaborates on the biblical episodes, but confirms the existence of an active Solomonic cult in his own age. Already visible are the elaborations upon his skills as a wiseman, magician, riddle and proverb maker. Josephus tells of a certain Eleazar who had cast out demons in the presence of the Emperor Vespasian and his soldiers by using a Solomonic ring and reciting Solomonic incantations (Josephus, *The Complete Works*, p. 173). Josephus recounts the story as proof of an active healing cult based on Solomonic powers administered through the famous ring.

Of equal importance is Josephus's account of the riddle contest between Solomon and Hiram, King of Tyre. He tells how Hiram first sent sophisms and enigmas for Solomon to solve, and how he was forced to hire the wise youth Abdemon to help him untangle those that Solomon sent in return. He mentions, too, how the friendly match led to increasing wagers and forfeits, resulting in heavy losses on both sides. Josephus does not specify the degree to which demonic agents were employed to abet the principals. That dimension was added from the Talmudic account of Solomon's struggle with Asmodeus. Dius and Menander of Ephesus had served as contributors to Josephus's account of the riddle contest with Hiram, Menander having translated the Tyrian Archives out of Phoenician into Greek. That fact signals the extent to which this story had been disseminated throughout the Near East to become part of Solomonic lore in the Greek and Roman worlds.

[7]The epic tradition began in the Talmudic accounts of Solomon as a magus figure who did battle with the spirit world and succeeded in subduing all the *shedim* with the exception of their prince Asmodeus. Only by getting him drunk could Solomon bind him with the magic

settled into typological representations of the perfect ruler, the just administrator, the wise sage and law-maker. Frankish kings, through this iconography of Solomon, came to view themselves as representatives of the Hebrew monarchy. Charles the Bold, in the Bible of San Paolo fuori le mura, illuminated at St. Denis in 869, is depicted as King Solomon.[8] In illustrations of the period, Solomon was shown as a judge in the temple, and in the years of the building of the great cathedrals he assumed a major place in the decorations as judge, king, and defender of Christian truth.

Solomon and Marcolphus as Early English Fiction

The edition to follow is presented, in the first instance, as a sample of early English fiction, and as a contribution to English incunabula. That Leeu selected the work for translation is, in itself, an indicator of at least his appraisal of a potential interest in such a work among English readers. Perhaps his estimate was made on

---

chain. A Faustian motif appears with the questions Solomon posed to these reluctant demons in his quest for the hidden secrets of the universe. Ultimately Solomon is tricked, exiled, and becomes a wanderer. His power could be regained only through a successful performance in a wisdom contest. Meanwhile, Asmodeus had gained access to the harem and to Solomon's magic ring.

These motifs are transformed into an epic traditon built around such elements as the seduction or the abduction of Solomon's wife, the search for her by a trickster brother named Kitovras in the Russian version, or Morolf in the German troubadour version. Solomon also joins in the quest for her return by disguising himself as a wandering beggar or pilgrim. The magic ring is produced in some versions in order to call supernatural powers to his aid.

In *The Myth of the Magus*, Elizabeth Butler deals with this dimension of Solomon's career, and in *Solomon and Solomonic Literature*, Daniel Moncure Conway reveals the extent to which the story of Solomon the wonder king who, under the influence of his pagan wives falls into apostasy, travelled by means of numerous oral cultures to places as far asunder as Ireland and eastern Asia. For a study of the Russian epic traditon and its origins, see Sir Mungo William MacCallum, *Studies in Low and High German Literature*.

[8]Stephen G. Nichols Jr., *Romanesque Signs: Early Medieval Narrative and Iconography*, pp. 85–86.

grounds no more solid than the popularity the work currently enjoyed in Flanders. But whatever the criteria of choice, it is clear that these entrepreneurial Flanders printers had much to do with the shaping of literary England in the last quarter of the fifteenth century, for it was here that most of the titles were chosen that were presented to the English book-buying public. These circumstances came about through the English alliance with Burgundy, an alliance confirmed by the marriage of Margaret, the sister of the English King Edward IV, to Duke Philip of Burgundy. Trade relations with Burgundian Flanders flourished thereafter, especially in the wool trade. Margaret's patronage encouraged William Caxton to set up his press and to translate popular French romances and mythological histories into English.[9] In due course a thriving book industry emerged that supplied the prospering English mercantile class with entertaining and instructive reading matter based largely on continental sources. After Caxton's removal to Westminster, Leeu was one of the Flemish printers who continued to supply England with translations of continental favorites, most of them former Caxton titles.[10]

We may attempt to characterize the tastes of the English common reader in terms of the titles of books that were published and circulated, although the limitations of this approach are readily apparent. Not all books were written with their specific tastes in mind, and not all books won general approbation. In these early years titles were selected and produced on a commercial risk basis. Each new title tested the interests of the reader at the same time that the supply of books also served to influence taste and to create demand. In that sense, *Solomon and Marcolphus* appeared on the English market as one title among many — a foreign import seeking the approval of the English reader. To be sure it might live to shape tastes and to have an important subsequent role in the shaping of native comic fiction. But it cannot

---

[9]Margaret Schlauch, *Antecedents of the English Novel 1400–1600*, p. 48. See also George Haven Putnam, *Books and their Makers During the Middle Ages*, Vol. II, p. 133.

[10]E. Gordon Duff, ed., *The Dialogue . . . Between . . . Salomon and Marcolphus*, p. xxiii.

be said that *Solomon and Marcolphus* was created by an author attempting to reflect English life. Were this the case, we might adopt C.H. Hereford's description of the early German readers of *Tyl Eulenspiegel* for an equally apt description of the English reader of *Solomon and Marcolphus*: "every line of Eulenspiegel vividly records the essential qualities of the society which made a hero of him: its gross appetites, its intellectual insensibility, its phlegmatic good humor, its boisterous delight in all forms of physical energy and physical powers, its inexhaustible interest in daily events of the bodily life, and the stoutness of nerve which permitted it to find uproarious enjoyment in mere foulness of speech."[11] Marcolphus answers to all of these, and the success of the book depends to a degree on the reader's capacity to laugh at scatological proverbs and dirty tricks played upon a monarch of mythological proportions. But it would be an error to profile the English book-reading public through the pages of this book, even though they had a capacity to be amused by its particular brand of humor.

To put matters in perspective, we note that the English reader received from Flemish and English presses during those first seventeen years of activity — from Caxton's first book in 1475 to the publication of *Solomon and Marcolphus* in 1492 — a wide variety of works, all of them seeking, in one way or another, to shape English tastes. These works included the sayings of philosophers, historical chronicles, parts of Ovid, Virgil, and Cicero in translation, Malory's *Morte Darthur*, *Godfrey of Boulogne*, *The Siege of Rhodes*, *The Knight of the Tower*, a few saints' lives, treatises on political wisdom, on manners, and the art of dying. There were early editions of Chaucer and Gower, and after 1492, an increasing number of theological and moral works.[12] Clearly, in the area of imaginative literature, the preference was for romance; indeed only a few works of non-romance fiction were offered, notably Caxton's translation of Aesop's *Fables* and the translation from the Dutch of *Reynard the Fox* that appeared in 1481. The conclusions to be drawn here are not self-evident. From time to time the

---

[11]C.H. Herford, *Studies in the Literary Relations of England and Germany in the Sixteenth Century*, p. 251.

[12]H.S. Bennett, *Chaucer and the Fifteenth Century*, pp. 205–14.

early printers selected popular non-romance works for translation and printing; *Solomon and Marcolphus* was among the limited number. In an indeterminate way, this little book swelled and diversified the list of titles of imported popular fiction. It was no doubt endorsed or criticized for much the same reasons that such a book would be judged today by readers unconcerned with matters historical, structural, political, or archetypal; it would have been found amusing, exotic, perhaps clumsy and unpolished in it execution, or crude and unedifying, depending upon the reader's moral, aesthetic, and literary disposition. Essentially, it would have been read as a contemporary book and judged for its capacity to entertain. But no statement of any kind has come down to us that expresses an opinion concerning this book or its reception by early English readers. Attempts to profile the common reader in terms of tastes and attitudes in order to speculate upon the reception of this book will also prove difficult. Even the most elaborate assessment of the age in terms of native humor, religious sensibilities, early interests in the new learning, education in the schools, and levels of literacy will only serve to split the field in a more speculatively detailed way between a certain propensity for rough humor, and a certain disdain for the uncultivated and the amoral. Little can be concluded from the fact that William Borde borrowed a few episodes in the 1540s to add to the *Jests of Scoggin*, or that the Puritan Richard Dering preached against the reading of such books in the 1570s, or that Archie Douglas, the fool of King James I, was credited with the authorship of the trick of the footprints in the snow by which King Solomon was led to the baking oven. That later jest collectors might borrow, Puritans protest, or king's fools plagiarize is hardly enlightening, except that in each reference there is at least confirmation that the work was remembered and that it left modest traces of itself in English culture.

There are, of course, arguments of a more general nature to be made concerning the place of *Solomon and Marcolphus* in sixteenth-century English culture. Speculation allows that with the new sensibilities occasioned by the arrival of humanist thinking, such medieval creations would rapidly fall from favor. Works of this kind would be too crude and unpolished to assume a place in the new order of the sonnet, the pastoral, the romance, or the novella. Social circumstances were also changing. The world of *Solomon and Marcolphus* was anti-clerical and anti-aristocrat in its satirical orientation, whereas the new English social order was far more concerned with city fops, misanthropes, and confidence men. Moreover, a work so vulgar could hardly be expected to survive the zealous scrutiny of the reformers. That was as demonstrably true in Germany as one suspects it would have been in England. Martin Luther in 1545 could still allude to the story of Marcolphus in the baking oven at a social gathering, and in the marriage sermon for Sigismund von Lindenau, he could tell his Catholic opponents, in reference to that same episode, to "take a look on Morulf's looking glass."[13] But within a few years German Protestant theologians such as Hieronymous Rauscher called this material unclean, and in 1601 Eucharius Eyering, in his *Proverbiorum copia*, complained that the stories of Marcolphus and Eulenspiegel were learned more readily than God's commandments.[14] But such speculation also brings us nearly full circle, for if Eyering is still protesting the popularity of the stories, he also confirms their staying power. Important, too, is the rich diversity of English culture during the sixteenth century and the persistence of numerous native traditions of literature, including the flourishing of the English jest book. That flourishing is no guarantee of the ongoing popularity of *Solomon and Marcolphus*, but it does suggest that the work's destiny in England was not determined by a general disapprobation of the genre. As Louis Wright says of the Elizabethans, "an age that could justify contemporary jest books as aids to health by reason of their alleviation of melancholy could easily find sermons in stone, and good in everything."[15] The statement merits retroactive application.

The book would also have had its place, on a different score, for the English were equally fond of neat sententious statements,

---

[13]Martin Luther, *Works*, Vol. 54, *Table Talk*, p. 389; Vol. 51, *Sermons* I, p. 361. See also John Kemble, *Anglo Saxon Dialogues of Solomon and Saturn*, pp. 69–70.

[14]Malcolm Jones, "Marcolf the Trickster in Late Medieval Art and Literature . . . " in *Spoken in Jest*, p. 165.

[15]*Middle-class Culture in Elizabethan England*, pp. 102–03.

books of proverbs, adages, and similes. One such, admittedly not published until 1547, was *A Treatise of Morall Phylosophie, contaynyng the sayinges of the wyse*; it went through eighteen editions in less than 100 years. *Solomon and Marcolphus* is a different kind of book, but it is not without a supply of proverbs and clever anecdotes. Louis Wright gives a full account of the report by Robert Laneham of the library of Captain Cox of Coventry in 1575, where there was found an extraordinary variety of popular literature including the continental romances, *Howleglass, Frier Rous, Gargantua, Skogan, The wido Edyth, The Ship of Foolz, A Hundred Mary Talyz*, to name but a tell-tale few. The jest books are well represented; it is a library in which Solomon and Marcolphus would have had a comfortable place.[16]

Turning from the few certainties that can be adduced about the tastes of the fifteenth- and early sixteenth-century common reader,[17] we may look next at the equally few conclusions that can be drawn from an examination of the influences of *Solomon and Marcolphus* upon English literature. One could argue that because this work contained the earliest English representation of a trickster hero projected through a series of comic episodes, it achieved paradigmatic status in relation to the many English jest books to follow in which the same formulas were employed. But during the thirty-four years between its appearance and the publication of *A Hundred Mary Talys* in 1526, there were three new continental jest book imports, all of them more likely to have captured the English imagination than *Solomon and Marcolphus*, each of them offering both episodes and structures for imitation, and none of them ultimately influencing the English writers to the point of generating close copies. In 1502, Wynkyn de Worde published *Robert the Devyll*, featuring a demon-possessed hero

---

[16]*Middle-class Culture in Elizabethan England*, p. 84.

[17]Richard Altick in *The English Common Reader* offers mostly disclaimers in dealing with reader tastes during this period. We do not even know "how large the literate public was in Caxton's time, or in the century that followed" (p. 15). What can be known is based largely on the activities of the printing houses themselves or on lists of books in wills, and on the presumed literacy rates in relation to the education system of the time.

whose exploits involved the supernatural. He was the first of the magician tricksters, and would be followed by Virgilius the Magician, Friar Bacon, John Faust, and Friar Rush. If a concatenation of literary fashions and opportunities in the Antwerp of 1492 caused Leeu to gamble on *Solomon and Marcolphus* in the English market, a similar concatenation caused the Antwerp printer Jan Doesborch to gamble on *Tyl Eulenspiegel* in 1519, and again on *Pfaffe Kalenberg* in 1520.[18] These were books about two popular buffoons whose careers in knavery are two of the most outstanding in the German jest-book tradition. They appeared in English as *Tyl Howleglass* and *The Parson of Kalenborowe*. Little more can be said about their reception in England than can be said about *Solomon and Marcolphus*, except that Tyl was more often mentioned, with all his advantages as an itinerant prankster, and that the work enjoyed a second edition, printed in London in 1528 by William Copland.

English jest books began to appear shortly thereafter, built for the most part around English-style jesters, some claiming historical origins, and featuring both native and imported jests often adapted in detail and temperament to the English setting. They were characterized by episodic structuring and some featured merry-minded protagonists credited with the authorship of the quips and jests they launched upon the unsuspecting. Others were merely collections of comic anecdotes without a central comic hero. They were much of a piece both in mood and structure with their continental predecessors, but given the generic simplicity of their procedures and the relative anonymity of their component parts, borrowed and adapted as though from a vast common fund of medieval European anecdotes and smart replies, there is little room for argument concerning specific models. They simply fed upon one another in random ways, repeating formulas that were part of the literary *Zeitgeist*, and nourishing a reading public with occasionally subtle and relatively harmless horseplay. In these books the English writers tamed all the farce of carnival laughter to the level of folklore.

---

[18]Margaret Schlauch, *Antecedents of the English Novel 1400–1600*, pp. 90–100.

New titles appeared at intervals throughout the century, and included *Wittie Questions and Quick Answers, Merie Tales of Skelton, Scoggin's Jests, The Sack Full of Newes, Mery Jests of the Widdow Edyth, Pasquil's Jests, Merrie Conceited Jests of George Peele, Tarleton's Jests,* and the *Merie Tales of the Mad Men of Gottam.*[19] In all of this, the place of *Solomon and Marcolphus* is both confirmed and ignored: confirmed because it was one of several in a sub-genre that must have enjoyed the favor of English readers, and ignored because there is so little evidence for showing direct influence upon the new native tradition. It was simply the first (or nearly the first, allowing for Aesop and *Reynard the Fox*) in a long line of imported and native jest cycles. But while Borde, for one, borrowed an episode or two for Scoggin, its early publication is no assurance that it was widely exploited for its forms, structures, or characterizations. Marcolphus was limited to a jesting relationship with an Old Testament king, which rather cramped his range of social currency and the style of his tricks. There is potential in him for a court fool prototype, but as I will point out later, Marcolphus in his carefree peasant guise does not fit the role either historically or in terms of his relations with Solomon. As a potential model, the book is an anomaly, for it features neither the court fool, nor a contemporary social type, nor the free-wheeling itinerant prankster. Given its limiting conventions, there is much about this little work that would not recommend it to the attention of English authors intent upon producing their own national version of the trickster.

Nevertheless, there is much that is hidden in those primitive forms and conventions, far beyond the appreciation of the Renaissance reader, that may prove of interest to the modern reader concerned with the evolution of literary genres, for *Solomon and Marcolphus* is a veritable laboratory of formal experimentation in which is to be seen the earliest developmental phases of certain structural motifs that were among the most important in the late Middle Ages in Northern Europe. Or to put it into different

---

[19]These have been collected by W. Carew Hazlett in the *Shakespeare Jest Books.*

terms, all that *Tyl Eulenspiegel* might have been as a formal prototype for the English jest book, *Solomon and Marcolphus* might
have been (and perhaps of necessity was) for *Tyl Eulenspiegel*.

Critical Approaches

Solomon and Marcolphus poses challenges to the literary critic both
for what it is and for what it is not. By its very nature, it resists
a number of conventional modes of investigation. It is not a
work that openly seeks, much less achieves, beauty, whether in
design, language, characterization, or ethos; the dimensions of
art celebrated in accordance with modern aesthetic appreciation
for the most part elude us. Nor does this work attempt to edu-
cate or elevate the spirit of the reader, except insofar as the entire
performance seems designed to elicit carnival laughter, abetted
by the grotesque and the scatological. There is little to say about
themes or messages of profound interest. Nor does it display the
genius and inventiveness of an author so individually inspired
as to leave us some sense of his identity; thus the avenue of
biographical criticism is also closed. The challenges of *Solomon
and Marcolphus* lie rather in complex critical demands pertaining
to its composite authorship, its relation to sources, its inform-
ing structures, its transmission through centuries, its relevance
to late medieval culture, and its potential for emblematic and
political meanings. Despite our limited purchase on issues of
aesthetics, higher thematic interests and authorship, it is possible to explicate *Solomon and Marcolphus* in terms of its materials,
its primitive forms, its temper or ethos, and the collective will
that both produced and received it, presumably as a reflection of
a mood that prevailed during the time it was conceived.

The first readers of *Solomon and Marcolphus* to uncover something in it of deep historical importance were those nineteenth-
century German and French philologists who recognized in the
work a piece of their linguistic patrimony.[20] Motivated by a cultural quest for sources and origins, they had as their main concern

---

[20] Among them are Walter Benary, whose edition of the Latin *Salomon
et Marcolphus* appeared in 1914, Johann Büsching, Friederich von der
Hagen, Emmanuel Cosquin, who set out to examine and describe all
of the surviving copies of the Latin *Solomon and Marcolphus*, Friederich

literary archeology — to find a locus of buried folklore motifs or an anthology of early proverbs, rather than to elucidate a work of creative literature with its specific forms and conventions. Through their intensive investigations, *Solomon and Marcolphus* found new merit as a literary artefact, and the way was opened to reading the work historically, that is, with a historically informed imagination whereby the sense of its otherness in time becomes part of the reading pleasure. A summary of their archival work and of their often ingenious and contradictory hypotheses will follow in the last half of this introduction, together with a resumé of new materials that have come to light in recent years. Valuable though all this is, the momentum of such historical inquiry can deflect the critic from the primary task of identifying the substance and design of the work within the classifications of literary structure. Therefore, we shall turn first to the literary dimensions of *Solomon and Marcolphus*, beginning with a consideration of its elementary structural components.

Simple Forms: The Proverb

I am indebted to the work of André Jolles, whose *Einfache Formen* was first published in 1930, for the notion of simple forms that provides a starting point for discovering the principles of composition that inform *Solomon and Marcolphus*. Indeed, Jolles' "simple forms," specifically the proverb, the riddle, and the jest, can be recognized as the basic building blocks of the work. Jolles applied the term "simple" to these forms to denote their stability and similarity through time and place as elementary word games or ploys that crystallize in language a response both cognitive and affective to a set of similar phenomena distinguished by the mind from the diversity of lived experience. Jolles thus highlighted their role as the verbal expression of experiences typical to the human psyche, what he called "mental dispositions," whose essence and power inhere as well in the language

---

Vogt, Gordon Duff, Ernst Voigt, Walter Hartmann, Alfons Hilka, Ernst Schaubach, Walter Schaumberg, Samual Singer, Arthur Ritter von Vincenti, and Alessandro Vesselofsky. Their contributions will be found in the accompanying bibliography.

forms that describe them.[21] Jolles saw in the fable, the joke, the riddle, the jest, and the proverb, vehicles that moved psychic experiences into social rituals, initiation processes, and belief and memory systems.

What Jolles did not explore were the recombinant possibilities within forms, their capacities for mutation and evolution into compound forms. Nor did he examine beyond a few brief allusive paragraphs the subversion of their initial functions through satire, parody, and irony, and their capacity to destabilize as well as to reify the orders of social and cultural practice. Thus while Jolles helps with understanding primitive structures, he does not elucidate the kind of compound forms seen in *Solomon and Marcolphus* — a work paradoxical insofar as its proverbs, riddles, and jests retain their defining characteristics, and yet are incorporated into larger organizational structures in ways that alter their original functions. In these transitions lies the structural novelty of the work, and while they may appear elementary in retrospect, they were for their time and place innovative achievements.

The contest in proverbs that frames the first part of the text may have emerged as a parody of a preceding agonistic dialogue of a serious nature, but it relies, nevertheless, upon elements that are independent of any organizational device, that is, upon a readily available stock of proverbs. To create the contest, the author(s) must first collect the proverbs and then separate them according to their contrasting qualities before arranging them in alternate pairs. These in turn must be assigned to the contrasting participants. In the process, the proverbs also assume a dialogic arrangement one to the other. The proverb, by incorporation into a dialogic contest, preserves its structural integrity as a proverb, yet undergoes a diminution of its apodictic and imperative functions because in essence it has become a counter in a game, invested with a potential for irony in its relation to the matching proverb that was not present in the simple form. In this way, the proverb moves into a compound form and is no longer received as advice but as a gaming gesture.

At the same time, the "Solomonic" proverb has been given new dramatic vigor by coming live from Solomon's mouth, just

---

[21]*Formes Simples*, p. 211.

as the low proverbs are assigned to an ugly, deformed peasant. More will be said later about the two characters' strange path through literary history to the present work. For the moment, we note that in the irresistibly symbolic contrast between king and peasant, the proverbs form a split field of wisdom representing the high or biblical and the low or rustic. Thus the proverb, once a simple, independent and authoritative form, in this compound framing structure, where it is relativized through dialogic arrangement, takes on new referential potential as a dialogic quip and an emblem of class standing, with all its attendant vulnerability to parody and social criticism. These transitions would have been inconceivable without a structuring idea based upon the exploitable potential within the proverb as a simple form.

The complex issues surrounding the final form of the proverb in *Solomon and Marcolphus*, that is, as a marker in a field divided along class lines, can best be illustrated if we begin with a more detailed look at the proverb as a simple form functioning in a dialogic contest. Definitions of the proverb can run to great length, but most contain variations on common criteria: proverbs are popular or learned sayings formulaic in nature; that is, the linguistic form (and there are many variations on this) is as essential to the proverb as the didactic message; proverbs touch on a wide variety of topics reflecting in resumé fashion the wisdom of collective experience; they are often uttered with authority and carry overtones of didacticism and instruction. Moreover, the combination of language, play, and common sense message serves to make the proverb memorable and apt for easy transmission from person to person and indeed from culture to culture.

The similarity in structure and content among proverbs from widely separated cultures suggests that the form is controlled by a quality of encounter between mind, experience, and verbal expression that is relatively constant. Yet debate will always remain concerning membership in the genre of highly complex formulations, or of simple statements of fact as opposed to sayings that offer some form of locution, or carry an imperative message. The problem is readily apparent in *Solomon and Marcolphus*. The English translation contains some ninety-one pairs of proverbs remaining from a Latin collection that was, in certain of the earlier manuscripts, fifty percent larger. Each unit contains two sayings that qualify, *ipso facto*, as proverbs for purposes of the contest. When some of these are singled out, however, they appear wanting in terms of basic form. If the Solomonic performance is taken as normative, a saying appears more proverb-like if it contains a simple locution whereby the abstract is given imagistic substance, a value is reduced to example, or the particular is given a general cast. Solomon says, "he that soweth wickedness shall reap evil," borrowing an agricultural figure to establish the causality between a quality of behavior and a quality of reward. Marcolphus replies, "he that soweth chaff shall poorly mow," which contains a lesson but no trope; he speaks literally of agricultural matters. In some of these instances, we may simply be seeing an inept translation which loses the word play or diction present in the Latin. In others, however, we can only conclude that Solomon surpasses Marcolphus in his capacity to think in figures, whereas Marcolphus is often so literal as to utter near tautologies. Yet in another sense, Solomon is as often surpassed by Marcolphus because each serious utterance gives the responding Marcolphus the opportunity for ironic allusion, either to the form or substance of Solomon's proverb. Indeed, in many instances, the intention of Marcolphus's performance seems to be to detrope Solomon's figure, deflating a significant portion of its power by disregarding its form in his parallel response.

An alternative reading is that each contestant merely reflects his world in parallel with the other, that is, in the official world of Solomon, the *quid pro quo* involves moral injunctions and rewards, whereas in the peasant's world, reciprocity takes place at the elemental levels of simple animal survival. It would seem for Marcolphus that "he that feedeth well his cow eateth often of the milk" carries no trope, the linguistic power of the saying lying rather in its diction and rhythm. Yet even such reduced forms carry a kind of consolidated and generalized wisdom and, in the cause and effect formula, conduct a miniature plot with its logic of closure. This unqualified assertion concerning feeding and milking may represent the minimal definition of the proverb as a simple form, even as it characterizes the sometimes simplistic yet profound wisdom of the folk.

In the difference between these two proverbs—the moral-figurative and the literal—may lie the whole matter of contention between the king and the peasant. The proverbs of high culture, including biblical ones, are authoritarian, sometimes even smug, a prescription for conduct without questioning. In Solomon's case, they are typically high-brow and dogmatic in terms of who shall prevail and who shall reap punishment. As such, they become targets for deflation. Such a challenge may be mounted by anyone who thinks himself marginal to the social hierarchy or who doubts the aptness of its system of rewards and penalties. That Marcolphus must play this role in relation to the world of the Solomonic proverb seems almost self-evident. We sense that the dialogic structure of the contest functions, not as the parallel recitation of proverbs in different registers, but as straight proverb, followed by one chosen for its quality of word play or formal echo, of flatness or insouciance, that will deflate the preceding one. Even though the proverbs in the work sometimes refer to each other only loosely or not at all, we continue to read for potential irony, potential referentiality. The dialogic patterns, the coincidences of language, and the contrasting personalities of the protagonists will not allow us to believe that the simple forms have not been appropriated by the strategies of parody.

We see in *Solomon and Marcolphus*, then, a work created out of a literary or social will to transform, using collective wit, an assembly of simple forms into an agonistic structure that may, in turn, serve ideological ends. Furthermore, given that the details of authorship will undoubtedly remain beyond discovery or documentation, we cannot but choose to concentrate upon the reading of those structures and their potential for emblematic or even political meaning. Yet in our wish to be responsible readers, we come back repeatedly to the question of whether the process of compounding forms represented here is formally or ideologically driven, or whether the two motivations can even be separated one from the other. What we want to resolve, or at least clarify as a question, is whether the creation of an agonistic and parodic structure is an expression of social unrest or subversive energy investing the work with implicit or explicit patterns of revolt, or whether these structures are the creations of the recreational mind intent merely upon realizing the recombinant possibilities suggested by the forms themselves.

The question is vexed by recent critical inclinations, which will be examined later, to see negotiations between authority and powerlessness in the reversed roles that are expressed by literary play and irony. In this light, all literary forms are potentially subversive in their constant susceptibility to variation. Critical faith in the subversive quality of all forms is further shored up by the belief that the only reason to vary forms would be to undermine the authority invested in them because that authority is aligned with dominant political, social, or ecclesiastical institutions. By that reading, the spirit of literary play itself becomes a carnivalesque gesture which is anti-authoritarian. And yet, *Solomon and Marcolphus* never seems to cooperate as fully as it might with this mode of analysis, its authorial history and the structure and probable uses of the text serving to undermine its purpose as purely ideological.

At the heart of the issue, of course, lies the concept of parody, a topic of much recent critical discussion, which has extended its applications from formal to political ones.[22] The concept is relevant to an assessment of the first part of *Solomon and Marcolphus* in relation both to the dialogic arrangement of proverbs and to the contest framing device. In the conventional sense, parody is a conscious adaptation of a previous style with the purpose of drawing ironic or sarcastic attention to the original. As a rhetorical device, it depends for its effect upon the surprising, unanticipated alteration of familiar structures, and in that sense, parallels such forms as the pun or the joke, the former because the word play throws up for comic display a standard word or word order, the latter because of its patterns of expectation and surprise. Parody usually makes its alterations to the familiar in terms of substituted or ironic content poured into a standard form, although the form itself can be subjected to playful variation so long as its essential identity is preserved. Stated differently, one can call attention to the proverb in a parodic way

---

[22]For one such study see Linda Hutcheon's *A Theory of Parody: The Teachings of Twentieth-Century Art Forms.*

only by citing that form in a manner that confirms its identity as a form.

The notion of parody has been broadened to include all manner of intertextual procedures based on imitation. Carried to extremes, the theory suggests that nearly all literature is parodic to the degree that it contains imitative or referential relationships to other texts. This is the crux of the matter, for when Marcolphus offers a proverb, even one in which we detect allusions to the preceding proverb, we can not always be quite certain that the relationship is parodic. To be so, Marcolphus must target either the content or the style of that proverb through imitation. Naturally, in a proverb contest there is implicit imitation because both speak in proverbs, but here, each draws from his own fund. Hence the imitation must consist of ironic choices. But in that regard, the evidence is ambiguous. When Solomon states that "the wicked man fleeth, no man following," by which he means that a man with a guilty conscience runs even when there is no one pursuing him, Marcolphus thinks in terms of flight, and replies that "when the kid runneth men may see his arse." These proverbs represent independent worlds, one moral, the other animal, brought into juxtaposition by a common action. Marcolphus causes us to ponder the significance of running and showing one's colors at the same time in relation to the man running out of a guilty conscience. It is an angular connection at best. Yet we sense that Solomon's proverb is diminished by the comparison. On other matters, however, the two are in full agreement, as when Solomon states "a woman strong in doing good, who shall find?" to which Marcolphus replies "who shall find a cat true in keeping milk?" Solomon answers "None," while to the first question Marcolphus replies "And a woman seldom." Here clerical anti-feminism makes temporary friends of the two contestants. If Marcolphus's cat is a substitution for woman, and the reference is lowered from human to animal, can it thus be said that there is parody? In form yes, but with the intent to draw ironic or sarcastic attention to the original, we are far less certain.

This ambiguity holds true for most of the pairings. Two proverbs coupled together does not necessarily imply parody;

a parodic association must be established by heightened referentiality. At what point parallel forms develop parodic relations,
however, is an engaging matter. The authors of *Solomon and
Marcolphus* were first collectors and then perhaps ironists. If the
latter, the exploitation of their materials was inconsistent. Their
game began in assigning high proverbs to Solomon and low
ones to Marcolphus, such as they were extracted from the current fund. It may have also stopped there, with the exception of a
few notional echoes that produce more playful pairings. Marcolphus wins the contest by volume, not by content, and just how
much damage he does to the Solomonic proverb along the way
is obvious in principle, but less demonstrable on a line-by-line
basis.

In similar fashion, we may ask whether the gaming structure,
the contest in proverbs, is the product of recreational or political energies. As stated earlier, given the class-related identities
of the contestants, we expect the proverbs to reflect their social
echelons. Those of Solomon are biblical, prescriptive, figurative; those of Marcolphus are empirical and touch generally on
matters earthy and local. That Marcolphus is so compulsively
scatological is, in itself, a sign that those who chose his material
wished to keep him low, potentially offensive, and a representative of his class. Whether this manner of representing the *rustici*
was essentially snobbish and disdainful or welcomingly indul-
gent may have some bearing on the question of parodic intent.
But the division of proverbs high and low, their class overtones,
and the agonistic structure suggest, if not parody, at least sharp
contrasts along ideological lines, played out in comic fashion,
with the victory going to the cultural underdog. That will prove
evidence enough of an ideological design within the work for
many readers.

Drawing for a moment on the historical section to follow, we
note that this part of *Solomon and Marcolphus* in all likelihood orig-
inated in the ecclesiastical schools of the eleventh century, where
Latin exercise patterns in the form of the *altercatio* or *disputatio*
comprised a seminal part of the curriculum and were doubtless

parodied by whimsical students of the time.[23] This form was, in
fact, fundamental to the organization of medieval discourse on
many levels from the early religious polemics in literary form to
scholastic argumentation. Thus, if parody perceived in *Solomon
and Marcolphus* is directed against biblical culture and the Latin
proverb, or against the figure of Solomon, it was carried out by
those who were the appointed curators of that language and culture, or by their pupils. Such is a reminder that parody both
destabilizes yet preserves and reifies the authority invested in
the form it imitates. That form was both a mere school exercise
and the rhetorical context in which Solomon participated as a
defender of the Christian faith — or such is the interpretation of
the iconographical representations of him opposite the Queen of
Sheba, with his fingers raised in scholastic debate fashion. By
a simple substitution, the debate becomes a comic one: Marcolphus the peasant stands in for the Queen and her riddles.
Until that fact was understood, the little grotesque figure sometimes posed near Solomon with his fingers also raised in debate
remained unidentified. But the extent to which this comic adver-
sary was adopted by the authors of *Solomon and Marcolphus* in
order seriously to call into question the conservative church culture represented by Solomon or merely to sport with the debate
form remains open to question.

Simple Forms: The Riddle and the Jest

In the second part of *Solomon and Marcolphus*, the adversarial
relationship between king and peasant continues but under entirely different circumstances, and in the transition, no allusion
is made to what has already transpired between the two opponents. We are challenged here with a new set of simple forms,
new principles for compounding these forms, and new criteria
for determining their ideological significance. Once again the
work commands our attention as a kind of textual laboratory
for tracing the continuum from simple to compound forms, and
specifically the migration of these forms into the realms of the

---

[23]For a discussion of the literary importance of the *plet* or *disputoison*,
see J.W.H. Atkins, ed., *The Owl and the Nightingale*, p. xlviii.

trickster protagonist and the subversive ideologist before return-
ing again into autonomous comedy. The essential structural unit
here, the simple form upon which this pathway is based, is the
riddle.

As with the proverb, many definitions of the riddle exist,
though again, as with the proverb, the range of variation on
the riddle form discourages hard and fast definitions. Closely
related to game structures, the riddle is played out between one
who questions and one who attempts to answer. The question
is a dark relation of words which must contain all the necessary
clues to the answer, but at the same time remain enigmatic, for
the object of the riddler is to baffle the analytical powers of the
opponent. Still the riddle must be fair. Not only must it have a solution (as Jolles says, a riddle without an answer is not a riddle),[24]
but it also demands of the one questioned that that solution be
found. Great importance can be attached to the abilities of those
who solve riddles, for these proving devices are often associated
with the identities of persons, groups, or group values. Riddles
may be used to hold or release power, to segregate members from
non-members, or to measure the preparedness of an initiate to
join a group. The questions of a catechism are, in essence, riddles
to a non-member who, upon answering them gains admission to
the religion whose mysteries these questions contain. Samson's
riddles were answered only through treachery. Odin may have
cheated by feigning to gamble his rulership on a riddle that had
no answer. And in the later Middle Ages, Marcolphus himself
was represented iconographically as enacting the solution to the
riddle associated with the clever peasant girl.

At the time when *Solomon and Marcolphus* was composed,
many riddles were available in folklore and literary anecdotes
that could be compounded into pranks that were built upon the
enigmatic use of words. Of particular interest is the way in which
the Marcolphus figure carries the simple riddle form into a new
semantic field, that of the trickster, which transmutes the riddle
into a new form altogether, namely the jest. At the beginning
of the second section, when Solomon goes hunting and comes
upon Marcolphus in his house attending to a pot of beans, the

---

[24]*Formes Simples*, p. 211.

king asks factual questions to which Marcolphus responds with riddles. No longer the quasi-mythological visitor who comes as a challenger from the East, this Marcolphus is a jester, full of quips, whose riddles are not only the simple forms in which he traffics, but also the building materials for the larger narrative and organizational structures that define the entire section. He is not interested in showing his prowess through resolving the riddles; the trickster mentality with which he is endowed needs tricks to be realized; thus the riddles become a template, as it were, for the construction of the jest by which Marcolphus triumphs at the king's expense. Even as they preserve their own definitions as simple forms, the riddles contribute to the formation of a jest cycle and, by extension, to the career of the trickster hero.

In one example of this, Solomon concludes his first encounter by posing to Marcolphus the famous riddle about covering the pot of milk with a product of the same cow, and implicitly from the milk of the same cow. But because of the ambiguity inherent in the wording of the riddle, a perverse answer, in addition to the conventional one (a flan), is possible. Marcolphus, in his trick, seizes the opportunity by substituting a piece of dried cow dung for the flan, thus turning the answer to the riddle into a jest. The static question-answer structure of the riddle is transmuted into an enacted problem-resolution structure driven by the motives of knavery. Once at court, Marcolphus plays out his innocence by insisting that he had every right to interpret the riddle thus — he was merely following instructions. This manner of disguising knavery with innocence will become the stock-in-trade of Tyl Eulenspiegel; indeed Marcolphus may well be the progenitor of this trickster. In the adaptation of the riddle to the jest, we glimpse an early instance of the trickster mind at work, compounding forms through his perverse processes of lateral and analogical thinking.

The waking contest to follow is a greater challenge in terms of the mutation of forms. The episode is framed as a game and structured with its own rules, prepared scenario, and objectives. Solomon and Marcolphus agree to a waking match in which, should it be Marcolphus who first falls asleep, he will forfeit his life. Just why he should take such a risk is irrelevant. What matters is that he has bound himself over to the game as though taking an oath, and if he loses by going to sleep, he can save himself only by changing the rules. This he does by coming up with riddle-like statements as evidence that he was thinking rather than sleeping. Solomon falls for the ruse. Bested in this round, Solomon himself abandons the rules of the game and now tells Marcolphus that unless he can prove his riddle-like sayings true he will lose his life. This gives Marcolphus the advantage, for although he was powerless against sleep, he knows the answers to the riddles and how to demonstrate them in the form of jests that would compromise and humiliate the king. Successful once again, Marcolphus protests his innocence after the fact by claiming to have done no more than he was told in order to save his life. From game to riddle and thence to a series of tricks, Marcolphus incorporates the simple into the complex with single-minded determination, completing the jest as a structure with its own teleological imperative toward closure.

The play of language in shaping tricks can work in two directions. When Solomon poses a riddle about something made from the same cow, Marcolphus finds an ironically literal solution. By contrast, when he tells Marcolphus not to spit "but upon the bare earth," Marcolphus finds a figurative answer by spitting on a bald man's head, which, because it grows no hair, might pass for the bare earth. In effect, literal language is turned into a riddle with a hidden answer that Marcolphus demonstrates through yet another nasty deed. This riddle-like handling of otherwise denotative language carries through to the end when Marcolphus secures from the king permission to choose the tree from which he is to be hanged. Solomon, in failing to see the riddle in the wording, permits Marcolphus to escape because the trickster knows that the ambiguity in the wording allows him to make no choice at all.

Turning riddles into jests or games is one form of compounding simple structures into complex ones. Collecting jests from other sources and arranging them into a cycle as though all were the deeds of a single protagonist is another. *Solomon and Marcolphus*, by all indications, features the earliest surviving example in medieval literature of this seminal literary idea. The component parts of the jest cycle, though crudely assembled in this prototype, are worth enumeration. First, the form requires recognition of the jest as a simple form suitable for grouping into collections. It next requires recognition of the entertainment value in assigning those jests to a popular protagonist who serves as maker and agent. The selection of jests is disciplined by the need to create a coherent, though often kaleidoscopic, collection of deeds informed by a single personality. Finally, as the logic of biography takes over, the collected deeds are compounded to form the life of the trickster, which is in effect the sum of the pranks he has engineered. In this way, simple jests, when gathered and adapted to new contexts, become the raw materials of the jest collection or cycle rationalized in the name and image of a central protagonist, a trickster whose career profile is that of the over-reacher whose increasingly audacious tricks bring him to a final demise.

Because jests require the agency of jesters, and jesters in time become volitional characters, it is not long before we are apt to forget the pathway from simple to compound and assembled forms and posit in its place an intentioned prime mover behind all that is done, attributing to him a will, a wit, and an *a priori* motive for his malignity. In other words, we fall for the fiction implicit in the compounded form of the trickster cycle. The critic looking for ideological warfare in literary forms will readily attribute to that malignant will all the political causes, all the ideologies, all the subversive impulses that seem justified by the trickster's deviancy, his targets, and the contents of his exploits. In this mutation of simple jest forms to create the trickster personality, the critical challenge to balance formal play fairly with ideological purpose clearly appears. The debate becomes a matter of reading the personality of Marcolphus either as the mere agent of formal play or as the first genius of the strategies of carnival liberation.

The jest itself as a simple form is hardly simple. Its intention is to outwit, fool, or deceive an unsuspecting victim. But it takes on its peculiar form in the nature of its planning. We have already noted that the jester so specializes in the devising of these little plots as often to lack any other dimensions to his personality. The skillful jest, the jester's *raison d'être*, has several components. The unsuspected event by which the appointed victim is surprised, injured, ridiculed, or otherwise outwitted must be imagined and projected into a future setting complete with enabling circumstances and conditions. This can be as simplistic and mechanical as placing a tack on a chair in anticipation of someone sitting on it, or as ingenious as relying upon the assertive, avaricious, compulsive, or naive conduct of the targeted individual himself to bring on the projected results. Other unwitting players may also be incorporated and through secondary trickery prepared for a role in the primary trick, as when Marcolphus lies to his sister Fudasa about his intentions to kill the king in expectation of her spiteful revelation of the secret before Solomon, all by way of proving to the king, as one of the conditions imposed during the waking contest, that women are never to be trusted. The trickster who draws his victims into the ruse by playing on their curiosity, cupidity, ambition, naivete, or arrogance is the master craftsman. Such pranks achieve a social purpose surpassing those that merely take advantage of the unsuspecting. The trickster plies his imagination, reads the nature of his target, prepares the conditions of the trick in conjunction with his reading of personality, creates the necessary words or gestures that call the other to play, and plans the ambiguities whereby he can assert his own innocence after the results are achieved. It is that combination of inventiveness, the pre-planned scenario, the controlling of circumstances, the daring employment of the victim as an unwitting contributor to his own humiliation, and the duplicity of the ensuing explanation that characterizes the jest as a simple form.

If the riddle is a dark relation of words, the jest is a dark or hidden relation of intentions that is similarly not without its clues and intimations. That Solomon, the world's wisest man, should fall for a dozen tricks in a row and still not understand Marcolphus's nature accounts for much of the incremental effect of the humor, for he is never without warning. If the riddle is an invitation to play through a set of verbal clues, the jest contains warnings to avoid play through a set of verbal or gestural clues. The trickster's character precedes him, and his behavior, though it does disguise his intentions and dissimulates his devices, constantly sends out hints to his purpose; the naive and unobservant king never catches on. Thus the gaming device weaves its way through the second half of *Solomon and Marcolphus*, the king's risk escalating as the humiliation meted out by each completed jest accumulates and provokes his growing wrath, if not his skepticism. It is that increase of anger, incited by the boldness of the trickster, that generates a sense of crisis and that leads to the climax and closure of a sequence of jests that might otherwise be added to indefinitely. In this simple way, the open-ended and cumulative structure of the collection is circumscribed by the qualities of an elemental plot.

The Jest Cycle and the Trickster "Biography"

In *Solomon and Marcolphus*, the cycle as a rogue biography is a brief one. To call it a biography at all is to signal its potential more than its reality, to anticipate its development in later tricksters rather than its present status. We have been observing a process in which a class of materials selected from diverse sources can be subordinated to a principle of organization based on the notion of the course of a single life. That life, moreover, is devoted entirely to a single mode of activity. The career of Marcolphus is restricted even further because although he makes and performs tricks in the best trickster tradition, he targets only one individual. Such a preoccupation severely limits the choice of tricks assigned to him and hence his development as a trickster protagonist. No other Teutonic trickster cycle is as confined and limited in its range, a reminder that *Solomon and Marcolphus* represents an early moment in the experimental compounding of these forms. The notion of the biography built around a coherent perception of the trickster personality is still in its nascent stages. Nonetheless, there emerges a sufficiently complete sense of Marcolphus as a character to permit his association with the trickster as an archetype, and as an embodiment of its associated social and psychological values.

A profile of that generic character is available in the collected traits common to individual tricksters, together with a frame of mind that accounts for his typically aggressive, devious, and deviant, behavior. The trickster is an outsider, a loner, a self-created outlaw primarily motivated by a compulsive will to play.[25] He

---

[25]For a more extended definition see Matthew Hodgart in *Satire*, pp. 20ff.

may be driven by his desire for food, sex, or shelter, but more often he is driven by a fascination with the disruptive little plots conjured up in his imagination and by a willingness to test his projected scenarios against the circumstances of social reality. Thus he toys with the margins of authority, the justice of the collective will, and the social constraints placed on personal liberty, designing offensive forms of play and directing them against figures of power. Marcolphus easily fits such a description, although one can see immediately in later tricksters how far the type was to develop from the agent who is the by-product of collected simple forms.[26]

The trickster rarely or never tells us about himself directly, but through his deeds. Hence all that can be posited about his mentality must be drawn from the tricks themselves and their relationship to the victims. Repeatedly we are teased by the question of motive, and instinctively we are inclined to read the tricks themselves as emblematic or subversive gestures. For those inclined toward this mode of analysis, a world proffering all manner of ideological readings opens before them, as we shall see below.

As far as Marcolphus is a man of the people and Solomon is the typological embodiment of the king, and as far as the pair are locked in a contest of wits and cunning, this work does provide an early paradigm of class conflict. Moreover, assuming that the trickster is an agent of freedom, seeking release for himself and by implication for his class from all manner of authority, we are inclined to assign to the representatives of authority within the text

---

[26]Karl Kerényi and Paul Radin on the one hand viewed the trickster as a primitive folk hero who finds repeated representation in the mythologies of the world. Carl Jung on the other hand saw in the trickster a projection of an early phase in the integration of the human psyche, a mythic embodiment of an abstract psychic state. These dimensions of the archetype need not detain us here, although Marcolphus qualifies in many ways for a place in this broader assessment of the type. See Carl Jung, *Four Archetypes: Mother, Rebirth, Spirit, Trickster*, pp. 135–52; Paul Radin, *The Trickster: A Study in American Indian Mythology*; in the latter appear the two following seminal essays: Karl Kerényi, "The Trickster in Relation to Greek Mythology," and C.G. Jung, "On the Psychology of the Trickster Figure."

those things from which Marcolphus is likely to be seeking freedom. Reflecting upon the probable circumstances of the work's genesis, we may presume that those projecting their sentiments of rebellion through a subversive peasant hero must in reality have been thinking in terms of ecclesiastical institutions, their restrictive forms, disciplines, and traditions, so that in Solomon we should see the authoritarian embodiment not only of the ruling classes and official culture, but also of intolerant Christian morality, the ecclesiastical schools, church hierarchy, and Latin culture in general. The capers of Marcolphus are thus a literary holiday, a moment of enforced license, an hour of carnival laughter. The issue once more is whether this hour of laughter is but for a moment, or for all time, whether it is tolerated recreational escape, or a surreptitious attack that seeks to nourish an underground rebellion destined, by slow degrees, to destabilize institutions or to reflect true social change. It is worth reviewing a number of critical perspectives on this issue.

Elements of Subversion

For Maria Corti, the importance of *Solomon and Marcolphus* can reside only in its contribution to the literature of rebellion and social change. In her reading of history, the evolution of societies comes about through the constant and inevitable assault upon whatever is deemed dominant, and this assault will often be carried out through the generation of counter-semiotic structures and discourses. One detects in Corti an implicit faith in that evolutionary process whereby inroads in the name of freedom, through the daring presentation of new forms, will be made against the established and thus tyrannizing forms of authority. In her words,

> each time there appears in a culture an ideology or a program which is in any measure deviant, a conflicting semiotic reaction is triggered off within the society between the "different," which requires new structuring models, i.e., new semiotic structures, and what has already been codified and which is thus with its differently orientated structures dominant.[27]

---

[27]Maria Corti, "Models and Antimodels in Medieval Culture," *New Literary History*, pp. 344–45.

Deviant works appear where there is a perception of injustice, or where there is already a *de facto* shift of power, in order to compel official institutions to reform their models of divine/human relations to include newly empowered sectors of the society. In this process, tricksters, by definition, serve the interests of the marginal, the emerging, or the oppressed, and thereby become Promethean, in spite of their amoral knavery. The lone peasant hurling himself against the presumptions of a king emblematizes for Corti the determined spirit of freedom seeking through wit to discredit and expose the grounds of the king's authority. In her terms, Marcolphus rises to heroic status almost as a cultural benefactor.

Corti's is an attractive thesis and one much in vogue. Because of the implicit conflict between dominant and deviant social structures perceived in *Solomon and Marcolphus*, the work may indeed be read politically as a contribution to the revisionist tactics sought by medieval authors. For those laboring under general persuasions concerning the political importance of the subversive, objections on structural and historical grounds will pose only temporary difficulties. Nevertheless, it should be objected that as a semiotic model for social change, *Solomon and Marcolphus* represents a rather unfocused performance. Solomon may be open to all kinds of political interpretations, but for all that, he remains remote and rigorously circumscribed by specific traditions and typologies. And if Marcolphus appears as a deformed peasant, an anti-prince, in order to match wits with Solomon, he nonetheless does so within an attenuated fairy tale structure in which, as the new contender for power through admission to Solomon's court, he tries his luck in the prescribed contest.[28]

---

[28] Jan de Vries remarked the frequency with which the wisdom contest as a means for entry to a new society was a part of the Solomonic tradition. In the riddles solved by the clever peasant girl in order to win a prince, or those solved by Solomon himself to regain his throne after a period of exile, the fairy tale motif persists. That same pattern is echoed by the appearance of Marcolphus at court in order to challenge Solomon in a wisdom contest. Many of these fairly tale motifs come from the East; they represented a means for social mobility without the use of power or arms. *Die Märchen von Klugen Rätsellösern*, pp. 312ff.

This motif contains a principle of social mobility alien to the logistics of the subversive. The crux of the matter will always come back to the intentions of licence and parody, whether they are meant to destabilize and alter the institutions they target, or to confirm them. There is the problem too of the trickster's volition, the trickster who emblematically attacks with apparent purpose, or the trickster who demonstrates nothing more than the urge to trick and who, for the author, may be little more than a convenient agent and principle of organization.

The Court Fool

Corti's theory works in concert with others concerned with demonstrating carnival and court fools as agents of destabilization and change in late medieval society. Long before these theories emerged, however, Enid Welsford made the association between Marcolphus and the court fool type. She did so by dividing her candidates into two categories, the mythological fool and the historical fool; Marcolphus clearly fits only the former category. Such creatures "of the popular imagination" performed in literary contexts much as their historical counterparts performed at court."[29] Welsford's inclusion of Marcolphus is, in a sense, confirmed by Borde and Croce who borrowed episodes from *Solomon and Marcolphus* in order to flesh out the careers of their court fool protagonists.[30] In a general way, the thesis can be endorsed, even though Marcolphus is quite early and himself shows no trace of origins in the court fool as such. To be sure, he quips and jests at court, plays upon the king's tolerances, refuses to mince his words, finds himself punished, and once or twice regains a kind of grudging favor. But he is never truly in the king's employ, nor is he granted licence in official manner. He does not indulge in the usual kind of banter or smart repartee that characterizes the court fool, and by no means can he be constructed as the wise fool who, out of his concern for ruler and state, seeks to introduce advice and policy under the cover of his disguise. In

---

[29] *The Fool: His Social and Literary History*, pp. 35–40.

[30] For further accounts of this Italian Marcolphus, see Enid Weslford, *The Fool*, p. 40, and Pierre Louis Duchartre, *The Italian Comedy*, pp. 255–57.

that regard, he may be related to a structural prototype only in the most general way; he is far from a literary representation of the court fool type.

Maurice Lever's *Le Sceptre et la Marotte* is a valuable contribution to the history of the court fool. Lever makes the important distinction between the natural fool, a kind of simpleton brought to court for his amusing horseplay and innocent rambling, and the "morosoph" or "fol-sage" who is essentially a counsellor in disguise, a man who, through his provocative play, attempts to alert and direct the prince.[31] Like Welsford, Lever claims Marcolphus for a court fool, but that Marcolphus fails to qualify for either class of Lever's fool is an indication of how awkwardly he fits the classification. Lever concludes that Marcolphus ridicules Solomon in exactly the way Shakespeare's buffoons humiliate their masters, "not because he is more intelligent, but because he is crazy (parce qu'il est fou)."[32] This is to diminish the trickster to a single aspect of the court fool. The fool may feign stupidity as a cover for his barbs, or he may be a true simpleton and survive the better for it, whereas the trickster may feign ignorance, but he can never be a fool and prosper. Low though he may be, Marcolphus is the height of intelligence, and the model of cunning. Lever's characterization of Marcolphus in terms of madness would appear to be a complete misrepresentation of him as a trickster protagonist.

Despite the many historical and typological difficulties, Michel Foucault, in *Histoire de la folie à l'âge classique*, goes on to adopt the court fool as the epitome of the transgressive individual in medieval society whose conduct expresses a free spirited form of resistance to authority. According to this thesis, every such court parasite seeks to destroy the host upon whom he depends for subsistence. Foucault makes much of the fool's "unreason," which he regards as a narrow category of deviancy tolerated by medieval authority but still able to undermine the tyranny of official culture.[33] Foucault invests a philosophical dimension in

---

[31]Maurice Lever, *Le Sceptre et la Marotte: Histoire des Fous de Cour*, p. 164.

[32]Maurice Lever, p. 166.

[33]*Histoire de la folie à l'âge classique*, p. 24.

the "unreason" of the fool, who becomes a central if not uniquely privileged creator of the counter-rhetoric and counter-gesturality that alone can bring human liberation. To Foucault, Marcolphus belongs by definition to the circle of the court fool as a figure of unreason. Putting aside the difficulties on historical grounds of investing in this generic type an ideology of revolution of twentieth-century making, the immediate problem is to locate specific instances of unreason in Marcolphus's conduct, whether literally or symbolically. He simply bests the world's wisest man in a social context conditioned only by his wit.

Carnival

Of all the purveyors of liberationist deviancy, no doubt Mikhail Bakhtin is the best known. He came to his theory of carnival essentially through his study of Rabelais, a study whose hidden purposes were influenced by the circumstances of Stalinist Russia under which he worked. Creating his own form of symbolic dissent, Bakhtin set about to show the ways in which late medieval society negotiated a degree of freedom from the totalitarian institutions of the age. Thus he unveiled a people's culture running parallel to the official ecclesiastical and feudal cultures. By means of laughter, the bawdy, the parodies of official rites and offices, the folk asserted a spirit of protest disguised as institutionalized merry-making. This politicized definition of carnival has contributed in a significant way to recent critical debate but it is not without its limitations as a critical concept. Bakhtin himself anticipated the objection that carnival was institutionalized in a way that authorized its transgressive practices by attempting to build that paradox into his theory as one of its strengths.[34] But the expressions of individualism that are absorbed into official culture may reveal more about the survival strategies of that official culture than about the liberationist tactics of the folk.

As a carnival text, *Solomon and Marcolphus* presents difficulties. The work was created in Latin, borrowed the forms of higher learning, and merely appropriated the deformed peasant to generate the contrasts necessary for laughter; it was by

---

[34]Linda Hutcheon, *A Theory of Parody: The Teachings of Twentieth-Century Art Forms*, pp. 74–76.

no means a production of the folk or of a people's culture. As a transgressive text, its survival rate should have been slim — official censorship would have seen to that — but the number of surviving manuscripts is substantial (attesting to the many more that have perished, due perhaps more to overuse than suppression) and most of those that have survived are to be found in monastery libraries. These doubts are aligned with the much greater one expressed by Umberto Eco that carnival was ever intended as a true act of political liberation.[35] Bakhtin was concerned with works in which the values and acts of carnival itself were represented: food, song, violence, laughter, blasphemy, and sex. He was interested in the open-ended, unstructured events of the people paralleled in literary forms. But Marcolphus is no self-indulgent creature driven by his sensual appetites. That is one reason for his initial invulnerability. He is reserved and analytical; there is no question of carousing laughter. Tricksters are loners. Neither anger nor self-righteousness figure in his moods, and the book itself, while cumulative, nevertheless follows the closure principles of the game and the trickster jest cycle. Marcolphus's gestures may be carnivalesque in value and effect, but his world is remote from the ethos of carnival.

Judgment in these matters ultimately returns to the pleasures and profits we desire in reading this little book. If our purposes as readers have become politicized, then *Solomon and Marcolphus* will easily submit to those purposes, although as readers, our generation may have sacrificed its pleasure to the virtues of purpose to the same degree that we have accused others of making their purposes the pursuit of pleasure. Who would have thought that we could learn to look for carnival with so much moral earnestness?

Misogyny

Much has been written on the issue of misogyny in medieval literature in recent years, and there is ample material in *Solomon and Marcolphus* to nourish the debate. Two of the jests in particular turn on allegations concerning women. Marcolphus states outright that women are not to be trusted and "proves" the point by

---

[35]Umberto Eco, "The Frames of Comic 'Freedom,'" in *Carnival*, p. 3.

goading his own sister into revealing a sworn secret. In another instance, he rouses the town women in anger against Solomon in order to force the king to break his promise never to speak ill of women. The episode begins with a critique of Solomon's famous judgment of the two women fighting over the infant. Women possess craft, Marcolphus argues. They can weep outwardly while they laugh in their hearts. They are in essence hypocrites and "have innumerable crafts." Solomon excuses them, justifies them, lays blame for their faults on others, and celebrates them as "honest, chaste, meek, loving, and courteous." The two men argue, and Marcolphus plans his ruse, namely to tell the women that new marriage laws have been enacted entitling men to seven wives. The women spread the news among themselves, then storm the palace. Solomon flies into a rage. Never does he speak of particular situations; he leaps to open generalizations concerning the entire gender and its ways. He calls them serpents, curses them, claiming in phrases redolent of proverbs that women are talkative and disobedient, that "an evil wife maketh a patient heart and a sorry visage," that she is "the beginning of sin" and the cause of death. He is interrupted by Nathan his prophet who tells him to make peace with the women. Solomon apologizes by explaining that he spoke not of all wives, but only of the "froward" ones. Whether his biblical flattery that a good wife "is a light shining brighter than the light of candles" will serve to convince readers of his sincerity, it persuades all the women present to say "amen" and to depart.

Readings of rhetorical intent have become so complex in these matters that these episodes could register both high and low on the misogyny scale. In a dramatic sense, the women are entirely innocent because they have been misinformed by the lies of a trickster. Moreover, Solomon was unfairly provoked to wrath by the circumstances engineered by Marcolphus in which the women are but unwitting pawns. Solomon apologizes, while Marcolphus is judged and banished. But few will absolve the clerics responsible for this relation of the matter, for surely their agenda was to rehearse the nasty things traditionally said about wives.

Both episodes were drawn from anecdotes appearing in variant versions in the *Gesta Romanorum*, as the section on sources will reveal, and furthermore, all these medieval renditions were based on classical originals. Thus it may be said that if there is a degree of anti-feminism here, it is not the original product of the society in which the work was written. These jests were a nod to the humor of the ancients. Of course, it will be argued with reason that such materials were transmitted, adapted, and thereby made a part of contemporary culture. Conventionally, we regard medieval clerks as indulging every possible way to malign or laugh at women, and as developing forms of literary humor throughout the period explicitly to promote an anti-feminist spirit. For instance, as early as the eleventh century, short poetic narratives began to appear in the forms of *ridicula* and *nugae*, both of which gained in sophistication during the century and prepared the way for the goliardic poetry of the twelfth century. To a degree, these carried the seeds of the fabliau. The *ridicula* belong to the tradition of learned poetry with its emphasis on stylistic control and scholarly allusions. A subversive quality is already apparent in the *ridicula* insofar as the narrators were willing to side with the knaves in their stories rather than with the establishment. These writers were interested in the nature of craftiness, the quality of wit (*ingenium*) and fraud (*fraus*).[36] *Ridicula* were recreational productions of the ecclesiastical schools just as *Solomon and Marcolphus* is thought to be, and they contributed a repertoire of tricks and anecdotes about human nature, including unflattering references to women, that nourished the fabliau, the sermon *exemplum*, the burle or jests, the riddle-narratives, the novella, and the fairy tale. As Wolterbeck confirms concerning "the dangers of wicked women, . . . nearly every late eleventh-century writer has at least one poem on the subject."[37] He adds the telling observation that the two biblical figures perceived at that time to be the greatest victims of women's deceptions were David and Solomon. Perhaps a key then to this baiting of Solomon on the question of women has less to do with outright misogyny and more to do with the king's reputation in the Middle Ages as a man who was cowed and compromised by his pagan wives, as a man who, for his

---

[36]Marc Wolterbeck, *Comic Tales of the Middle Ages*, p. 124.

[37]Marc Wolterbeck, p. 115.

uxoriousness, was led into apostasy. Yet we do not sense that Marcolphus was setting out to correct historical wrongs after the fact with a preliminary lesson.

The matter of misogyny, or at least the distrust of women, would be easier to deal with historically in relation to *Solomon and Marcolphus* if the gestation period of the work could be brought forward to the period of the fabliau. The entire matter could be taken into the age of the Wife of Bath who protested at the end of the fourteenth century that "it is impossible / That any clerke wol speken good of wyves."[38] In another sense, however, the conditions of genesis are never the whole matter where works have passed, as popular literature, through several generations of readers in several different social periods. In that regard, these two episodes take on a kind of rhetorical neutrality that will be interpreted in accordance with the values, perceptions, and conditions of each generation of readers. To elucidate that point, the critic must profile each period from the eleventh to the sixteenth century in terms of its literary treatment of women and the evolving controversy — one that was carried on in Tudor England, for example, from Edward Gosynhill's *Schole house of women*, first published in the 1540s, which Louis Wright describes as "a diatribe against the vanity, talkativeness, extravagance, faithlessness, and general frailty of women from Eve to Jezebel,"[39] to Joseph Swetnam's spiteful *The Araignment of Lewd, Idle, Froward, and unconstant women*, published in 1615. To the extent that *Solomon and Marcolphus* was read in England during that century, it could have been perceived as a minor contribution on the pejorative side to the controversy over women in much the same way that it stands to have been received by the readers of the French fabliau, or of the German Shrovetide plays, for both literary forms were notorious for generating laughter at the expense of wives.

And yet, according to many observers, the anti-feminist discourse in late medieval literature rarely carried the message of wholesale attack. The manner of slighting women often carried

---

[38] Geoffrey Chaucer, "The Wife of Bath's Prologue," ll. 688–89, p. 114.

[39] *Middle-class Culture in Elizabethan England*, p. 468.

sub-textual messages as powerful as the surface rhetoric of diatribe. Brent Pitts, in his introduction to *The Fifteen Joys of Marriage*
[Les XV. Joies de Mariage] demurs as follows:

> one is compelled to say at the very least that the author's satire
> on women, though coarse and cruel at times, seems anti-feminist
> with a difference. For if woman in the *Fifteen Joys* is portrayed as a
> conniving, often oversexed termagant, the husband receives a few
> hard knocks as well: he is shown as a tightfisted, preoccupied bore,
> slow-witted, easily swayed, and not too famous a lover at that.[40]

Derek Brewer believes that the anti-feminism, the black humor, the laughter at victims, whether wives, priests, or husbands,
in the medieval comic tales are all offset by resolute optimism
revealed on all sides, by cheerfulness in the face of adversity.[41]
After the many terrible things Markolf says about women in the
Fastnachtspiel by Hans Folz, he calls an end to the bickering and
invites the women to dance in an obvious gesture of renewed
mutuality.

One may go further to proclaim that men in groups gather to
make light of what they most fear and least understand. Small
consolation, perhaps, to those who are the object of their abuse.
But the matter brings out a profound paradox in our modern
approaches to medieval culture, which is the difficulty of dividing laughter both by class and by gender. Bakhtin, who was
interested in class, made very little mention of the laughter generated in medieval literature about members of one class by other
members of the same class. Bahktin states:

> The popular tradition is in no way hostile to woman and does not
> approach her negatively. In this tradition woman is essentially
> related to the material bodily lower stratum; she is the incarnation
> of this stratum that degrades and regenerates simultaneously. She
> is ambivalent.[42]

In the fabliau, this "ambivalence acquires an ambiguous nature;
it presents a wayward, sensual, concupiscent character of false-
hood, materialism and baseness. But these are not abstract moral

---

[40]*The Fifteen Joys of Marriage*, p. xviii.

[41]*Medieval Comic Tales*, p. ix.

[42]*Rabelais and His World*, p. 240.

traits of the human being." They are, for Bakhtin, part of a general pattern that always re-endorses women as the "foil to . . . avarice, jealousy, stupidity, hypocrisy, bigotry, sterile senility, false heroism, and abstract idealism."[43] Woman is the eternal creative principle and the grave of man, unconquerable by any force of humor. Laughter merely confirms her creative and dominant nature.

This sets up a distinct critical orientation for approaching *Solomon and Marcolphus*. In the huddle of the monastery or the boy's school a little sniggering ritual about the cunning power of wives individually or in groups will automatically reverse itself in the processes necessitated by comic justice, becoming as it does a lesson in the virtues of women. Solomon is part of this discourse in which maligning women becomes part of the praise. Marcolphus is, as we expect him to be, low, married to a hag, brother to a sister of dubious mores, and a rustic incapable of noble sentiment. The question is whether the true Solomon is he who begins and ends with the praise of women, or the angered Solomon provoked out of his cool diplomatic façade by knavery.[44]

Of interest is not only the degree of misogyny expressed, but the fashioning of the wife in Solomon's ideal portrait of her, for if we attribute the vision of the wicked wife to the clerics who compiled the text — to their perverse anti-feminist sentiments — we must attribute to them at the same time the vision of the good wife. The proverbial phrasing is rather empty, but the sentiments are telling, for they concentrate on the necessary, positive, guiding role of the wife in a domestic setting. She is the joy of her husband if her life is "grounded upon a sure stone without and the commandments of God ever in her mind." Woman is credited with God-given power to exercise moral judgment. The domestic scene is, admittedly, the only one she is granted, but it is there that love, creativity, and mutuality will be found, and the

---

[43]Ibid.

[44]There is a precedent for both aspects to his character as it is conveyed in biblical proverbs, some of which caution against the ways of women, while others, namely the last half of Proverbs 31, are dedicated to the praise of virtuous women.

responsibility is given to the woman to become a good housewife and to follow a religious and social option. She is cast as an ideal, not in remaining always subjugated, virginal, cloistered, but in finding fulfillment in the family. This is perhaps no improvement for some readers, but Solomon has turned the diatribe against *die böse Frau* into a little sermon on domestic tranquility, achieved not through strict obedience, but through a spirit of love and of duty to God. These attitudes foreshadow Reformation views in which women find fulfillment in the family. As Sigrid Brauner states with regard to Luther's views:

> woman has to entice men to righteous behavior by her own pious example: through submissiveness, humility, and the inner beauty of the soul. This moral and spiritual power of the married woman is not only based on her spiritual equality as affirmed by Saint Paul in Galatians, but on Luther's new understanding of the state of matrimony as the primary institution for leading a religious life and one that is superior to the monastic one.[45]

Solomon and Marcolphus passes in its history through many fields of readership. These are culturally defined, beginning with the climate of the eleventh-century *ridicula* and ending with modern views concerning medieval misogyny. Yet exploring these fields may still leave us wide of the ideological context in which the work was conceived. All humor based on generalities, including humor at the expense of women, is in its own right one of the simple forms generated by the human psyche.[46] It was as apt to surface in Old Testament proverbs as in recent popular humor. Identifiable groups, especially powerful or threatening ones, are subject to stereotyping at the cost of misrepresenting both the group and its individual members — especially the more vulnerable ones. There are social circumstances in which even those targeted can laugh at the stereotype, recognizing in it exaggerated elements of truth, while asserting, of course, one's own independence from the stereotype, and revelling in the capacity

---

[45]"Martin Luther on Witchcraft: A True Reformer?" in *The Politics of Gender in Early Modern Europe*, p. 34.

[46]Matthew Hodgert has traced the controversy over women as far back as the sayings of the Vizier Ptah-Hotep, active around 2500 BC. *Satire*, p. 81.

to strike back in kind. Bakhtin saw the treatment of women in the fabliau in those terms.

With regard to the expression of humor in the milieu in which *Solomon and Marcolphus* was first conceived, there were questions of an even more fundamental kind, for in the monasteries and ecclesiastical schools, there was first the issue of whether laughter itself in any form should be tolerated. If there is a measure of freedom-seeking in this Latin exercise book, it may well be an escape from the very strictures that prohibited laughter altogether. Ernst Robert Curtius outlines the debate in his *European Literature and the Latin Middle Ages* where he cites numerous passages from the early theologians, pointing out that the "question to what extent clerics might jest occupied one of the most important thinkers and scholars of the twelfth century, Walter of Chatillon." The question was debated throughout the entire period in which *Solomon and Marcolphus* was in circulation, ending in the Counter-Reformation climate of Jansenism, and Rance's "malheur a vous qui riez!"[47] *Solomon and Marcolphus*, assembled from the stock in jests inherited from the ancients, more or less as it was found in companion collections, was a gesture toward the courage to laugh. The misogynist overtones of the work are a dimension of that courage, and a small piece of the multifaceted tradition of rhetorical strategies built around the question of women that persisted throughout the High Middle Ages.

Intertextual Readings

One final quality of recognition encouraged by *Solomon and Marcolphus* — and yet another pleasure of the text — is the intertextuality relating not merely to the tracing of sources in philological fashion, but also to the similarities in motifs between texts not demonstrably related in a linear or evolutionary way. In this sense, *Solomon and Marcolphus* could be said to preserve vestiges or to remember traits by processes beyond historical demonstration. We have been concerned so far with the contribution to Western letters implicit in the experimental arrangement of

---

[47] *European Literature and the Latin Middle Ages*, p. 422.

simple into complex forms represented by this work to the exclusion of historical processes that led to its origins and transmission. The comparative process inhabits a kind of middle ground between critical approaches to the work as a cradle of new structures, and the work as a product of former traditions. That Marcolphus, all deformed and hairy, should arrive a wanderer from the East, that he should concern himself with riddles, or that he consumed the blood of that same vulture whose heart Solomon had eaten to gain wisdom — all suggest echoes of works no longer extant, although the motifs can be found in various literary analogues.

There is for instance the Russian tale of the boy Solomon and the blacksmith's son, with its origins in eastern folklore.[48] Its climax is a wisdom contest through which the exiled young Solomon seeks to demonstrate his right to the throne against the pretensions of a low-class usurper. The power negotiations through a wisdom game structure involving high- and low-born players, despite the reversal of the roles, invites reflection. Just how Solomon found himself banished and a blacksmith's son put in his place is a curious story. At the age of three, the precocious child had furnished evidence to his father David of his mother's infidelity. The queen, incensed, sought to have the child slain. The commissioned servant motif is invoked, and true to the tradition, the servant takes pity on the child. He is to have the child's heart roasted for eating as proof of the killing, but a substitute is supplied, as in the story of the birth of Saturn, with which this tale has affinities. We register in passing the roasted heart motif, although how it may have been metamorphosed into the vulture heart requires considerable imagination.[49] Meanwhile, to deceive the king, a smith's son had been put in Solomon's place. David detects the fraud and demands the return of his own child. Fearful for his life, Solomon temporizes and in the fashion of Hamlet takes on the guise of the trickster by using his

---

[48]The story was given in resume by Jan de Vries in *Die Märchen von Klugen Rätsellösern: eine vergleichende Untersuchen*, pp. 312ff.

[49]Malcolm Jones traces the motif of drinking vulture's blood to gain wisdom to the story of Sigurd. *Marcolf the Trickster in Late Medieval Art and Literature*, p. 187.

quips and riddles for a façade. We may be tempted to think in terms of a remote common source that by other channels nourished the comic transformation we are concerned with in this edition, still carrying as it does a few nearly pointless vestiges of its narrative ancestors. But the advantage of intertextuality is that one does not have to create such hypothetical links; one merely relishes the resonances like music, all the way back to the Bengalese *Vikramaditya*.[50]

Marcolphus as a proto-court trickster is not without his many and diverse ancestors. Of gate crashers, cadgers of meals, and entertainers at banquets there are many tales among the ancients. Such characters turn up in Athanaeus, Plutarch, Xenophon, Lucian, and Plautus. Xenophon relates how a certain Philip takes on the philosopher Socrates at Callia's dinner party and gains the upper hand through repartee and mimicry. In Lucian's *Feast of the Lapithae* the buffoon Satyrion takes on the cynic philosopher Alcidamus and draws him by degrees into a boxing match. The Romans enjoyed the satiric value in pitting a lowly entertainer against a respected man of wisdom and in seeing wisdom defeated by craft.

Such tales provide engaging examples for comparison, albeit of a general kind, whereas the affinities between *Solomon and Marcolphus* and, for example, the tale of the tenth-century Arabian court trickster Nasr-ed-Din, or Si-Djoha are more specific.[51] Here we see the life of a trickster through the collection of his exploits, a presumably independent discovery of the jest cycle principle. Si-Djoha's personality itself becomes the means for harmonizing and rationalizing the collection. Moreover, he gains entry to the court of Timur-leng (our Tamburlaine) by answering a riddle that, unresolved, carries the death penalty. It is as though a common store of motifs, a common vocabulary of characters and devices, was available to authors across the known world to be drawn upon in recombinant ways. The riddle carrying the threat

---

[50] Alexandre Vesselofsky in *Les Légendes slaves sur Salomon et Kitovras et les légendes occidentales sur Marcolphe et Merlin*, traces this story to the *Vikramaditya, Les Récits du trone*, Paris, 1883, but I have not been able to examine this work.

[51] Enid Welsford, *The Fool*, pp. 29–34.

of death is a generic motif and has little to do with the extreme penalty imposed as part of the waking context in *Solomon and Marcolphus*. But the recognition is sustained by the conjunction of common character types and common principles of organization — works that represented a common level of achievement in remote centers during a general moment of literary time.

For many years subjected to the vagaries of manuscript copy and dissemination, and yet benefiting by the accretions and corrections that entered through that same process, *Solomon and Marcolphus* arrived at a state of relative stasis by the fifteenth century. It passed thereafter, in several languages, through several generations of readers during two centuries of rapid economic and cultural change. Given such dynamic circumstances, the book must have met with varied reception from hearty endorsement of its humor to moral disdain. We may hypothesize that without firsthand knowledge of the crude reality of former times, or without the benefit of later critical and historical methods, no ideal reader could exist. But the book defines its own terms of laughter, its own conventions, as all works of the past must do, instructing all readers alike. Its simple strategies for laughter are universally accessible. A book we may examine for historical and critical purposes, the sixteenth-century reader must have perused as a representation of a comic encounter between the life of the fields and of the courts, much as this distinction was still recognized in that age. We, by contrast, are the beneficiaries of a rich repertoire of analytical considerations that for us may alone redeem this little book. As an object of literary study, it is almost without equal, for it is a laboratory of forms, a potential study in radical deviancy, a portrait of the trickster, a record of early humor, a glimpse into the medieval literary mind at play, and as the subsequent section will demonstrate, the object of one of the most intensive philological quests on record.

The Cultural and Literary History of
Solomon and Marcolphus

Early References to the Solomonic Dialogue

Solomon and Marcolphus, as a comic text, is almost certain to
have borrowed features from serious wisdom matches featuring Solomon as a principal polemicist or contestant. Locating
the scattered references to that tradition will serve as a point of
departure for the historical survey to follow, which traces the
origins of the forms, names, motifs, and episodes that appear in
the present text. By dint of a single surviving title, the Solomonic
dialogue tradition can be traced back at least as far as the late fifth
century. Pope Gelasius, pontiff from 492 to 496, was a zealous
prelate whose writings were largely aimed at the suppression
of heresy and the eradication of all vestiges of pagan religion.
(To him we owe the demise of the ancient Roman feast of the
Lupercalia). His concerns included books he thought unfit for
Christian readers; among them was a *Contradictio Salomonis*. The
title confirms a dialogic format, but what the work discussed
remains open to speculation. Josephus is but one witness among
several concerning the Solomonic cults popular in the Near East
during the centuries around the beginning of the Christian era.
During that period and after, proverbs continued to be collected
in Solomon's name. Talmudic texts associated him with tales
of magic, riddles, and demonic lore; little wonder that Gelasius
was concerned if the book in question dealt with such matters as
these. An alternative hypothesis is that Solomon had assumed
a theological or doctrinal voice in opposition to a non-Christian
debater, as he was to do in later dialogues. Erika Schönbrunn-
Kölb argues for the defacing or mutilation of biblical texts as the
reason for suppression. For her, the fifth century *contradictio* was
a wisdom contest involving a parodic handling of Old Testament
proverbs.[52] This is an attractive thesis, and if true, would suggest that an irreverent contest involving proverbs may not have
been original to *Solomon and Marcolphus*. Such wisdom contests
may go back to the early centuries of Christianity. Solomon's

---

[52] "Markolf in den mittelalterlichen Salomondichtungen und deutscher Wortgeographie," in *Zeitschrift für Mundartforschung*, p. 100.

opponents may have assumed demonic guises following the Talmudic tradition, or they may have appeared as social equals the equivalent of Hiram, King of Tyre with whom Solomon matched wits in riddle contests.

While the tradition of Solomonic dialogues in Latin was undoubtedly perpetuated during the earlier centuries of the Latin West, the earliest and only surviving texts in the tradition were two poems of 164 and 331 lines respectively written in a West Saxon dialect by unknown clerics around the year 900.[53] It is from these marginal and possibly atypical vernacular poems that all impressions must be derived, whether of their immediate continental sources, or of the larger tradition. In both poems Solomon debates with a visiting Chaldean prince whose name happens to be Saturn, seeking to bring him over to Christianity. In the first poem a verbal contest between two cults takes place; Saturn pledges thirty pounds of gold and his twelve sons if Solomon succeeds. Already one recognizes the buried allusions to earlier Solomonic lore, namely, the gambling of riches in riddle contests, and Solomon's role as polemicist against the old pagan gods. In this poem, the dialogic dimension gives way to a didactic one as Solomon delivers a discourse on the Pater Noster and the special uses of its individual parts as incantations to ward off evil. The second poem is finer stylistically and presents a true dialogue in which Saturn represents the angry despair and moral confusion of the worldly, non-Christian heart, while Solomon, through the procedures of the dialogue, gives instruction in the saving wisdom of Christianity. Much more complex than a simple contest between two belief systems, one pagan, the other Christian, the poem is a dialogic *gradus* or pathway to hope and salvation that culminates not only in Saturn's defeat, but more importantly in his joyful acceptance of Christianity. In this encounter, Mary Wallis sees two protagonists functioning not only according to their typologies established by myth and history, but also according to an epic motif in which an outsider arrives to challenge the ruler of an unstable court. This challenger is often an adventurer, an exile, who evinces not only superior prowess, but also

---

[53]Robert J. Menner, ed., *The Poetical Dialogues of Solomon and Saturn*, p. 6.

superior intelligence which he demonstrates through trickery, dark questions, riddles, and destabilizing plots.[54] Identification of this motif clarifies Saturn's origins as a wanderer from the East and his alien status in Solomon's world. The motif is related to Marcolphus's behavior as an intruder into Solomon's court where he first seeks power through victory in a wisdom contest and then vengeance through discrediting Solomon in the eyes of his subjects. Marcolphus's conduct parallels the intrigues of the court challenger, thereby fixing a curious degree of continuity at the mythological level in light of these hints in the Anglo-Saxon poems.

The most pertinent detail for our purposes appears at line 180 of the second poem: it is the first literary allusion to Marcolphus. The Saturn of this work is said to be the Prince of Chaldea, a man from the East who had disputed with the sages of the Philistines, who knew the history of India, and who possessed the sciences of the Greeks and Libyans. This Saturn had travelled throughout the world and knew "marculfes eard," the land of Marculf. For the author of this poem, Marculf was associated with eastern places and mythologies and is represented as a source of Saturnine wisdom somehow linked to the magic of Chaldea and the Roman paganism that Solomon must defeat. There is reason to think that the models for these poems derived from Byzantine sources, and were originally associated with Hebrew folklore and the Talmudic traditions.

To John Kemble and Walter Schaumberg we owe an ingenious explanation of the name Markolis in the role of Solomon's opponent and, by extension, of the channels whereby the name of an ancient deity is remembered in the name Marcolphus. The reference in the second Anglo-Saxon poem to the land of Marculf which Saturn had visited on his way to Solomon's court is one of the most important pieces of evidence. Another is the translation by St. Jerome around the year 400 of Proverbs 26:8 which Jerome gives as: "sicut qui mittit lapidem in acervum mercurii."[55] The

---

[54]Mary Wallis, *Patterns of Wisdom in the Old English "Solomon and Saturn II,"* pp. 160ff. See also Note 28 above.

[55]J. Levy, *Neuhebräisches und Chaldäisches Wörterbuch*, Vol. III, p. 261.

Revised Standard Version reads "like one who binds the stone in the sling is he who gives honor to a fool." But the reading is contested. Another is "putteth a precious stone in a heap of stones." The heap of stones draws attention because in the Midrashic tradition this heap was called a "markolis." By this it may be reasoned that for Jerome, Markolis and Mercury, the Roman god, were the same person. Schönbrunn-Kölb discovered in the seventh-century encyclopedic work of Aethicus Cosmographicus a reference explaining the association between Markolis and a heap of stones, and between the heap of stones and the god Saturn. Aethicus notes that the Turks, in worshipping Saturn, built piles of stones called "morcholon."[56] It is supposed that Markolis was the Hebrew version of the god Mercury, that he became the object of worship after the Roman conquest of Palestine late in the first century, and that he was honored, as Hermes had been, by erecting herms or statues where roads crossed. The name passed into Jewish folklore and accounts for Jerome's translation of Markolis's stone heap into Latin as Mercury.

There is but one caveat to be mentioned in the matter, namely that the *Cosmography* attributed to the fictive Aethicus is not, according to Peter Dronke, to be viewed merely as a representative eighth-century encyclopedia, but rather as a Menippean enterprise in which the author, presumably an Irish cleric, in pre-Rabelaisian fashion, offers a "send-up of accepted wisdom about strange places, people, and times." Dronke sees the work as one of "exuberant impishness,"[57] so that nothing of a factual nature can be taken entirely at face value without corroboration in other sources. Nevertheless, the speculation in the *Cosmography* concerning Markolis appears to have substance; traces of support in other sources do occur.

This issue is dealt with as well by Robert J. Menner, *The Poetical Dialogues of Solomon and Saturn*, p. 363.

[56] Walter Schaumberg, *Untersuchungen über das deutsche Spruchgedicht Salomo und Morolf*, pp. 52–59. See also Charles H. Herford, *Studies in the Literary Relations of England and Germany in the Sixteenth Century*, p. 125.

[57] Peter Dronke, *Verse with Prose from Petronius to Dante: The Art and Scope of the Mixed Form*, pp. 14–19.

The same tradition appears to have survived in Asia Minor where the stone heaps called "morcholon" were transferred to the worship of Saturn. The evidence can be variously interpreted. Kemble, the nineteenth-century editor of the Anglo-Saxon *Solomon and Saturn* poems, uncovered an important clue as to how Saturn and the god Morchol may at one point have been associated. In a manuscript in the British Library, London, Kemble found the following passage: "appellaverunt lingua sua morcholon id est stellam deorum, quod derivato nomine Saturnam appellant."[58] The word "morcholon" meant in Turkish "star of the gods" and by derivation, the name Saturn also meant the same thing; thus the association between the two. This does not account for all of the substitutions and associations along the chain, but it does suggest an early origin for the name Marcolphus, and it allows for early associations between a variation of this name and the Saturn who appears in debate with Solomon in the ninth-century poems. Saturn seems to be a temporary substitution for Markolis-Marculf in the tradition. The antiquity of the name Markolis itself lends support to the idea that by a parallel tradition a Markolis figure, as a representative of pagan beliefs, had been a Solomonic sparring partner in wisdom debates going back many centuries. Those early associations were, in all likelihood, obscured by the passage of time, so that the name Marculf, Latinized into Marcolphus, could pass into the comic tradition in the form of a common Germanic name suitable for a peasant protagonist. The name Morolf also survived by different channels (no doubt from the same early sources) as Solomon's brother in a Middle High German minstrel epic.[59]

---

[58]John Mitchell Kemble, *Anglo Saxon Dialogues of Solomon and Saturn*, p. 119. From Cotton-Caligula A. 3 fol. 4 in the British Library, London.

[59]The name Marcolf-Marcolphus has raised the interest of many scholars, and the question of its origin and meaning has produced a number of engaging solutions. The name has existed for centuries in the North. In the Old English poem *Widsith*, Mearchealf is the name of the ruler of the Hundings. This poem dates to the seventh century but may have echoes going back to a minstrel who lived in the fourth century. See *The Cambridge History of English Literature*, Vol. I,

Medieval Proverbs

Precisely when this Marcolphus figure, as Solomon's antago-
nist, became the deformed peasant and reciter of folk proverbs
is a matter of continued speculation, but if a remark made by
Notker Labeo (952–1022), the celebrated monk of St. Gall, is in

---

p. 36. J.J. Eschenburg thinks Marcolphus was named after the seventh-
century Frankish monk Marculphus. Le Roux de Lincy believes the
name was derived from Marcus Cato. Friedrich J. Mone thinks it was a
Dutch word meaning chatterer or mimic. J.M. Kemble associates Marcolf with Markwolf or boundary wolf—one that guards boundaries.
Konrad Hofmann proposes that it came from the Mahol of I Chronicles
4:29 whose sons faced Solomon in a wisdom battle. F. Liebrecht thinks
that Marcou comes from Markolf, a species of *Häher*, the jay, in its role
as a forest spirit. Walter Schaumberg corroborates the theory that it
was derived from the Hebrew Markolis. For these listings see Biagioni,
Marcolf und Bertoldo, p. 5. Erika Schönbrunn-Kölb conducted a thorough examination of the question and states her belief that whatever
the validity of the theories of eastern or southern origins, the name in
northern countries achieved its currency because of its correlation with
the jay, the *Eichelhäher*. In Bk. 23, sect. 120 of Albert the Great's *Man
and the Beasts* (de Animalibus), p. 297, written between 1258 and 1262,
he states "characteristically this bird scolds everyone and everything in
sight; besides, it possesses a talent for mimicry which prompts some
people to call it marcolphus." In modern German this is Morkolf, the
mocking jay, having the origin of its name in the common romance verb
"moccare," to mock and mimic. This word thus adds itself to the list of
roots for Marcolf the mocking jester. Of note, however, is that Marcolf
was not always a jester, although he has those properties in the German epic as well as in our own textual tradition. The jay theory cannot
account for a serious Marcolf in the earlier Solomonic debate tradition,
and presumably it has nothing to do with the "marculfes eard" of the
Anglo-Saxon poems, even though the name appears to have a "Ger-
manized" spelling. The fact remains that in the mind of the folk in the
North the name of the bird might very well have become associated
with the jester and would acount for such references as "bruder Marolff
der Holtzvogel" in Fischart's *Geschichtsklitterung*. One final reference
suggests that the name raised curiosity even in the fifteenth century. In
Gregor Hayden's version of Marcolphus's genealogy he says that the
father of Marcolfum was Merkel, and that his grandfather was Markart.
See the *Dictionary of the Middle Ages*, p. 146. In the Cracow University
Library manuscript 1950 he is also called Marquart.

reference to our text, then Marcolphus was performing in his comic peasant role as early as the year 1000. I cannot determine which scholar first located this reference, but it has been quoted in articles and introductions going back well into the nineteenth century. Notker wrote a commentary on Psalm 118 that made a detour into the question of secular stories and the way they obstruct spiritual teaching. Such "fabulationes" are told by the loquacious heathens and worldly story-tellers. In the course of this discussion Notker mentions in passing: "was ist es anderes als dass man sagt dass Marcolf gegen die 'proverbia Salomonis' streite? An alledem sind nur schöne Worte ohne Wahrheit."[60] "What else is it [but lies] when Marcholfus [Notker's spelling] speaks against the proverbs of Solomon? These are but beautiful words without any truth in them." In these sentences we have a clear reference to Solomon and Marcolphus in confrontation in which the latter opposes Solomon's proverbs with words that are beautiful but untrue. Everything about this statement points to the tradition of our text, except for the description of the folk proverbs we associate with Marcolphus as being either beautiful words or lies. Notker, we assume, would make a distinction between low, rustic statements and lies. The question is whether, in the context, Notker is referring in the second sentence specifically to Solomon's proverbs and Marcolphus's replies, or, more generally to the stories of the heathens which he might well refer to as lies because they were "fabulationes" or fiction rather than history and thus unprofitable. Our only option is to imagine that Notker was speaking of the same kind of *Contradictio Solomonis* that Schönbrunn-Kölb described as the source of Gelasius's objections, namely a work in which an opponent makes light of Solomonic wisdom by twisting the biblical proverbs into clever and blasphemous parodies. That fits my sense of the statement made by Notker, but the authorities are in disagreement. Cosquin thought that Notker was objecting to Marcolphus's mockery of the scriptures,[61] while Singer held that

---

[60]Qtd. in modern German by W. Benary, *Salomon et Marcolfus*, p. vii, from Paul Piper, *Die Schriften Notkers und seiner Schule*, Vol. II, p. 522.

[61]Emmanuel Cosquin, "Le Conte du Chat et de la Chandelle dans l'Europe du Moyen Âge et en Orient," p. 384.

"beautiful words" refers only to the heathen story-tellers, and that Notker is surely referring to the first part of *Solomon and Marcolphus*.[62] Ultimately the question may be purely academic, for if Notker is not referring to our text, he is surely referring to one that is closely related. I see in his concern an attitude that may in fact have encouraged the creation of the earliest version of the work presented here, one in which Marcolphus performs less objectionably because he represents the proverbs of the folk, as opposed to more direct and potentially more blasphemous parody of the scriptures. The ambiguity concerning the parodic intent of *Solomon and Marcolphus* discussed earlier in the introduction may be traced back to this substitution of contents.

That the time of Notker is the right one for this kind of conception or substitution to have taken place receives further support from two pieces of circumstantial evidence. In another St. Gall manuscript from that same period, there appears one of Marcolphus's proverbs in its original vernacular version, "sô daz réchpocchilin flîet, sô plecchet imo ter ars";[63] it appears in *Solomon and Marcolphus* as "si fugit capreolus, albescit ei culus." The proverb is neither beautiful nor a lie, but a saying of the folk based on animal behavior. What is significant is that clerics were recording such material and that it was being translated into Latin. Further supporting evidence of this trend is the work of one of Notker's disciples, Egbert von Lüttich (Egbert of Liège), who collected and translated into Latin what we may term the popular wisdom literature of his age. His collection of proverbs, both learned and popular, he called the *Fecunda ratis* (Loaded Raft); it was in circulation by 1023. The most striking fact, for our purposes, is that it contains approximately one-seventh of the proverbs recited by Marcolphus. Singer has no doubt that our text came first, and that Egbert drew upon it directly for his collection, thereby confirming the claim that *Solomon and Marcolphus* is the earliest collection of European folk proverbs. This theory raises but one question, namely why Egbert, with his

---

[62]Samual Singer, *Sprichwörter des Mittelalters*, Vol. I, p. 55.

[63]Samuel Singer, Vol. I, p. 34; last page of MS. 111, St. Gall, in K. Müllenhoff and W. Scherer, *Denkmäler deutscher Poesie und Prosa aus dem VIII–XII Jahrhundert*, Vol. I, p. 59; Vol. II, p. 135.

encyclopedic interest in proverbs, would have taken so small
a sampling. But whether these two works drew directly from
each other, or whether they are related through intermediary
sources, they would appear to belong to a common cultural moment during which the folk proverb first came to the attention of
the learned world as a possible tool of pedagogy.

In his introduction, Egbert provides not only important insights into his own purposes for collecting proverbs, but conceivably a rationale for the creation of the first part of *Solomon
and Marcolphus*. His stated purpose was to create an "opusculum
rustici sermonis," a collection of folk wisdom which he claims
to have gathered directly from the people.[64] Moreover, it was
his conviction that such proverbs, translated into Latin, would
facilitate the learning of Latin for students drawn from the lower
classes. Egbert taught at the cathedral school in Liège. His
purposes extended beyond popular pedagogy, however, for he
made of the *Fecunda ratis* a compendium of proverbs drawn from
several language groups, but principally French and German,
as well as from the Bible, classical authors, the Church fathers,
and possibly from other collections of proverbs. As an omnium
gatherum, the work crosses cultural boundaries, giving a kind
of official Latin status to materials deemed culturally "low," as
later critics point out.

If Notker's objection to Marcolphus was based on the recitation of folk proverbs, we would have in Egbert's work a radical
departure from the sentiments of his teacher. But I think, rather,
that Egbert had grace in his enterprise, and that the compilers
of *Solomon and Marcolphus* may have worked under that same
dispensation. Our interpretation of this work could be influenced by the knowledge that it was not designed as a gesture
of rebellion against official learning and culture, but rather as a
contribution to that learning in the form of a pedagogical work
for the learning of Latin made more enjoyable and accessible by
intermixing a bit of the familiar with the biblical in a way that
calls attention, not to the glibness of Solomon, but to the humor-
ous qualities of folk wisdom, and that the framing structure of

---

[64]Werner Lenk, "Zur Sprichwort-Antithetik im Salomon-Markolf-
Dialog," p. 153.

the dialogue or disputation was resurrected from the Solomonic tradition merely to form a comic framing device.

In the earliest versions of *Solomon and Marcolphus* there would have been only the proverbs and the names of the players; the descriptions of the characters, their origins and pedigrees would have been added as further embellishments to the framing device. That a few fifteenth-century manuscripts exist without this material suggests that it was added later, and that some copies continued to be made from the earlier versions. The juxtaposing of high and low proverbs in such collections as Egbert's, together with his concern for the learning of Latin, constitute a formal idea in the making that might have resulted in the production of a school manual that only had currency in the schools during its early years, and that during a later period it caught the popular fancy largely through translation into the vernacular. For these several circumstantial reasons it would appear that the first part of *Solomon and Marcolphus* may be dated to the first half of the eleventh century.

The place of origin is also a matter of conjecture, but the proverbs themselves have been thought to provide certain clues. Samuel Singer examined the sayings common to the *Solomon and Marcolphus* textual tradition (the number of proverbs in all the surviving manuscripts is larger than in any single manuscript) and the *Fecunda ratis* in order to produce a complete set of analogues and their regional frequencies. Of the thirty-one of Marcolphus's proverbs cited by Egbert, eighteen he traced to French sources, six to German sources, while seven were of indeterminate origins.[65] Perhaps all that can be deduced is that French-speaking areas had the richer tradition of proverbs, rather

---

[65] In addition to Singer, *Sprichwörter des Mittelalters*, Vol. I, p. 34, several scholars late last century and early this century took up the challenge of determining the geographical origins of our text through lexicographical evidence. The diversity of their findings, however, leaves the question largely unresolved. Because such words as "bergarius, follus, ingenium, merda" and "pensare" appear in the Latin text, it was reasoned that a French genesis alone could account for their presence. Cosquin added other words: "leccator" for Fr. "lecheor," "trufator" for Fr. "trufeor" (cheater), "bosa" for Fr. "bouse" (cow pie), and "nutritura" for Fr. "nourreture" (education). But Cosquin goes on to show

than that our text was of French origins. As a subsequent section will point out, there was a tradition of "villain" proverbs in
France perhaps as old as the eleventh century, and by the early
thirteenth century one of the participants was the peasant Marcolf or Marcoul. But the French may only have borrowed the
name insofar as the proverbs cited in the two traditions reveal no
readily identifiable co-ordinates. Concerning *Solomon and Marcolphus*, one compromise might be to assign origins to a place
in one of the bordering areas, such as Flanders. Lüttich, at the
time Egbert was writing — between 1010 and 1024 — was part of

---

how Latinized French words entered general Latin usage. Moreover,
he argues that clerics travelled widely and found their Latin in many
places. Walter Benary added even more words of French origin to the
list, but denied that such evidence would establish the place of origin.
There can be no doubt that some of the proverbs in our collection were
of French origin, but in fact the most popular proverbs had versions
in all the major European languages and most of them had also been
translated into Latin.

The matter is complicated by the probability of intermediary Latin
collections — even of the folk proverbs — such as the *Fecunda ratis*, which
was part of the process of Latinizing folk culture in the schools. Walter
Schaumberg favors collections by Jourdain de Blavies and Apollonius
of Tyre. Benary is partial to the collection by Heinrich Bebel, and to the
proverbs found in the *Altfranzösische Sprichwörter*, edited by Zacher and
Tobler. For further research into the matter of the early proverb, recommended authors include Heinrich Bebel, Johann Agricola, Gruterus,
and Sebastian Frank. In none of these works are direct sources to be
found, however; these are collections compiled later than *Solomon and
Marcolphus*, offering parallel proverbs that may go back to common
sources. A sampling of these relationships will be pointed out in the
textual annotations.

If lexicographical clues point to French origins, other evidence points
to German inspiration. The transformation of Marcolphus into a peasant
is in keeping with other such characters in German literature, although,
to be sure, there were the early "villain" proverbs in French. The first
vernacular language in which this work appeared was German by almost two centuries. These early translations may have nourished the
Latin tradition in detail and episode. Finally, nearly every surviving
manuscript of the text has been located in libraries across southern and
central Germany, in Vienna, and Berlin.

France, linguistically, but part of Germany politically.[66] If Egbert drew his proverbs directly from the folk, they may have constituted a mixture of Walloon, Flemish, and German materials. The Latin world crossed boundaries in any case, allowing for the author to be a French monk or cleric teaching at an ecclesiastical school in Germany. This was the solution favored by Singer.[67] But the question of place remains open to speculation.

Presumably by the mid-eleventh century the idea of juxtaposing folk and official proverbs had become something of a mode, because at least three new collections — all appearing before 1055 — in practice or in open protest, opposed the alternating high-low proverb organizational principle. Wipos in his *Proverbia Henrici*, Otloh of St. Emmeran in his *Liber proverbiorum*, and Arnulfus in the *Cleri delicie* may have been responding to this trend when they insisted upon representing only the proverbs of official culture, for these alone were worth emulation. Arnulf speaks in his preface of "clerus" and "rusticus" as contrasting styles, and describes the latter as "ethnicorum infructuosa loquacitate," the "useless talkativeness of the people."[68] He compiled only biblical, classical, and patristic sayings.

By the eleventh century as well the literary dialogue form, already a fertile medium for doctrinal debates, tests of wit and wisdom, and explorations of vexing life problems (as in Boethius and Augustine) begins to serve increasingly as a repository of popular wisdom, no doubt at times in opposition to the more conservative among the learned. This growing populist interest found a place among clerics like Egbert who collected local vernacular maxims and translated them into Latin for use in the schools. The conjunction of circumstances that enabled them to incorporate such popular proverbs into their Latin dialogues is likely complex, having to do with a changing social awareness among the clergy, political and economic shifts, and the inevitable attractions of the creative imagination through which

---

[66]Samuel Singer, *Sprichwörter des Mittelalters*, pp. 66.

[67]Samuel Singer, pp. 34, 65.

[68]R.N.B. Goddard, "Marcabru, *Li Proverbe au Vilain* and the Tradition of Rustic Proverbs," p. 65, and Werner Lenk, "Zur Sprichwort-Antithetik im Salomon-Markolf-Dialog," p. 153.

ideas are born for recombining cultural elements into new forms of expression.

The formula involving Solomon and Marcolphus the peasant in dialogue, together with the formula of the proverb contest, once established, became literary "ideas" and models apt for adaptation and representation in other media such as the graphic arts. Marcolphus's repertoire of proverbs, tricks and riddles, in particular, must also have been appropriated by writers in different burgeoning national vernacular literatures. Tracing those many channels of borrowing and influence would result in a book-length study of the character of Marcolphus as a pan-European cultural phenomenon. Moreover, determining just how the textual tradition under examination here made its contribution to that highly diversified phenomenon would pose difficult challenges. The degree to which borrowers might draw upon the structural matrix while substituting local matter serving to disguise their debts is but one dimension of the problem. Nevertheless the impression remains that the Latin *Solomon and Marcolphus* was seminal to all that was subsequently developed in the name of Marcolphus. Among those formal ideas described in the first part of this introduction that made themselves available for imitation and exploitation were Marcolphus the rustic proverb maker, Marcolphus the maker and solver of riddles, and Marcolphus the enacter of tricks which in turn form a plot and a trickster biography. Here was a comic prototype waiting for variant representations as knave, comic debater, or court fool. Some of these developments will be outlined briefly in the final sections of the introduction; a sense of their scope is important to an appreciation of the place of *Solomon and Marcolphus* in later centuries in the context of the parallel traditions for which our text was the presumed prototype, or at least the source of procedures and character types. Before turning to that survey, however, there are four allusions, taken by many scholars for early references directly to *Solomon and Marcolphus*, that deserve evaluation. These references are, in effect, the only markers of the passage of our text from its earliest manuscript phases down to its appearance in typeset form in the last quarter of the fifteenth century. Apart from them, nearly everything that we must suppose about its evolution, the addition of the second part, and the place this work enjoyed among medieval readers, must be deduced through an examination of the text itself or from the very fact of its survival.

Four Ambiguous Early Allusions

The four following references are included for discussion here because, beginning with the nineteenth-century scholars interested in *Solomon and Marcolphus*, they have been repeatedly listed as a testimony of its passage through Europe during the twelfth and thirteenth centuries. Duff and Benary invoke them, for example, in the introductions to their respective editions. They were led to believe that all of the four allusions to the protagonists can only refer to the text edited here, whereas I am convinced that the first three refer to a much older tradition in which Marcolphus was still one of the *shedim* attempting to conquer Solomon in a contest of riddles.

The Provençal poet Raimbout d'Auvergne (or d'Orange), active between 1150 and 1173, sought to compliment the wisdom of his mistress by stating that it surpassed the wisdom of both Solomon and Marcolphus.[69] What forms hyperbole will take! The sense of the poem, however, is that these men were equals, and that the one was as wise as the other, which would preclude reference to the Marcolphus we know. Moreover, it would have been poetically indelicate to have compared a mistress for any reason at all with the misshapen peasant who utters foul proverbs.

A second reference from the same period may help to clarify the first. William, Bishop of Tyre, in his *Historia rerum in partibus transmirinis gestarum* (Bk. XIII, ch. 1), written between 1181 and 1184, comes to a discussion of the *Jewish Antiquities* of Josephus; in the context of that discussion he mentions Hiram, King of Tyre, who had exchanged riddles with Solomon, and in the course of that exchange had employed Abdemon to help

---

[69] Raimbout's name is variously spelled: one such is Rambout d'Arenga. For materials and texts see K.A.F. Mahn, *Gedichte der Troubadours in provenzalischer sprache*, Vol. II, p. 219. Raimbout claimed that his mistress was wiser than "Salemos ni Marcols" and later "Salomon sage e com Marcun." The spellings are of potential significance.

him. William states, "this [Abdemon] is perhaps the same person called Marcolf in the vulgar, about whom there are amazing stories of solving Solomon's riddles, and in his turn offering riddles of his own to be solved."[70] Clearly this reference is not to our text, but to another tradition in which Marcolf had taken over the role of Abdemon as an extraordinary maker and solver of riddles. Yet the reference is valuable to us in several ways: it links Marcolphus to a former tradition with Talmudic and supernatural overtones; it suggests the survival into the medieval period of a work that may have raised the objections of Gelasius and Notker; it confirms the early association between Marcolphus and riddle making, and for the part they come to play not only in the jest section of our text, but in the representations of Marcolphus in medieval art.

A bit of marginalia in the *Apology* of Guido de Bazoches, written before 1203, is but further confirmation of the persistence of the riddle match between equals associated with Solomon and Marcolphus, but with a new dimension added. Guido tells a version of the cat and the candle story by which Marcolphus, in the second part of our text, proves to the king that nature is stronger than nurture. Guido makes no mention of Marcolphus in the text, and thus the reference by itself does not prove that the second part of *Solomon and Marcolphus* was already compiled by that date. Someone annotating the text at an indeterminable moment simply states in the margin: "de Salomone rege et Abdemone Tyrio, qui Marculphus vulgariter appellatur."[71] Two or three conclusions can be drawn: that the story of the cat and the candle was known to the annotator as part of the Solomon and Abdemon tradition; that it was from this tradition that it was borrowed by the authors of the second part of our text; that whatever Abdemon was to this earlier tradition was taken over by Marcolphus because he was essentially the same person in the vernacular traditions; that by the time of the annotations the second part of our text was known; and that a recognition of the same story in the two works provoked the comment in

---

[70]William of Tyre, *Historia rerum in partibus transmirinis gestarum in Recueil des Historiens des Croisades*, vol. I, pt. 1, p. 557.

[71]Robert J. Menner, *The Poetical Dialogues of Solomon and Saturn*, p. 29.

the margin. In short, Guido is not referring to our text, but the marginalia may be, and in a way linking it to the older version featuring Abdemon.

A fourth allusion appears early in the thirteenth century in the works of the Swabian poet Freidank. He says, simply, "Salmon wîsheit lêrte, Marolt daz verkêrte," that Salmon taught wisdom, but that Marolt perverted it.[72]   In effect, as textual critics, we are where we were two centuries earlier with the complaint of Notker. "Verkêhren" meant then, as it does now, to invert or turn upside down, but also to transform or pervert. This may carry the sense of deformation through parody, and thus to pervert wisdom by perverting forms in which such wisdom is conveyed. But there is little to preclude the possibility that he is talking about related traditions in which Marcolphus fills Abdemon's role, or argues with Solomon the Christian polemicist, or perverts the biblical proverbs, given that Marcolphus's performance in our textual tradition hardly suggests that his primary function is the perversion of wisdom. Thus it must be concluded that while these several allusions from early witnesses pertain to Solomon and Marcolphus in "dialogue," there is little about them assuring us that they refer specifically to the comic Latin text under study here. Yet if they do not, they are in reference to a parallel textual tradition of which no traces are known to survive.

Sources and Analogues of Marcolphus's Jests

A history of the origins of *Solomon and Marcolphus* is really two histories, for the second part containing the twelve jests was initially a separate work that, sometime before 1300, was attached to the first part. The date is an approximate one, however, based only on the fact that the first translation of *Solomon and Marcolphus* into German dates to that era, and that it contained the two parts. Much has been made already of the necessary steps whereby the collecting of jests might be turned into a trickster cycle, and a trickster "biography." The historian, for lack of direct evidence, must attempt to fit the phases of development and the use of materials into a general time frame largely by coordinating them with parallel literary developments. A sense

---

[72]*Friedankes Bescheidenheit*, ed. H.-E. Bezzenberger, p. 81, ll. 3–6.

of those levels of development can also be intuited from such elements as the alignment of Marcolphus with Abdemon in the references cited above, the depiction of Marcolphus in various iconographical contexts, the arrival in the West of the materials of the Solomonic epic in which his brother Morcolf had a role, and in the borrowing of Marcolphus's tricks by contemporary jestbook writers. For example, the second half of the thirteenth century produced the first iconographical representations of Marcolphus as a trickster; the first of these to co-ordinate with episodes in our text date to the early fourteenth century. Clearly the depiction of Marcolphus the trickster and riddle solver was by then well established and much in vogue, and it is difficult to imagine that *Solomon and Marcolphus* did not make a contribution to the phenomenon. Finally, the German trickster cycles such as *Tyl Eulenspiegel* had their origins around the mid-fourteenth century, and there is evidence that the Tyl redactor knew the *Solomon and Marcolphus* material, and that he was willing to borrow.[73] Just how much these new cycles were informed by the structural ideas pioneered in our textual tradition is open to speculation, but my belief is that by this time our text had achieved its complete design and thereafter became highly influential. When all these kinds of indirect evidence are assembled, it would seem that the riddle tradition featuring a potentially god-like, sage, or demonic Marcolphus evolved into a popular jest cycle during a period when such materials were being collected generally, and before the national trickster figures emerged as cycle protagonists, perhaps just before the iconographical representations of Marcolphus came into vogue. That would push the date for the first experimental assembly of a trickster jest cycle back to 1250; it may have been earlier.

---

[73]These two works appear to make contact only in episode No. 57 of the Tyl cycle where Tyl is caught for theft and threatened with hanging. He, like Marcolphus, accepts the punishment with provisions for one final wish—which is solemnly granted, provided he ask neither for money nor escape, but only for some good after his death. Tyl then requests that all who contributed to his hanging be obliged to kiss his bare arse before dining. Unwilling to meet this condition, the officials release him.

The scribes who first assembled the second part were, in the first instance, collectors, for all of the jests, or at least their defining motifs, are known from earlier sources. Their practice was to create through appropriation and adaptation; that was a basic literary procedure. Indeed, early readers may have enjoyed a dimension largely lost to us, namely of reading with knowledge of the sources from which the jests were taken.

Two examples will serve to illustrate the typical relationships between episodes as they appear in *Solomon and Marcolphus* and in contemporary collections. The *Gesta Romanorum*, according to the best conjectures, was assembled around 1300.[74] It is not a jest cycle featuring a central protagonist, but a collection of anecdotes purporting to be of Mediterranean provenance, many of them deriving from the work of the ancient Romans. In this compendium are to be found versions of the two anti-feminist episodes: Fudasa's revelation of a sworn secret, and the provocation of the women with the lie about permitting men to have seven wives. The differences between them are an assurance that neither work was an immediate source for the other, but the representation of identical motifs is equal assurance that they belong to a common source.

Paralleling the Fudasa episode, *Gesta Romanorum* (No. CXXIV) offers the story of a knight in disgrace who is told by the king that his reinstatement may be earned only if he can demonstrate the nature of true friendship, true happiness, and true enemies. The knight solves the riddle much as Marcolphus did, by creating circumstances in which his wife would betray him, thereby revealing that a man's wife can be his worst enemy. When a pilgrim arrives at the knight's castle seeking lodging, the knight and his wife plot to kill him for his money. Secretly, however, the pilgrim is told to flee, while in his place the knight kills a calf, hides its parts in a sack in the stable, and then shows a sum of money to his wife. On the day of reckoning at court, the knight presents himself with his dog, his baby, and his wife, and, through their unwitting collaboration in a prepared scenario, he regains the king's approbation. First he wounds the dog, trusting that the creature would nevertheless come back to him, then he presents his child as a prattler and jester who brings true pleasure and happiness. Finally, he strikes his wife a blow on the cheek for allegedly looking lasciviously upon the king. In revenge she reveals the homicide. The calf parts are exhumed, the ruse is exposed, the wife is maligned, and the knight is reinstated for his cleverness and wisdom. Here is another enacted riddle solution converted into anti-feminist trickery. But the number of substitutions necessary to link the two versions to a common source surpasses the imagination.

The second anti-feminist story also has a parallel in *Gesta Romanorum* (No. CXXVI), this one having a rich pedigree in classical sources. Marcolphus demonstrates the inflammable nature of women by tricking them into storming Solomon's palace in protest. In the *Gesta*, a boy attends the Roman Senate with his father and hears its secrets. His mother, driven by curiosity, not only cajoles but even beats the boy in order to make him reveal what he has heard. To pacify her, he concocts a story about how the Senate debated whether it was better for a man to have many wives, or for a wife to have many husbands. This news is immediately spread among the women, a march on the Senate ensues, the boy's ruse is revealed, and his perspicacity commended. A brief consultation of H. Oesterley's list of analogues reveals half a page of them. They include the version in the *Saturnalias* of Macrobius, I.6, taken in turn from the *Attic Nights of Aulus Gellius*, I.23, and a section in Marcus Cato's speech against Galba.[75] The story was told by Johann Enenkel as one of the events of the

---

[75]Hermann Oesterley, ed., pp. 732–33; Aulus Gellius, *Attic Nights*, vol. I, xxiii, pp. 105–09. On stories about keeping secrets from women see also Luigi Biagioni, *Marcolf und Bertoldo und ihre Beziehungen*, p. 59. The *Gesta* itself, though composed early in the fourteenth century, is known to us only from versions produced late in the fifteenth century. The 181 stories that constitute the vulgate can be traced back only to the Cologne editions printed by Ulrich Zell in 1475. The 1473 edition by Ketelaer and De Leempt of Utrecht contains only 150; that by Arnold Ter Hoener of Cologne offers 151. Because several of the stories appear to have been taken from the *Moralities* of Robert Holkot, who died in 1349, one may conclude that the *Gesta* was still evolving as a collection at mid-century and may have remained in a transitional state until well

reign of Domitian (81–96 AD) in his thirteenth-century *Chronicle*. These analogues merely prove a common interest in the material; for actual sources we are no closer than when we began, thereby allowing us to posit either a significant number of intermediary sources, or a considerable degree of adaptation on the part of a single author.

Similar problems arise with the search for sources of the other ten jests. Analogues are common. Many of them are of eastern origin and may have been transmitted to the West as Solomonic lore, perhaps as parts of the riddle books hypothetically described above. In the case of the riddle responses concerning the activities of Marcolphus's father, mother, sister, and brother, Biagioni not only found a parallel in the editions of *Tyl Eulenspiegel*, but also in stories from Morocco, Tangiers, Bengal, and Kashmir.[76] One parent goes to separate earth from earth, while the other goes to join earth to earth: one goes to help with a birth, the other with a burial. In all cases we are dealing with a question-and-answer sequence of ancient origin. It is related to the motif of the clever peasant girl who wins a royal marriage by proposing and explaining these cryptic sayings. A close parallel may be found in the tales of Imriolkais ben Hodja (Hodschr) el Kindi, an early Arabic poet.[77] A slave, laden with gifts, is sent in search of a bride, asks the leading questions to a young girl about her family, and receives enigmatic answers which he reports to his master; in this way the girl wins courtly favor. The magician Merlin was known to have employed this routine as well.[78] Much later Frederick II of Prussia is alleged to have asked such questions of a twelve-year-old peasant boy and to have received the well-worn replies.[79]

---

into the fifteenth century. In effect, then, because our own text grew in precisely the same way, at the same time, we have the challenge of comparing two early texts, in terms of their origins, only through late versions.

[76] Luigi Biagioni, *Marcolf und Bertoldo*, pp. 50–51.

[77] Biagioni, p. 51.

[78] Alfons Hilka, *Neue Beiträge zur Erzählungsliteratur des Mittelalters*, p. 8.

[79] Biagioni, p. 52.

Just as the *Gesta Romanorum* is important to our textual tradition as a source of comparative episodes, the co-existing Middle High German minstrel epic or *Spielmansepos* of *Solman und Morolf* is important, not only as a part of the general Solomonic culture in medieval Europe, but as a potential locus of comparative elements. At a rather late moment in the manuscript tradition of the Latin *Solomon and Marcolphus* there appears to have been an attempt at a *rapprochement* of the dialogue and the epic, either by making them into a narrative sequence, the former an introit into the latter, or by borrowing episodes from the epic to fill out the jest cycle.[80]

As stated earlier, versions of this epic circulated throughout Europe in several vernaculars. In fourteenth-century Portugal it was known as *Livro velho de linhagens* and in France as *Li Bastars de Buillon*. The German redaction was a poem of 4210 lines composed in a unique five-line stanza. Like the Latin *Solomon and Marcolphus* it existed for some three centuries before the time of the first surviving texts. It was first published in printed form in Strasbourg by Matthias Hupfaff in 1499, and bears the title, *Dis buch seit von Kunig Salomon und siner huxzfrowen Salome wie sy der Kunig fore nam und wie sy Morolf Kunig Salomon bruder wider brocht* (This book tells of King Salomon and how Salome, his wife, forsook him for King Fore, and how Morolf, Salomon's brother, brought her back). In this saga, Salome escapes with her lover after feigning death during four days through the use of a magic root. Morolf was all along convinced that her death was a ruse and attempted unsuccessfully to wake her by burning her hand. After her burial and escape, Morolf disguised himself as a peddler and travelled the land until he found her. The sign was the scar on her hand, revealed as she was buying gloves from him. The king, informed of this, disguised himself as a pilgrim in order to gain entry into his rival's castle. Morolf took soldiers and lay in ambush in a nearby forest. The queen recognized Salomon through the disguise and betrayed him to King Fore, who then asked Salomon what he would do were their places exchanged. Salomon, in a sportive vein, answered that he would allow the

---

[80]Walter Schaumberg, *Untersuchungen über das deutsche Spruchgedicht Salomo und Morolf*, pp. 3–8.

captive to choose the tree on which he wished to be hanged. Fore agrees and allows the king to set the matter in motion. This is not an occasion for wandering endlessly without choosing a tree, but for making the three blasts on his trumpet that would signal Morolf to attack. The epic concludes with Fore's death by hanging and Salome's by bleeding.[81]

Morolf plays the trickster in his search for Salome, and this role is even more pronounced in earlier versions of the epic. A Russian version is known in which Solomon's brother, there called Kitovras, reveals characteristics that relate him to a wily supernatural predecessor. Morolf the brother may have his origins in the same Markolis who was Solomon's ancient opponent. Other motifs may be identified in passing: the trumpet blast of Roland, the sleeping potion of Juliet, and the escape ruse of choosing the tree. This last motif was itself a substitution within the epic tradition for other closing mechanisms, but it was likely through the medium of this epic that it came to serve as the closing device of the second part of *Solomon and Marcolphus*. Many of them are ancient motifs; the story of Somadera or the sleeping lady who feigns death through the use of a potion goes back to the *Panchatantra*. The epic is also connected with the Arabic tales of the stolen bride and the exploits necessary to bring her back. These were used to reshape the ancient story of the wandering Solomon. It is thought that the German version of the epic had its origins during the closing years of the twelfth century, thereby offering itself as another potential source insofar as the idea of the trickster Marcolphus may have been wholly or in part inspired by the epic figure of Morolf.

If the Latin *Solomon and Marcolphus* was paralleled by a vernacular epic from as early as 1200, it was paralleled by itself from about 1300 in the form of a vernacular translation entitled the *Spruchgedicht Salomo und Morolf*. This was the leading translation among several to follow.[82] This translation marks a new career for the text as a *Volksbuch* outside the Latin schools, a form that

---

[81]Gordon Duff, ed., *The Dialogue . . . Between . . . Salomon and Marcolphus*, p. xvii.

[82]During the era of early printed books this work went through many printings in several centers. The most attractive of these editions was

may have been more open to the incorporation of new jest material. It is even conceivable that the cycle continued to grow in the vernacular, and that certain episodes were afterwards translated into Latin. The hanging tree ruse may have found its way into the cycle through the *Spruchgedicht* because in certain of the vernacular manuscripts this episode is made the means for Morolf's return to court, whereupon the king, admitting defeat, decides to heap honor and riches upon Morolf and his wife. In some of these versions the scribe attaches an abbreviated version of the entire epic to the end of the jest cycle.[83] Morolf, the one-time peasant trickster, goes on to serve the king in precisely the same way that Salomon's brother does in the *Spielmansepos*. This creation of a continuous narrative out of two works lacking a common ethos but sharing the two central characters illustrates a dimension of medieval literary thinking. Not only were episodes transferable, but whole works could be joined together with only a minimum of accommodation.

The prose *Volksbuch* became, in turn, the source of at least two further versions in the vernacular, both of them in verse. The first was by an anonymous author, the second was by Gregor Hayden, written for the Count Palatine Friedrich von Leuchtenberg, who died in 1487.[84] A third version entitled *Frag und antwortt Salomonis und Marcolfii* was published in Nuremberg by N. Ayrer around 1482; this work appears to be a new prose translation from the Latin. Only the first third of a single copy survives, but it is important as the only vestige of the work used by Hans Folz in writing his Shrovetide play, the text of which is translated in an appendix to this book. This brings us to the fifteenth century

---

published in Strasbourg in 1499 by Christian Müller, for it was accompanied by 47 woodcuts, 8 of which are reproduced in the present edition.

[83] The linking of the two traditions may be seen in the Cracow University Library, MS. 554, which features a version of the epic with numerous variations of its own attached to our text. In this collection Marcolphus is called Marchlandus and Solomon's wife is called the Queen of Ethiopia. It is a free reworking of the epic in Latin. See Walter Benary, ed., *Salomon et Marcolfus*, p. xxiii.

[84] Gregor Hayden's poem was edited by Felix Bobertag in the *Narrenbuch*, as well as by Friedrich von der Hagen in 1811.

and the earliest period from which copies survive of *Solomon and Marcolphus*.

Manuscripts and Early Printed Editions

Most, but not all, of the surviving manuscripts contain the two parts of the text. Munich Codex Lat. 5015, originating in the Benediktbeuern Monastery and bearing the date 1443, contains only the first part and bears the title *Conflicta verborum inter regem Salomonem et rusticum Marcolfum facta*. Did the scribe fail to complete his work, or was the copy perhaps made from an early original lacking the second part? Because the section also lacks the physical description of Marcolphus, and makes no mention of Polycana his wife, it would seem that it came from a source created before the second part was added. By contrast, another manuscript, Munich Codex germ. 3974, contains both parts, yet lacks these same descriptive passages in the first part.[85] These variations are reminders that the surviving copies reflect many divergent channels of copy and diffusion.

The number of late fourteenth- and fifteenth-century manuscripts of this work still in existence early in the twentieth century appears to have been about sixty — a substantial number. These were located and described by a diligent group of philologists seeking to establish the history of this textual tradition as an important segment of the Latin medieval heritage. Given the havoc which time and two intervening European wars may well have played with this fund of documents, we can be grateful for their efforts. These works were located for the most part in libraries in southern and eastern Germany, Austria, and Poland. Emmanuel Cosquin set out to examine as many manuscripts of the work as possible, and left accounts, together with those of Johannes Bolte, Reinhold Koehler, M.P.A. Becker, and Ernest Schaubach, who wrote a doctoral dissertation on this material for the University of Leipzig in 1881.[86] Walter Benary, in the intro-

---

[85]Full bibliographical descriptions of twenty-four of the approximately sixty surviving manuscripts of *Solomon and Marcolphus* were compiled by Walter Benary, ed., pp. xiii–xxv.

[86]Emmanuel Cosquin, "Le Conte du Chat et de la Chandelle," pp. 377–80.

duction to an edition of one of the Latin manuscripts, provided a stemma based on his careful reading of previous investigators and on his examination of some twenty-four of the total number. Benary's purpose was twofold: to establish the variations among the surviving manuscripts in an effort to determine their order of filiation, and to find the most complete and uncorrupted manuscript available to serve as the copy text for a critical edition. His findings produced a tri-partite stemma in which the German manuscripts formed one group, and the Latin manuscripts two further groups going back to a conjectural common source. Manuscripts in the two Latin groups differed from one another both in matters of style and in the number of proverbs they included in the first part. Benary noted that in the manuscripts belonging to the group designated "X" the second part begins with the words, "Igitur rex Salomon quodam die cum venatoribus suis . . . " whereas the same passage in his group "Z" begins, "Rex igitur quondam . . . "[87] This scheme has received general approbation; no more recent scholar has sought to challenge or verify his work through a more extensive examination of the original documents. Benary's work, in any case, appears careful and thorough and for that reason has inspired no objectors. The entire matter of the relationships between these manuscripts has little bearing on an edition of the English text except to reveal something of the process by which Benary established his ideal text. It is worthy of note that his choice comes from his group "X" whereas the English text was derived from a source in group "Z." Benary's edition, thus, serves as a control text for determining the degree of corruption that has crept into the Latin source used by the English translator. These comparisons have occasioned several explanatory notes in the annotations following the text.

Benary's edition is based on a handsome copy in the Würzburg University Library. It was produced in 1434, and prior to 1497 it was in the Neumünster Monastery in Würzburg.[88] It has the particular virtue of containing 142 proverb pairs, making it the most complete of all the surviving copies. That this number dwindles

---

[87]Walter Benary, ed., *Salemon et Marcolfus*, p. xxix.

[88]Walter Benary, ed., p. xv.

to 91 in the Latin edition published by Leeu suggests a degree of diminution and impoverishment of the textual tradition in the "Z" group. Of these 91 survivors, several have suffered corruption in the process of transmission. The Würzburg text is thus of much value in making corrections in the notes. At the same time, some of the variations are not the result of error, but of alternate readings.

In situating Leeu's Latin edition in the schema, one sees that it belongs to a group of editions produced in the Low Countries by such printers as Richard Paffroet, and that all of these have as their closest relative the early printed editions produced in Leipzig. This has been determined by the similarities these books reveal in terms of the numbers and correspondences of the proverbs. If we turn to the manuscripts in order to establish a potential source for the Leipzig editions we are on more speculative grounds. In looking at all of the manuscripts described by Benary, we note that the one he designated "Q" is also "missing" fifty-one proverbs, of which fifty are in common with the fifty-one that differentiate our English translation from the Würzburg manuscript. Before 1914 this manuscript was in the Royal Library in Berlin, bound together with plays by Terence, the *Facetiae* of Poggio and other fragments of comic material, and dates to the second half of the fifteenth century. Possibly this, or a closely related copy, served the Leipzig printers, thus forming the link between the English *Solomon and Marcolphus* and the manuscript tradition.

In addition to the early manuscripts there were a great many printed editions, again testifying to the enduring popularity of this work even in Latin during the last quarter of the fifteenth century. The earliest of these appears to have been printed in Cologne in 1473. This edition is characterized (as are those that followed) by the title *Dyalogus Salomonis et Marcolphi*. The later Dutch printings, including those by Leeu, belong to a second group, distinguished by the title *Collationes quas dicuntur fecisse mutuo rex Salomon . . . et Marcolphus*. To this group belong the editions by Konrad Kacheloffen in Leipzig, and those by Paffroet in Deventer, Holland. The Latin editions of Paffroet and Leeu feature a woodcut of the ancient Greek fabulist Aesop, depicted as a squat, rude-looking slave figure; this portrait was no doubt borrowed in order to represent the peasant Marcolphus. These are only a few of the twenty-three incunabula editions identified by Gordon Duff: others include Nürnberg, 1482; Augsburg, 1490 and 1493; Venice, 1492; three by Paffroet; six by Jacobus de Breda; one by Leeu in Antwerp; and a second in Antwerp by Felix Baligault. Still more followed after the turn of the century in Venice in 1502; in Cologne in 1510; in Landeshut in 1514; and again in Paris in 1515.[89] The Latin text was in its prime, it would seem, for in the fourteen years between 1488 and 1500 Jacobus de Breda and Richard Paffroet printed no less than eight editions in their corner of Europe.

Caxton, it will be recalled, specialized in titles with a potential for popular appeal: readable histories, tales, and romances, rather than theological treatises, editions of the classics, or of the church fathers. Gerard Leeu appears to have followed his example. In 1492–1493 he produced four books in English: *The History of Jason*, *The History of Knight Paris and the Fair Vienne*, *The Dialogue of Solomon and Marcolphus*, and *The Chronicles of England*. All but the *Dialogue* were reprints of former Caxton editions. So close an affiliation with Caxton titles led Gordon Duff to posit that *Solomon and Marcolphus* was conceivably yet another Caxton translation.[90] There are difficulties, however, for Caxton left Antwerp in 1476, a date too early for him to have had at his disposal a version of the printed Latin text corresponding to the English version. It is true that Kacheloffen, the Leipzig printer, did not date any of his editions, but they could not have appeared earlier than 1476. The English translation coincides too well with Leeu's Latin edition to have been the work of Caxton some eighteen to twenty years earlier.[91]

---

[89] Gordon Duff, ed., *The Dialogue . . . Between . . . Salomon and Marcolphus*, pp. 34–46.

[90] Gordon Duff, ed., p. xxiii.

[91] Leeu was, himself, one of the more important printers of his age. He began his career in Gouda in 1477 and left for Antwerp in 1484. His death in 1493 came about not long after the production of the English *Solomon and Marcolphus* as the result of a quarrel with his typesetter, Henric van Symmen. As the story goes, Henric dealt him a fatal blow on the head following an argument over wages. In *The Chronicle of*

For the fifteenth-century printers, *Solomon and Marcolphus* provided an opportunity for adding woodcut illustrations and engravings, several of which are reproduced in this edition. In the English edition Leeu replaced the borrowed illustration of Aesop used in his Latin edition with a new woodcut apparently created specifically for this new translation. Solomon raises a finger in debate as Marcolphus stands before him, pitchfork in hand, seconded by his wife with her walking stick. His heavy face, rude clothes, and broken shoes create the image of the peasant rather than of the grotesque. This woodcut eventually made its way to England where William Copland made use of it to illustrate his edition of *Howleglas*. The figure of Solomon is entirely out of place, not to mention Polycana, and Tyl was never described as a rude peasant. But perhaps an association between them as tricksters was pretext enough. It was by a similar degree of license that Aesop, the trickster of Thrace, was pressed into service as a likeness of Marcolphus.[92] This completes the synopsis of historical and philological evidence relating to the origins and development of the *Solomon and Marcolphus* textual tradition. There remains but a survey of the parallel manifestations of Marcolphus — with or without Solomon — in European culture that may have some bearing on the understanding of this work.

Representations of Solomon and Marcolphus in Medieval Europe

Rustic Proverbs in France

A glance at the French folk proverb tradition will reveal just how fashionable the form remained in the twelfth century and after. Taking up the narrative where we left off with Egbert and his opponents, we discover that even though the works of Otloh, Wipo,

---

England, his final book, one finds a touching colophon: "Emprentyd by maistir Gerard de Leew, a man of grete wysedom in all maner of kunnyng; which nowe is come from lyfe unto deth, whiche is grete harme for many a poure man. On whos sowle god almyghty for hys hygh grace have mercy. Amen." Gordon Duff, ed., p. xxiv.

[92]Herodotus, [History of Greece], Bk. II, ch. 134, vol. I, p. 437.

and Arnulf carried implicit or explicit protests against the rustic proverb, Egbert was not without his followers. The most important was Serlo of Wilton, an Anglo-Norman who studied in Paris, taught at Oxford, and died in a Cistercian monastery near Blois in 1181.[93] In his collection of some one hundred French proverbs with their several different Latin translations, Serlo established his debt to Egbert by presenting several proverbs in the same order that they are to be found in the *Fecunda ratis*. Moreover, the multiple translations clearly reveal his pedagogical intent; his was an exercise book in turning French proverbs into good Latin. R.N.B. Goddard thinks that the *Proverbia rusticorum*, from the early thirteenth century, and *Li proverbe au vilain*, dating to the period from 1179 to 1191, were created for the same purpose, namely to teach Latin composition and versification.[94]

Li proverbe au vilain has been associated with Nureddin, and the *Proverbia rusticorum* has been traced to the region of St. Omer. The former is possibly the work of Philip, Count of Flanders. There is a thirteenth-century manuscript in the Bodleian Library, Oxford that contains a work entitled *Li proverbe que dit li vilains*, which was compiled from sources in some way related to Li proverbe au vilain.[95] The differences between these two survivors of an earlier original indicate the probable loss of a number of interim versions. Both show that low-life protest against high culture in proverb form was an idea well established in the medieval world by the end of the twelfth century. Goddard points to passages in Marcabru (active from 1125 to 1150), Philippe de Thaün's *Computus* (ca. 1119), Cercamon (active from 1137 to 1148), Girart de Roussillon (ca. 1150), and Wace's *Brut* (ca. 1155) in which rustic proverbs are employed as an affront to the manners of the nobility, or as an attack upon the pretenses and illusoriness of chivalric culture.[96] This dichotomization of society is customary in the collections to follow in which Solomon and Marcolphus appear as representatives of the two estates.

---

[93] R.N.B. Goddard, "Marcabru, *Li Proverbe au Vilain*, and the Tradition of Rustic Proverbs," p. 65.

[94] R.N.B. Goddard, p. 65.

[95] Bodleian Library, Oxford, Rawl. c. 641.

[96] R.N.B. Goddard, p. 64.

One of the earliest to be written was the poem entitled *Ci com-mence de Marcoul et de Salemon que li quens de Bretagne fist* (Here begins [the proverbs] of Marcoul and Salemon, written by the Count of Brittany); the count was Pierre Mauclerc, who died in 1250, and the poem likely dates to the period from 1216 to 1220.[97] Admittedly these little gnomic verses are remote in spirit from the *Solomon and Marcolphus* tradition, but they are a testimonial to the diversity of literary expression featuring these two person-ages which had been attained by 1225. In the fifty-nine stanzas of six lines each that make up the poem there is a debate between high culture and low in which Salemon speaks for the values of courtly love and chivalry while Marcoul speaks for the laboring poor. Neither speaker is characterized in detail, and there is no acrimony in their exchange. At one point Salemon says, "poor suffering men are often covetous," to which Marcoul replies, "they aren't too ashamed; they learn this from their betters." Salemon is not a pompous lord, and Marcoul is not a crafty "vil-lain." They merely speak in statement-counterstatement fashion, moving from topic to topic.

En cortoisie a paine
Mais bien fait qui la meine,
      Ce dit Salemons;
Mois et jor et semaine,
Travail est dure paine,
      Marcoul li respont.

There is suffering in following courtesy,
But whoever leads this life does well,
      This Salemon says.

---

[97]G.H. Crapelet, ed., *Proverbes et dictons populaires*. The "Marcoul et de Salemon que li quens de Bretaigne fist" contains 35 proverbs and counter-proverbs, the latter characterized by their obscurity and low humor. Marcoul is Solomon's fool-like companion. The fourteenth-century manuscript version begins:

Ci commence de Salemon
et de Marcol son campaignon
si orrez la desputoison
quentrax font par quel occoison.

Month and day and week
Labor brings great suffering,
    Marcoul to him replies.   [my translation]

This poem participated in a formula that would remain current throughout the following two centuries, and that would have its imitators in England. This group, in effect, forms a parallel tradition of Solomon and Marcolf poems in the vernacular dealing with class distinctions and the misunderstandings that separated them. There is an indication that the French poets took the oppositional pairing from the Latin tradition and used it for their own social purposes.

A second French poem, written before the third quarter of the thirteenth century, entitled *De Marco et de Salemons*, juxtaposes the boring proverbs and commonplaces of the latter with Marco's observations on the ways of prostitutes.[98] former poem. Mauclerc's verse form, aa, "Ce dit Salemons," aa, "Marcoul li respont" is echoed here in an aab refrain, ccb refrain pattern. In this work we see the beginning of a tradition, for it is closely related to others from the period.[99] New uses were being found for these social

---

[98]"De Marco et de Salemons," in *Nouveau Recueil de Fabliaux et Contes Inédits des Poètes Français des XIIe, XIIIe, XIVe et XVe siècles*, Dominique-Martin Méon, ed., vol. I, pp. 416–36.

Chargiez a jument	Load a mare,
Ou plane, o argent	With feathers or with money,
Hei ne chault loquel,	She doesn't care which,
Ce dist Salemons.	Salemon offers.
Pute ne tient conte	A whore doesn't care
Qui sor son cul monte,	Who shows his ass.
Tuit li sont ignel	They are all the same to her,
Marcoul li respont.	Replies Marcoul. [my translation]

[99]For further information see Erika Schönbrunn-Kölb, "Markolf in den mittelalterlichen Salomondichtungen," pp. 94ff. Other poems inventoried in this tradition include "Veez cy une desputacoun entre Salomon ly saage, et Marcoulf le Foole," found in a fifteenth-century manuscript dating to the reign of Henry VI of England, in the British Library, London, "Les dictz de Salomon avecques les responces de Marcon fort joyeuses." These copies taken in conjunction with close parallels found in the Trinity College Library, Cambridge, suggest a degree of

opposites in medieval literature. By the year 1250 these characters were functioning in concurrent roles as different as the king
and brother in the troubadour epic, the nobleman and churl in the
French poems, the debating figures in ecclesiastical iconography,
in addition to the roles they play in our textual tradition.

Iconographical Representations

We are already familiar with Marcolphus in the role of proverb-
maker, trickster, and Solomon's crafty brother in the epic, but
when we consider the iconographical representations we must
add to the list, scholastic debater, megaphallic grotesque, and the
solver of traditional riddles. Many of these identifications have
only been made in recent years, in part due to the discovery of
the necessary clues in the literary record.

One of the earliest of these portrayals is found on the right
lateral portal of Chartres cathedral. Here one finds the balanced
columnar statues of King Solomon and the Queen of Sheba representing the historical encounter of biblical origins and a host
of binary associations signalling Christian and pagan wisdom in
confrontation. It is the figure forming the plinth under Solomon
that attracts our attention, for in the program of iconographical
associations, this can only be Marcolphus seated in the position
of the *spinario of* classical inspiration extracting a thorn from his
foot. Here is a complementary program of opposites. The boy
pulling the thorn is *rusticitas* to Solomon's *urbanitas* and may
carry overtones of the fool or jester to the wise king. According to Sarafin Moralejo Alvarez, the *spinario* motif was widely
imitated by twelfth- and thirteenth-century sculptors.[100]

Another even more revealing representation of Marcolphus in
association with Solomon and the Queen of Sheba appears just

---

popularity enjoyed by this French poetic genre in England, one that
forms a link with later representations of Marcolf as a court fool.

[100]Serafin Moralejo Alvarez, "Marcolfo, El Espinario, Priapo: Un Testimonio Iconografico Gallego," p. 337. The spinario with his large genitals
has a wide representation in Western art, and that the figure could be
identified with Marcolphus was but another way in which analogical
thinking produced new manifestations and transformations of artistic
and literary motifs.

to the south of the famous western pilgrimage route to Compostella on the porch door of the Cathedral of Orense in Galicia. According to Moralejo Alvarez it was the work of an artist in the circle of Master Mateo, sculpted shortly after 1200. Again the king and queen are in debate, here lifting their fingers according to the custom.[101] Just to the right of Solomon is a small grotesque with a large head and dwarfish body who likewise lifts his fingers in gestures of formal debate. He has been identified as Marcolphus, depicting both the debate tradition and the association with the megaphallic grotesque. It is a moot point whether these representations are more closely inspired by the demonic or Abdemon tradition, or by the comic rustic of our text and of the French proverbs, or if they are, in fact, a fusion of the two.

Marcolphus was also known in England, beginning with the record of a decorated room in the Westminster palace of Edward II called *camera Marculfi*. It was created around 1252 for Henry III and, presumably, offered scenes from the life of Marcolphus. But no clues remain as to what was actually depicted there.[102]

Within a few years, Marcolphus as an enactor of riddles made his debut in English manuscripts and registers, on choir stalls, and cathedral roof bosses. The first of these is found in the *Ormsby Psalter*, a work from the first quarter of the fourteenth century. It contains three illuminations based on the deeds of Marcolphus, all of them illustrating Psalm 52 concerning the ways and thoughts of the fool. Among them is a representation of him clad in a fishnet and riding on a goat. At the same time he holds one foot in the air while the other drops to the ground, and he raises his fingers in the position of the scholastic debate, yet again a conflation of two traditions. Solomon looks on from his palace window, in another illustration, as a servant seeks to contain two dogs on a leash — conceivably an allusion to the hare and the hounds episode whereby Marcolphus regains entry to the court.[103]

---

[101]Serafin Moralejo Alvarez, p. 331.

[102]E.W. Tristram, *English Medieval Wall Painting*, p. 575.

[103]I am indebted to the innovative article by Malcolm Jones, "Marcolf the Trickster in Late Medieval Art and Literature," for much of this

Marcolphus riding the goat makes reference to the much studied riddle motif known as the clever peasant girl. It has many variants and a long-standing European history.[104] It is based on a girl's solution to a royal decree "to appear before the king neither riding nor walking, neither on horseback nor on foot, neither naked nor clad, neither barefoot nor shod, neither on the road nor off the road, neither with nor without a gift."[105] The riddle is a form of bride-selection of a democratic kind often featured in fairy tales. The clever girl wins a royal husband by simply doing everything half way in order to do neither one thing nor the other. Malcolm Jones found this same motif carved on a Worcester Cathedral choir stall and in *A Register of Writs*, now in the Pierpont Morgan Library, featuring an image labelled "Marculf" in which a long-haired figure sits astride a goat wearing fishnet clothing.[106] The same motif reappears in the *Douai Psalter*, again accompanying Psalm 52. In the same work, Marcolphus is seen baring his posterior to the king; it is a reference to the baking oven episode introduced to illustrate Psalm 97:6 concerning the sounding of trumpets![107]

---

information about the iconographical representations of Marcolphus in England.

[104]See Jan de Vries, *Die Märchen von Klugen Rätsellösern*, passim. This motif can be found in Celtic and Romance language versions, in Germanic, Slavic, and Finno-Ugric accounts, not to mention Arabic, Asian, and African analogues, making it one of the most successful riddle-narratives ever composed.

[105]Malcolm Jones, "Marcolf the Trickster in Late Medieval Art and Literature," p. 150.

[106]Malcolm Jones, pp. 149–50.

[107]The same gesture appears in a Franco-Flemish *Book of Hours* (British Library, London, Add. MS. 36684) made ca. 1325 for Marguerite de Beaujeu. Jones also located Marcolphus clad in netting in the *Smithfield Decretals* (1330–1340, British Library, London, MS. Roy, 10 E IV), on a capital in the north choir aisle of York Minster (ca. 1395), and on misericords in Worcester, Beverley, and Norwich. That Marcolphus as a master of riddles was a popular subject for illustration is further confirmed by an inventory from 1364 of tapestries belonging to Louis I d'Anjou, and by an account of the wardrobe expenses of Edward III for

These few examples point to the widespread interest in Marcolphus in his divergent roles during the late Middle Ages. Always he is the trickster, the debater, riddle-solver, fool, or rural clown, and the materials that nourished these representations derive from a variety of sources going outside the traditions revealed in our text. Yet there are correspondences both in general type and in specific episodes, providing clues that *Solomon and Marcolphus* was in circulation and nourishing this general flowering of the character type — a type who had first been turned into a comic rustic within the tradition of our text, then given back to the general culture as a prototype of the trickster with his unique set of identifying characteristics.

Marcolphus in England

If Marcolphus was known in England iconographically, he was also known in early literary texts, albeit in minor roles. No English author actually succeeded in producing a major text around him, and hence his foothold in English literary culture remained slight. Cultural trade routes between England and France were active in the years before and after 1300, so that it should come as no surprise that the French *De Marco et de Salemons* in which Marco reports on the behavior of prostitutes found its way to England. It was surely this poem, or one similar in form and content, that served as a model for the deaf and blind poet Hendyng. According to R.M. Wilson, his proverbs were written in the Midland dialect toward the middle of the thirteenth century.[108] It was no doubt due to Marcolf's reputation as a proverbs maker that Hendyng styled himself as "Marcolves sone."[109] His primary interest was in English content — pithy sayings and folk proverbs — and in the French formulas such as the stanza and refrain patterns. One stanza will serve to illustrate his materials and methods.

1349 where there is listed a *dorsaria* or wall hanging featuring Marcolf. Malcolm Jones, p. 150.

[108] Richard Middleton Wilson, *Early Middle English Literature*, p. 190.

[109] British Library, London, MS. Harley 2253. See also Charles H. Herford, *Studies in the Literary Relations of England and Germany in the Sixteenth Century*, p. 265.

If you have bread and ale,
Don't put all of it away in your pouch,
     But share some of it around;
Be generous with your provisions,
Then when food is being handed around
     You will never go without.
It is better to give an apple than to eat it.
                              Quoth Hendyng.[110]

This is good honest English fare, less cynical and bawdy than the French source. The sense of dialogue is much diminished and the notion of a contest between voices has disappeared. French authors had accommodated the dialogue to a rigid stanza pattern, and it was this form that Hendyng had borrowed; the contents he supplied from his own store.

A century or more later, in the *Order of Fools*, Lydgate adapted to his own purposes the French figure of Marcoul.[111] His source is *Les Dicz de Salemon et Marcoul*, also known as the *Disputacion de Salemon le saage et Marcolfe le fiole* (a title with several variant spellings). Lydgate expanded upon a quality latent in Marcolphus, namely that of the court fool. John Audley of Haghman had also described Marcolphus in these terms.[112] But for Lydgate the moralist, the antics of his Marcoul and the tradition he represented were unacceptably scatological, immoral, and ultimately mad. This was one possible line of criticism that may have undermined his later reception in England. As Solomon's fool, his position at court is under royal protection, but for his madness he is made the founder of The Order of Fools. Lydgate surrounds him with a Christian moral order by making him, not a character of subversive license, but a sinner to be condemned as the instigator of all manner of vice. In passing from pagan debater, peasant wit, and court fool to the emblem of wicked-

---

[110]John Michell Kemble, *Anglo Saxon Dialogues of Solomon and Saturn*, p. 273.

[111]John Lydgate, "The Order of Fools," pp. 449ff. See Charles H. Herford, p. 269.

[112]Gordon Duff, ed., p. xviii.

ness, Marcolphus sheds all of his carnivalesque dimensions. The trickster outsider, if taken back into the Christian collective, can only become an allegorical "Sinner."

Once again the historical survey brings us to the end of the fifteenth century, the period during which the English translation of *Solomon and Marcolphus*, by the channels already accounted for, was placed on the English book market. Sometime between 1527 and 1529 the English printer Richard Pynson made another small contribution in the form of an edition of *The sayinges or proverbes of King Solomon with the answers of Marcolphus translated out of frenche into englysshe*.[113] This small quarto of only four leaves contains forty-six stanzas translated from a French collection of 1509 by Johan Divry called *Les Ditz de Salomon et de Marculphus, translatez du latin en francois avec les ditz des sept sages et d'autres philosophes de la grece*. This is a humble production. Divry himself says, presumably without false modesty, that the Latin was far better than his French version. It probably did little to encourage an ongoing interest in the general tradition.

The English preferred trickster heroes from their own traditions, such as Scoggin, whom Welsford nevertheless calls an English Marcolphus.[114] That Scoggin borrows the footprints in the snow episode leading to the hanging tree ruse suggests that the author had Leeu's edition before him. He also makes crafty use of the hare and the hounds device, and in the search for a tree to be hanged from, Scoggin leads the king's troops on a long chase.[115] This was probably the highest moment of Marcolphus's

---

[113]Imprinted at London in flete street by Richard Pynson, ca. 1527–29.

[114]Enid Welsford, *The Fool*, p. 42.

[115]Authorship is traditionally assigned to William Borde, active as a writer and physician late in the reign of Henry VIII and during the reign of Edward VI; he died in 1549. Borde's objective was to regroup disparate jests and traditional comic material around the memory of a famous historical jester. He chose a court fool of the preceding century mentioned in Holinshed's *Chronicles*. Scoggin was an Oxford student whose merry wit recommended him to Edward IV, whom he served as court jester in the 1480s (Holinshed, vol. I, p. 110). This account of Scoggin is corroborated by John Bale in his *Scriptorum illustrium majoris Britanniae catalogue*. Borde's book is first mentioned in the Stationer's

career in England. He was to make a brief return in Birck's Latin play *Sapientia Solomonis*, performed in the presence of Queen Elizabeth in 1575–1576 by the boys of Westminster.[116]

Register in 1565–1566 in an entry by Thomas Colwell. He was the successor to Robert Wyer, who had published other books by Borde. He was probably the first publisher of Scoggin sometime in the 1540s. The first surviving copy of this work dates only to 1626, presumably because all former copies had been literally read to pieces. Some of the jests of Marcolphus lived on in Scoggin.

[116]R.H. Goldsmith, *Wise Fools in Shakespeare*, pp. 28ff.

Editorial Procedures

This edition has been prepared from the photographic facsimile made by the photographers of the Clarendon Press in 1892 for the edition of E. Gordon Duff. The remarkable clarity of that reproduction has obviated the need to expose the sole surviving copy of the original to further manipulation. That facsimile, reproduced here, is of interest insofar as Leeu had a new typeface specially cut for his English books, with a few unique characteristics such as the flourishes on the letter "d" when appearing at the ends of words, making it look like an "o" with a bow on top. There are compositor habits to be observed as well, and a few eccentricities such as the substitution of "y" for "g" and "u" for "n" appearing so often as to be doubted that it was done in error, and some entertaining errors such as "be heggyd" for "he beggyd." These anomalies and errors have been addressed in the list following the text entitled "Analysis of the Vocabulary of the 1492 English Text." Given that there are no variant editions to consult, meanings must be gleaned from this text alone through an examination of contexts and conventions and, to be sure, through the consultation of such works as *The Oxford English Dictionary*. Such strangers as "nevyrhtelesse" and "retonruyd" can easily be reduced to "nevertheless" and "returned," and only a few words do not find representation in the dictionary, such as "tapettys" and "kyndrebede," the former by context having to do with tapits (carpets) or tapestries, and the latter with either kindred or childbed. Not a great deal hangs on these words in any case.

Such presumed errors as "chamigyd" for "changed" (elsewhere spelled "chungyd") and "shalve" with its broken "b" meaning "shall be," as well as compressed words such as "pmysed" for "promised," or "shephde" for "shepherd" were not difficult to resolve. This list serves a double purpose, however, for the interpretations of words not only clarify the original text, but they serve as part of a new base text from which the modernized version has been drawn.

That modernization entails the regularization of the spelling of words that have modern equivalents, and the glossing of words that have no modern equivalents. Hence, all words, whether errors in the original, or words that have fallen from common usage, must be mediated through the modernized text either as errors or anomalies silently corrected to modern equivalents in the base text, or as words with glosses. Given that the intent of the modernized text is to reflect the full vocabulary of the original, most of the unfamiliar and archaic words are carried over to the modernized text and glossed where necessary. But there remained a small category of potentially unfamiliar words and practices idiomatic to the original text that are not errors that have nevertheless been incorporated into the list of annotated vocabulary of the original in order to introduce them silently into the base text for modernization. Among them are "thandys" for "the hands," "therte" for "the heart," "tho" for "then," "brotyll" for "brittle," "ierirho" for "Jericho," words the antiquity of which did not seem worth preserving where modern equivalents were so clear. These rather more arbitrary editorial decisions are not numerous. Other common variants such as "he" and "to" for "the" seemed pointless to keep and gloss. This analyzed vocabulary list thus contains virtually all the interpretations of dubious or corrupt words in the original that have been incorporated into the modernized text. Otherwise, this modern edition presents only an orthographical normalization and a rationalized re-punctuation of the original.

The desirability of modernized punctuation becomes self-evident after a brief examination of Leeu's text, especially for those readers inexperienced in finding their way by instinct through the mazes of early syntax. Nearly any sentence will illustrate the point: "Moost myghty prynce to whom goold/sylver/

preciouse stones and alle rychesse of the world tho you are brought/ye do alle thyng as ye woll.and non ayensayth youre pleasure: ye have a Quene and many Quenys. and ovyr that ye have cocubynes or paramours withoute numbre or as [sic] asmany as you pleasyth/for ye have all that ye wol: So may not every man do/ No narrative intent could be clearer once all the parts are examined and grouped, but it is a halting business the first time through. I think there is little that an editor can do to misguide the reader in reducing such material to modern phrasing, but much that can facilitate the reading.

Beyond such changes as these, only a few modern conventions have been introduced such as setting off direct discourse in quotation marks, and formatting the dialogue in the first part on the model of a dramatic text with each new speaker's entry on a separate line, and with the speaker's name followed by a colon. Finally, the names of the principal characters have been standardized to Solomon, Marcolphus, Fudasa, etc. throughout the text and the introduction, despite the several variants that appear in the text.

Establishing a modern version based on Leeu's original is a task not without pitfalls, but it is a relatively forthright process compared to the evaluation of Leeu's text in relation to its immediate and remote Latin sources. Leeu's own Latin edition has been taken for the copytext used for the translation for the several reasons already set out in the introduction. The translator commits minor lapses, but on the whole remains faithful to what he found in the Latin. For purposes of comparison I have used photoprints of the *Collationes* published by Leeu in 1488–89 and of the same work published by Paffroet in 1488, both of which were obtained from originals in the Cambridge University Library. The few departures from these texts have been recorded in the textual annotations.

The more difficult challenge arises with the degree of corruption reflected in the English translation by comparison with such earlier versions as the Würzberg manuscript of 1434 edited by Benary. It is then that one sees how much deterioration had afflicted the tradition, and indeed how much uninspired tampering had been employed to make new sense out of passages that had drifted from their former meanings. To be sure, the integrity of the English text as set by Leeu must be respected, and hence there is no prospect of "improving" the text itself through editorial intervention. Several of the proverbs, in particular, for this reason, defy real comprehension. The only remedy available remains the textual annotations in which solutions are sought both from within the *Solomon and Marcolphus* tradition, and from the cultural record beyond.

Among the more cryptic passages in the text are the concluding words of several of the trick episodes. Marcolphus makes use of a live rabbit to distract the guard dogs in order to regain Solomon's court. When the king asks how he got in, he replies, "Am I in comen?" which is as much as to say, it was so easy I hardly noticed I was even here. The Latin source says more specifically, "calliditas non parva" (by no insignificant cunning I managed to get in). The English turns direct statement into irony. Going further back, the Latin MS. of 1434 says "calliditas, non misericordia." Along the way a word substitution had taken place. Here is an allusion to Solomon's cruelty. These one-line conclusions function like little bridges to subsequent episodes, but they are so condensed as to leave the sequence with a sense of incompletion.

This is even more pronounced in the case of the episode in which Marcolphus spits on the bald man's head. The redactors of the later Latin editions sensed that problem and tried a bit of unhelpful *amplificatio*. The situation has produced an impasse insofar as the outraged knight wants Marcolphus punished, or at least expelled from the court, while Marcolphus insists on his good intentions based on a literal understanding of the instructions given. Thus he replies, "and be it peace in thy virtue, and I shall be still," which is a reasonable rendering of "et fiat pax in virtute tua, et tacebo." The earlier MS. offers merely, "Fiat pax! Tacebo" (You be quite and I'll be quiet). It is brief but clear and stands as a self-contained closural gesture.

The greatest challenge, however, lies with the proverbs that tease us with a tolerable degree of sense, but that nevertheless raise doubts. Where no corruption in the source is detected, one can only turn to other contemporary sources in hopes of finding traditional meanings. Many such readings have been included in the textual notes. Where there is corruption in the immediate source, clarification can usually be found in the MS. of 1434, which has always been the first locus of consultation. A scant few proverbs remain that defy glossing in terms of the minimum criteria we associate with proverbs. Some remain oblique due either to corruptions that have rendered them meaningless to us, or to changes in cultural values that produce much the same effect.

The matter of the sources and analogues of the various jests has been discussed in the introduction. The annotations contain a broad variety of gleanings relating to remote sources and parallel motifs in an effort to establish the currency and traditions of each, in light of the fact that immediate sources appear to be beyond recovery.

Analysis of the Vocabulary of the 1492 English Text

The first column denotes page and line numbers in the original text. The second column contains the words as they appear, many revealing errors in typesetting or orthographical anomalies. The third column lists the modern equivalents. These have been incorporated into the base text used for the modernized version on the facing pages.

page	line	
132	1	comynicacion: communication
	4	bnt: but
	10	fadres: father's
	11	theste: the East
	17	Thls: This
	17	Marcolf: Marcolphus
	18	T___: The
	19	filf: full
	20	myddys: midst
	21	yes: eyes
	27	ef: of
	29	hasny: hose
134	3	ont: out
	6	brostelys: bristles
	11	yreu: iron
	25	beholde: beheld
	27	thereo: thereto

page	line	
136	2	gate: begat
	15	tha: that
	28	unswere: answer
138	6	yawe: gave
	13	potfnll: potful
	19	browyn: brewed
	20	shabbe: shall be
140	2	yevyng: giving
	17	ony: honey
	21	au: an
142	3	yate: gate
	4	yeue: given
	9	vultier: vulture
	13	Wyl-thon: Will thou
	15	ether: other
	27	maist: master
144	3	Connsell: Council
	18	moee: more
	28	he: the
146	3	be heggyd: he begged
	6	thandys: the hands
	29	trefore: therefore
148	21	aGeldyd: a gelded; corruption of word for "dimwitted"
150	8	te: the
	13	lyke: alike
	22	breeche: breeches
	23	therte: the heart
	24	thars: the arse
	26	lyke: alike
	27	lyke: alike
152	1	inda: Judah
	2	n: and
	14	shephde: shepherd
	26	wynes: wines; corruption of word for "wives"
	29	thrusty: thirsty
154	1	fayre: fair

page	line	
156	1	pmysed: promised
	5	comth: cometh
	7	fight: sight
	9	thau: then
	9	to: then
	22	tho: then
158	29	Barsebea: Bathsheba
160	13	woll: wills
	16	his: her
162	12	chamigyd: changed
	15	chungyd: changed
	26	pre: prove
164	8	therhe: the earth
	16	shalve: shall be
166	5	iu: in
	10	retonruyd: returned
	27	Tho: Then
168	10	nevyrhtelesse: nevertheless
	28	bote: both
170	23	or: ere
172	2	Tho: Then
	7	Tho: Then
	15	afore or: afore ere (redundant)
174	5	Tho: Then
	19	yede: gede
	23	ayen be: again by
	28	tapettys: tapits? tapestries?
176		[no corrections]
178	9	vertn: virtue
	18	bodyr: mother
180	16	curtayse: courteous
	17/18	brotyll: brittle
182	3	pciouse: precious
	5	whitoute: without
	5	On: In
	11	forwyth: forewits
	13	of: or

page	line	
	16	gladynd: glad end
	26	or: ere
184	9	Tho: Then
	24	othre: others
	29	mastres: mistress
186	1	thau: then
	10	mayndehede: maidenheads
	17	g-sente: consent
188	1	se: so
	5	axyd: asked
	21	thaue: have
	23	tho: then
190	8	tho: then
	14	skorue: scorn
	23	tho: to
192	15	Tho: Then
	24	Tho: Then
194	28	kyndrebede: kinderbed? kindred?
196	21	unto: until
	21	comen: came
198	10	well: will
	16	josaphath: Jehosaphat
	17	ierirho: Jericho

Bibliography

Alanus de Insulis (Alan of Lille). *Doctrinale altum parabolarum*. Deventer: Jacobus de Breda, 1499.

Albert the Great. *Man and the Beasts*. Trans. James J. Scanlon. Binghamton, NY: Medieval and Renaissance Texts and Studies, 1987.

Alter, Robert, and Frank Kermode, eds. *The Literary Guide to the Bible*. Cambridge, MA.: Harvard University Press, 1987.

"Altfranzösische Sprichwörter." See Adolf Tobler.

Altick, Richard D. *The English Common Reader*. Chicago: University of Chicago Press, 1957.

Anglo Saxon Dialogues of Solomon and Saturn. See John Mitchell Kemble.

Atkins, J.W.H., ed. *The Owl and the Nightingale*. Cambridge: Cambridge University Press, 1922.

Bakhtin, Mikhail. "From the Prehistory of Novelistic Discourse." *Modern Criticism and Theory*. Ed. David Lodge. London and New York: Longman, 1988. 125–56.

———. *Rabelais and his World*. Trans. Hélène Iswolski. Cambridge, MA: MIT Press, 1968.

Bebel, Heinrich. *Proverbia germanica*. Ed. W.H.D. Suringar. Leiden: E.J. Brill, 1879.

Beecher, Donald. "Intriguers and Tricksters: Manifestations of an Archetype in the Comedy of the Renaissance." *Revue de littérature comparée* LXI, No. 1 (1987), 5–31.

Benary, Walter, ed. *Salomon et Marcolfus*. Heidelberg: Carl Winters Universitätsbuchhandlung, 1914.

Bennett, M.S. *Chaucer and The Fifteenth Century*. Oxford: Clarendon Press, 1947.

Bezzenberger, H.E., ed. *Frîdankes Bescheidenheit*. Halle: Buchhandlung des Waisenhauses, 1872.

Biagioni, Giovanni Luigi. *Marcolf und Bertoldo und ihre Beziehungen*. Doc. Diss., Cologne University. Cologne: Druck K. Utsch, 1930.

Bladé, Jean François. *Contes populaires de la Gascoigne*. 3 vols. Paris: Maisonneuve frères et C. LeClerc, 1886.

Bletz, Zacharias. *Die dramatischen Werke*. Ed. E. Steiner. Frauenfeld: Huber and Co., 1926.

Boas, Marcus, ed. *Disticha Catonis* (Distiches of Cato). Amsterdam: North-Holland Co., 1952.

Boeckl, Joachim G., et al. *Geschichte der Deutschen Literatur von 1480 bis 1600*. Berlin: Volk und Wissen Volkseigener Verlag, 1983: IV. 85–87.

Braekman, W.L., and P.S. Macaulay. "The Story of the Cat and the Candle in Middle English Literature." *Neuphilologische Mitteilungen* 70 (1969): 690–702.

Brandstetter, Renward, ed. "Marcolfus: Ein Fahsnacht spil zu Lucern gespillt Aa. 1546." *Zeitschrift für Deutsche Philologie* 17, Halle (1885): 421–24.

Brauner, Sigrid. "Martin Luther on Witchcraft: A True Reformer?" *The Politics of Gender in Early Modern Europe*. Ed. Jean R Brink et al. Vol. XII, Sixteenth Century Essays and Studies. Kirksville, MO, 1989. 29–42.

Brewer, Derek. "Notes toward a theory of medieval comedy." *Medieval Comic Tales*. Totowa, NJ: Rowman and Littlefield, 1973. 140–49.

Brückner, W. *Volkerzälung und Reformation*. Berlin: E. Schmidt, 1974.

Burke, Peter. *Popular Culture in Early Modern Europe*. London: Temple Smith, 1978.

Büsching, Johann G., and Friederich H. von der Hagen, eds. *Deutsche Gedichte des Mittelalters*. Vol. I. Berlin: Realschulbuchhandlung, 1808.

Butler, Elizabeth M. *The Myth of the Magus*. Cambridge: Cambridge University Press, 1948.

Camporesi, Piero. *La maschera de Bertoldo: G.C. Croce e la letteratura carnevalesca*. Torino: Einaudi, 1976.

Catholy, Eckehard. *Das Fastnachtspiel des Spätmittelalters: Gestalt und Funktion*. Tübingen: Max Niemeyer Verlag, 1961.

"De Certamine Salomonis et Marcolfi." See Thomas Wright.

Chaucer, Geoffrey. *The Riverside Chaucer*. Ed. Larry D. Benson. 3rd ed. Boston: Houghton Mifflin, 1987.

Clavicula Salomonis. See Shelomo Mafteah.

Conway, Moncure Daniel. *Solomon and Solomonic Literature*. New York: Haskel House Publishers (1899), 1973.

Collationes quas dicunter fecisse mutuo rex Salomon . . . et Marcolphus . . . . Daventer: Richard Paffroet, 1488.

Corti, Maria. "Models and Antimodels in Medieval Culture." *New Literary History* 10 (1979): 339–66.

Cosquin, Emmanuel. "Le Conte du Chat et de la Chandelle dans l'Europe du Moyen Age et en Orient." *Romania* 159, Vol. XI (July 1911): 371–430; *Romania* 160, Vol. XI (Oct. 1911): 481–531.

Cotgrave, Randle. *A Dictionary of the French and English Tongues.* London: 1611. Ed. William S. Woods. Columbia: University of South Carolina Press, 1968.

Crapelet, George H., ed. *Proverbes et dictons populaires.* Includes *Les proverbes de Marcoul et de Salemon.* Paris: Imprimerie de Crapelet, 1831.

Croce, Giulio Cesare. Bertoldo e Bertoldino. (In Appendix: *Dialogus Salomonis et Marcolphi, El dyalogo di Salomon e Marcolpho.*) Rome: G.A. Cibotto Canesi, 1960.

———. *La Sottilissime astuzie di Bertoldo: Le Piacevoli ridicoloso simplicita de Bertoldino.* Turin, 1978.

Curtius, Ernst Robert. *European Literature and the Latin Middle Ages.* New York: Harper and Row, 1963.

de Vreese, Willem, ed. *Dat Dyalogus of Twisprake tusschen den wisen coninck Salomon ende Marcolphus.* Leiden: E.J. Brill, 1941. [From the Antwerp edition of van Henrick Eckert van Homberch, 1501.]

de Vries, Jan. *Die Märchen von Klugen Rätsellösern: eine vergleichende Untersuchung.* Helsinki: Suomolainen Tiedeakatemia, 1928.

Die Deutschen Dichtungen von Salomon und Markolf. See Friederich Hermann Traugott Vogt.

Diogenes Laertius. *Lives of Eminent Philosophers.* Trans. R.D. Hicks. 2 vols. London: William Heinemann, 1925.

Divry, Jehan. *Les Ditz de Salomon et de Marcolphus.* Paris, 1509.

———. *The sayings or proverbes of King Solomon with the answers of Marcolphus translated out of frenche into englysshe.* London: Richarde Pynson, ca. 1527–29.

Dronke, Peter. *Verse with Prose from Petronius to Dante: The Art and Scope of the Mixed Form.* Cambridge, MA, Harvard University Press, 1994.

Duchartre, Pierre Louis. *The Italian Comedy.* Trans. Randolph T. Weaver. New York: Dover (1929), 1966.

Duff, E. Gordon, ed. *The Dialogue or Communing Between the Wise King Solomon and Marcolphus.* London: Lawrence and Bullen, 1892.

Eco, Umberto. "The Frames of Comic 'Freedom.'" *Carnival.* Ed. Thomas A. Sebeok. Berlin: Mouton, 1984.

Ehrismann, Gustav. *Geschichte der Deutschen Literatur bis zum Ausgang des Mittelalters.* Munich: C.H. Beck'sche Verlagsbuchhandlung, 1959.

El dyalogo di Salomon e Marcolpho. See Ernesto Lamma.

Elliott, Robert C. *The Power of Satire: Magic, Ritual, Art.* Princeton, NJ: Princeton University Press, 1972.

Enenkel, Johann. *Werke, Weltchronik.* 3 vols. Hannover and Leipzig: Hahnsche Buchhandlung, 1900.

Erasmus, Desiderius. *Adagiorum chiliades quatuor.* Lugduni: apud haered. Sebast. Griphii, 1592.

Erb, Ewald, et al. *Geschichte der Deutschen Literatur von der Anfängen bis 1160.* Berlin: Volk und Wissen Volkseigener Verlag, 1965. Vol. I, pt. 2, 787–96.

Eyering, Eucharius. *Proverbiorum Copia.* Eisleben: Typis Grosianis, 1601.

Fecunda ratis. See Ernst Voigt. See Egbert von Lüttich.

Fifteen Joys of Marriage, The. Trans. Brent A. Pitts. New York: Peter Lang, 1985.

Fischarts, Johann. *Geschichtsklitterung.* Ed. A. Alsleben. Halle a/s: Max Niemeyer Verlag, 1891.

Flögel, Karl Friedrich. *Geschichte des Grotesk-Komischen.* Ed. Max Bauer. 2 vols. Munich: G. Müller, 1914.

Florileg of St Omer. See Ernst Voigt.

Foucault, Michel. *Histoire de la folie à l'âge classique.* Paris: Gallimard, 1976.

Frag und Antwortt Salomonis und Marcolfii. Nürnberg: Marcus Ayrer, ca. 1482.

Frantzen, Johan Joseph A.A., and A. Hulshof, eds. *Drei Kölner Schwankbücher aus dem XVten Jahrhundert.* Utrecht: A. Oesthoek, 1920.

Frîdankes Bescheidenheit. See H.-E. Bezzenberger.

Friend, A.C. "The Proverbs of Serlo of Wilton." *MS* 16 (1954): 179–218.

Frye, Northrop. *Words With Power.* Markham, Ont.: Viking Press/Penguin Books, 1990.

Gellius, Aulus. *The Attic Nights of Aulus Gellius.* Trans. John C. Rolfe. Cambridge, MA: Harvard University Press, 1927.

Gesta Romanorum. See Wynnard Hooper and Charles Swan.

Gesta Romanorum. See Hermann Oesterley.

Gesztelyi, Tamás. "Zur Frage der Darstellung des soganantes Salomourteils." *ACD* XXV (1989): 73–84.

Goddard, R.N.B. "Marcabru, *Li Proverbe au Vilain,* and the Tradition of Rustic Proverbs." *Neuphilologische Mitteilungen* 88 (1987): 55–70.

Goldsmith, R.H. *Wise Fools in Shakespeare.* Liverpool: Liverpool University Press, 1958.

Gratius, Ortvinus. *Epistolae obscurorum virorum*. Ed. Francis G. Stokes. London: Chatto and Windus, 1925.

Gubernatis, Angelo de. *Zoological Mythology, or The Legends of Animals*. London: Trübner and Co., 1872.

Guerrini, Olindo. *La vita e le opere di Giulio Cesare Croce*. Bologna: N. Zanichelli, 1879.

Hagen, Friedrich von der, ed. "Salomon und Markolf." *Narrenbuch*. Halle: Rengersche Buchhandlung, 1811.

Hagen, Friedrich von der, and Johann Büsching. *Literaturischer Grundriss zur Geschichte der Deutschen Poesie von der ältesten Zeit bis in das Sechzente jahrhundert*. Berlin: Duncker und Humblot, 1812.

Hansen, Elaine Tuttle. *The Solomon Complex: Reading Wisdom in Old English Poetry*. Toronto: University of Toronto Press, 1988.

Harris, J. Rendel, ed. *Odes of Solomon*. Cambridge: Cambridge University Press, 1909.

Hartmann, Walter, ed. *Salomon und Markolf*. Halle: Gräfenhainichen Schulze, 1934.

Hayden, Gregor. "Salomon und Markolf." *Narrenbuch*. Ed. Felix Bobertag. Berlin and Leipzig: Kürschners Deutsche National-Literatur, 1884: II. 296–361.

Hazlitt, W. Carew, ed. *Shakespeare Jest-Books* (London, 1864). Rpt. New York: Burt Franklin, n.d.

Heitz, Paul. *Strassburger Holzschnitte zu Dietrich von Bern Herzog Ernst–Der Hürnen Seyfrid-Marcolphus*. Strasbourg: J.H.E. Heitz, 1922.

Heitz, Paul, and F. Ritter. *Versuch einer Zusammenstellung der deutschen Volksbücher*. Strasbourg: J.H.E. Heitz, 1924.

Helgason, Jón, ed. *Hervararsaga: Heiðreks Saga*. Copenhagen: J. Jørgensen and Co., 1924.

Henning, Wilhelm, ed. *Die Geschicht des Pfarrers vom Kalenberg, Hans Clawerts wirkliche Historien, Das Lalebuch: Drei alt-deutsche Schwankbücher*. Munich: Wilhelm Heyne Verlag, 1962.

Herford, Charles H. *Studies in the Literary Relations of England and Germany in the Sixteenth Century*. Cambridge: Cambridge University Press, 1886; rpt. New York: Octagon Books, 1966.

Herodotus. *[History of Greece]*. Trans. A.D. Godley. Cambridge, MA: Harvard University Press, 1963.

Hilka, Alfons. *Neue Beiträge zur Erzählungsliteratur des Mittelalters*. Breslau: G.P. Aderholz, 1913.

Hodgart, Matthew. *Satire*. New York: McGraw-Hill, 1969.

Hofmann, Konrad. "Über Jourdain de Blaivies, Apollonius von Tyrus, Salomon und Marcolf." *Akademie der wissenschaften Münich: Philosophisch-philologische classe.* Munich, 1871. I: 415–48.

Holingshed, Raphael. *The First and Second Volumes of Chronicles.* 2 vols. London: at the expenses of J. Harison, G. Bishop, R. Newberie, H. Denham, and T. Woodcocke, 1587.

Hooper, Wynnard, and Charles Swan, eds. *Gesta Romanorum.* London: Bohn, 1876.

Huizinga, Johan. *The Waning of the Middle Ages.* London: E. Arnold and Co. (1924) 1955.

Huschenbett, Dietrich. "Von dem König Salomon und Markolf und einem Narren." *Zeitschrift für deutsche Philologie* 84 (1965): 369–408.

Hutcheon, Linda. *A Theory of Parody: The Teachings of Twentieth-Century Art Forms.* New York: Methuen, 1985.

Jesus the son of Sirach. *The Wisdom of . . .* often referred to as *Ecclesiasticus.* Ed. W.O.E. Oesterley. London: Society for the Promotion of Christian Knowledge, 1916.

Jolles, André. *Einfache Formen.* Tübingen: Max Niemeyer Verlag, 1930.

———. *Formes simples.* Paris: Éditions du Seuil, 1972.

Jones, Malcolm. "Marcolf the Trickster in Late Medieval Art and Literature or: the mystery of the bum in the oven." *Spoken in Jest.* Ed. Gillian Bennett. Sheffield: Sheffield Academie Press, 1991.

Josephus, Flavius. *The Complete Works of Josephus.* Trans. William Whiston. Grand Rapids Michigan: Kregel Publications, 1981.

Jung, Carl. *Four Archetypes: Mother, Rebirth, Spirit, Trickster.* Trans. R.E.C. Hull. Princeton, NJ: Princeton University Press, 1970.

———. "On The Psychology of the Trichster Figure." In Paul Radin, *The Trickster.* New York: The Philosophical Library, 1956, 195–211.

Kanjur: Tibetan Tales ("The Wise and the Foolish"). Trans. A.K. Gordon. London: Luzac, 1953.

Karnein, Alfred, ed. "Salman und Morolf." *The Middle High German Epic.* Halle: Max Niemeyer Verlag, 1968.

Keller, Adalbert von, ed. *Fastnachtspiele aus dem fünfzehnten Jahrhundert.* 3 vols. Stuttgart: Litterarischer Verein, 1853; rpt. 1924 and 1965.

Kemble, John Mitchell, ed. *Anglo Saxon Dialogues of Solomon and Saturn.* London: Printed for the Aelfric Society, 1845–47.

Kerényi, Karl. "The Trickster in Relation to Greek Mythology." In Paul Radin, *The Trickster.* New York: The Philosophical Library, 1956: 173–91.

Lamma, Ernesto, ed. *El dyalogo di Salomon e Marcolpho.* Bologna: Romagnoli, 1886.

Langland, William. *Piers the Plowman* (C text). Ed. Derek Pearsall. London: Edward Arnold, 1978.

Lathrop, Henry Burrowes. *Translations from the Classics into English from Caxton to Chapman 1477–1620.* New York: Octagon Books (1932) 1967.

Lefebvre, Joël. *Les Fols et la Folie: Étude sur les genres du comique et la création littéraire en Allemagne pendant la Renaissance.* Paris: Librairie C. Klincksieck, 1968.

Lehmann, Paul. *Die Parodie im Mittelalter.* Munich: Drei Masken Verlag, 1922.

Lenk, Werner. "Zur Sprichwort-Antithetik im Salomon-Markolf-Dialog." *Forschungen und Fortschritte* Vol 39, No.5 (1965): 151–55.

Le Roux de Lincy, Antoine. *Le Livre des proverbes français.* 2 vols. Paris: A. Delahays, 1859.

Lever, Maurice. *Le Sceptre et la Marotte: Histoire des Fous de Cour.* Paris: Fayard, 1983.

Levy, Jacob. *Neuhebräisches und Chaldäisches Wörterbuch.* 4 vols. Leipzig: F.A. Brockhaus, 1876–89.

Li proverb au vilain. See Adolf Tobler.

Luther, Martin. *Works,* vol. 34, *Career of the Reformer* IV. Ed. Lewis Spitz. Philadelphia: Muhlenberg Press, 1960.

——— . *Works,* vol. 51, *Sermons* I. Ed. John W. Doberstein. Philadelphia: Muhlenberg Press, 1959.

——— . *Works,* vol. 54, *Table Talk.* Ed. Theodore Tappert. Philadelphia: Fortress Press, 1967.

Lüttich, Egbert von. *Fecunda ratis.* Ed. Ernst Voigt. Halle a/s: Max Niemeyer, 1889.

Lydgate, John. "The Order of Fools." *Minor Poems.* Ed. H.N. Mac-Cracken. London: K. Paul, Trench, Trübner; Oxford: Oxford University Press, for the EETS, 1934.

MacCallum, Sir Mungo William. *Studies in Low German and High German Literature.* London: Kegan Paul, Trench and Co., 1884.

Mafteah, Shelomo. *The Greater Key of Solomon* (Clavicula Salomonis). Chicago: DeLaurence, Scott and Co., 1916.

Mahn, Karl A.F. *Gedichte der Troubadours, in provenzalischer sprache.* 4 vols. Berlin: F. Duemmler, 1856.

Makarius, Laura. "Le Mythe du 'Trickster'." *Revue de l'Histoire des Religions* 175 (1966): 17–46.

Martini, Fritz. *Das Bauerntum in Deutschen Schrifttum zum 16. Jahrhundert*. Halle a/s: Max Niemeyer Verlag, 1944.

Master Tyll Owlglass. Trans. K.R.H. MacKenzie. London: George Routledge and Sons, n.d.

Mauclerc, Pierre, Count of Brittany. *Proverbes de Marcoul et de Salemon. Proverbes et dicton populaires*. Ed. G.H. Crapelet. Paris: Imprimerie de Crapelet, 1831.

McCown, Charles, ed. *The Testament of Solomon*. Leipzig: J.C. Hinrichs, 1922.

McGlinchey, James M. *The Teaching of Amen-em-ope and the Book of Proverbs*. Washington: Catholic University of America Press, 1939.

Menner, Robert J., ed. *The Poetical Dialogues of Solomon and Saturn*. London: Oxford University Press, 1941.

Merlini, Domenico. *Saggio di ricerche sulla satira contro il villano*. Torino: E. Loescher, 1894.

Méon, Dominique Martin, ed. *Nouveaux Recueil de Fabliaux et Contes Inédites des Poètes Français des XIIe, XIIIe, XIVe et XVe siècles*. 2 vols. Paris: Chasseriau, 1823.

Minnis, A.J. *Medieval Theory of Authorship: Scholastic Literary Attitudes in the Later Middle Ages*. Philadelphia: University of Pennsylvania Press (1984), 1988.

Moralejo Alvarez, Sarafin. "Marcolfo, El Espinario, Priapo: Un Testimonio Iconografico Gallego." *Primera Reunión Gallega de Estudios Clasicos*. Santiago: Sociedad Española de Estudios Clasicos, Sección Gallega; Santiago de Compostella: Universidad de Santiago, 1981. 331–55.

Morawski, Joseph de, ed. *Diz et proverbes des sages*. Paris: Les Presses Universitaires de France, 1924.

———— . *Proverbes français anterieurs au XVe siècle*. Paris: É. Champion, 1925.

Müllenhoff, K., and W. Scherer, eds. *Denkmäler Deutscher Poesie und Prosa aus dem VIII–XII Jahrhundert*. Berlin: Weidmann, 1892.

Nichols, Stephen G., Jr. *Romanesque Signs: Early Medieval Narrative and Iconography*. New Haven: Yale University Press, 1983.

Odes of Solomon. See J. Rendel Harris.

Oesterley, Hermann, ed. *Gesta Romanorum*. Hildesheim: Georg Olms Verlagsbuchhandlung (1872), 1963.

Oesterley, W.O.E. *The Wisdom of Egypt and the Old Testament*. London: Society for the Propegation of the Gospel, 1927.

———— , ed. *Wisdom of Solomon* (O.T. Apocrypha). New York: Macmillan and Co., 1917.

——, ed. *Ecclesiasticus*. See Jesus the son of Sirach.

A Pleasant Vintage of Till Eulenspiegel. Trans. Paul Oppenheimer. Middletown, CT: Wesleyan University Press, 1972.

Paris, Gaston. *La Littérature française au moyen age (XIe – XIVe siècles)*. Paris: Hachette (1888), 1905.

——. "La femme de Salomon." *Romania* IX (1880): 436–43.

Petsch, Robert. *Das Deutsche Volksrätsel*. Strasbourg, 1917.

Piper, Paul, ed. *Die Schriften Notkers und seiner Schule*. Freiburg i/B and Tübingen: J.C.B. Mohr, 1982–83.

Proverbes et dictons populaires. See George H. Crapelet.

Putnam, George Haven. *Books and Their Makers During the Middle Ages*. 2 vols. New York: Hillary House Publications (1896–97), 1962.

Rabelais, François. *The Histories of Gargantua and Pantagruel*. Trans. J.M. Cohen. Harmondsworth: Penguin Books, 1970.

Radin, Paul. *The Trickster: A Study in American Indian Mythology*. New York: The Philosophical Library, 1956.

Remnant, G.L. *A Catalogue of Misericords in Great Britain*. Oxford: Clarendon Press, 1969.

Rylaarsdam, J. Coert. *Revelation in Jewish Wisdom Literature*. Chicago: Chicago University Press (1946), 1957.

Sachs, Hans. *Werke*. Ed. Bernhard Arnold. Berlin and Stuttgart: W. Spemann, 1884–85.

"Salman und Morolf." See Alfred Karnein.

Salomon et Marcolfus. See Walter Benary.

"Salomon und Markolf." See Friederich von der Hagen.

Schade, Richard Erich. *Studies in Early German Comedy 1500–1650*. Columbia, SC: Camden House, 1988.

Schaubach, M. Ernst.*Die Erhaltenen Deutschen und Lateinischen Bearbeitungen des Salomon-Marcolf-Dialoges*. Doc. Diss., University of Leipzig. Meiningen, 1881.

Schaumberg, Walter. "Untersuchungen über das deutsche Spruchgedicht Salomo und Morolf." *Beiträge zur Geschicht der deutschen Sprache und Literatur*. Eds. Hermann Paul and Wilhelm Braune. Tübingen: Max Niemeyer, 1876; rpt. New York: Johnson Reprint Corp., 1967. II: 1–63.

Schlauch, Margaret. *Antecedents of the English Novel*. London: Oxford University Press, 1963.

Schönbrunn-Kölb, Erika. "*Markolf* in den mittelalterlichen Salomondich-tungen und in deutscher Wortgeographie." *Zeitschrift für Mundart-forschung* No. XXV (1957): 92–128; 129–174.

Schulz, Ernst. *Die englischen Schwankbücher.* Palaestra, No. 117. Berlin: Mayer und Müller, 1912. 1–126.

Seiler, Frédéric. *Deutsche Sprichwörterkunde.* Munich: Beck, 1922.

Serlon de Wilton. *Poèmes Latins.* Ed. Jan Öberg. Stockholm: Almquist and Wiksell, 1965.

Shakespeare Jest-Books. See W. Carew Hazlitt.

Shapiro, Norman R., ed. *The Comedy of Eros: Medieval French Guides to the Art of Love.* Urbana: University of Illinois Press, 1971.

Singer, Samuel. *Sprichwörter des Mittelalters I von den Anfängen bis ins 12. Jahrhundert.* Bern: Verlag Herbert Lang und Cie., 1944.

Slethaug, Gordon E. "Parody." *Encyclopedia of Contemporary Literary Theory.* Ed. Irena R. Makaryk. Toronto: University of Toronto Press, 1993.

Solomon and Saturn (Anglo Saxon Dialogues). See Robert J. Menner and Arthur Ritter von Vincenti.

Strayer, Joseph R., ed. "Solomon and Marcolf." *Dictionary of the Middle Ages.* New York: Charles Scribner's Sons, 1988. II: 366–70.

Suchier, Walther. *L'Enfant Sage.* Halle a/s: Max Niemeyer, 1910.

Suidas. *Lexicon.* Ed. Ada Adler. Stuttgart: Teubner, 1961.

The Comedy of Eros: Medieval French Guides to the Art of Love. See Norman R. Shapiro.

The Dialogue or Communing Between the Wise King Solomon and Marcolphus. See E. Gordon Duff.

The Testament of Solomon. See Charles McCown.

Tobler, Adolf, ed. *Li proverb au vilain.* Leipzig: S. Hirzel, 1895.

Tobler, Adolf, and Julius Zacher, eds. "Altfranzösische Sprichwörter." *Zeitschrift für deutsches Altertum* 11 (1859): 114–44.

Tristram, Ernest William. *English Medieval Wall Painting: The Thirteenth Century.* Oxford: Oxford University Press, 1950.

Vesselofsky, Alexandre. *Les Légendes slaves sur Salomon et Kitovras et les légendes occidentales sur Marcolphe et Merlin.* Saint Petersburg, 1872.

Vikramacarita (Sinhasana-dvatringaka). Trans. Franklin Edgerton. Cambridge, MA: Harvard University Press, 1926.

Vincenti, Arthur Ritter von, ed. *Die Altenglischen Dialoge von Salomon und Saturn.* Leipzig: A. Deichert'sche Verlagsbuchhandlung, 1904.

Vintler, Hans. *Die Pluemen der Tugent*. Ed. Ignaz Zingerle. Innsbruck: Wagner, 1874.

Vogt, Friedrich Hermann Traugott. *Die Deutschen Dichtungen von Salomon und Morkolf*. Halle: Max Niemeyer, 1880–1934.

———. "Zur Salman-Morolfsage." *Beiträge zur Geschichte der deutsche Sprache* VIII (1882): 313–23.

Voigt, Ernst. See Egbert von Lüttich.

———, ed. "Das *Florileg* von St Omer." *Romanische Forschungen* VI (1897): 557–94. [Ed. of Codex 115, St. Omer, ca. 1136–40.]

Waddell, Helen. *The Wandering Scholars*. London: Constable and Co., 1927; Garden City, NY: Doubleday and Co., 1961.

Waller, A.R., and Sir A.W. Ward, eds. "From the Beginnings to the Cycles of Romance." *The Cambridge History of English Literature*. Vol. I. Cambridge: Cambridge University Press, 1933.

Wallis, Mary. *Patterns of Wisdom in The Old English "Solomon and Saturn II."* Doc. Diss., University of Ottawa, 1991.

Walther, Hans. *Proverbia sententiaeque Latinitatis Medii Aevi: Lateinische Sprichwörter und Sentenzen des Mittelalters in alphabetischer Anordnung*. Göttingen: Vandenhoeck und Ruprecht, 1963–67.

Weise, Christian. *Comoedie vom König Salomo*. Ed. Ludwig Fulda. Kürschner Deutsche National Literatur. Stuttgart: J.J. Göschen, 1903, Vol. 39.

Welsford, Enid. *The Fool: His Social and Literary History*. Garden City, NY: Doubleday and Company (1935), 1961.

Werner, Jakob. *Lateinische Sprichwörter und Sinnsprüche des Mittelalters*. Heidelberg: C. Winter, 1912.

Wesselofsky, Alessandro. "*El dyalogo di Salomon e Marcolpho*." *Giornale storico della letteratura Italiano* VIII (1886): 275–76.

William of Tyre. *Historia rerum in partibus transmirinis gestarum*. In *Recueil des Historiens des Croisades*. Paris: L'Académie des Inscriptions et Belles-Lettres, Historiens Occidentaux, 1844. Vol. I, pt. I.

Williams, James G. "Proverbs and Ecclesiastes." In *The Literary Guide to the Bible*. Eds. Robert Alter and Frank Kermode. Cambridge, MA: Harvard University Press, 1987.

———. *Those Who Ponder Proverbs: Aphoristic Thinking and Biblical Literature*. Sheffield: Almond Press, 1981.

Wilson, Richard Middleton. *Early Middle English Literature*. London: Methuen and Co., 1939.

Wolterbeck, Marc. *Comic Tales of the Middle Ages*. New York: Greenwood Press, 1991.

Wright, Louis B. *Middle-class Culture in Elizabethan England.* Ithaca, NY: Cornell University Press (1935), 1965.

Wright, Thomas, ed. "De Certamine Salomonis et Marcolfi." *Early Mysteries and other Latin Poems of the Twelfth and Thirteenth Centuries.* London: Nichols and Son; Paris: Techener, 1838.

Wuttke, Dieter. "Die Druckfassung des Fastnachtspiels von König Salomon und Markolf." *Zeitschrift für deutsches Altertum und deutsche Literatur* XCIV, Vol. 2 (July, 1965): 140–70.

Zabara, Joseph. "The Book of Delights" (S'cha 'aschuim) [edited by M.I. Abrahams]. *Jewish Quarterly Review* VI (1894): 518–613.

Zacher, Julius, and Adolf Tobler, eds. See "Altfranzösische Sprichwörter."

From *Salomon et Marcolphus collocutores*, ca. 1580, in the Bodleian
Library (Donca 125).

Aesop as Marcolphus from *Salomonis et Marcolphi dyalogus*, Antwerp:
G. Leeu, 1488. Cambridge University Library.

**Collationes quas dicuntur fecisse mu~
tuo rex Salomon sapientissimus
et Marcolphus facie defo~
mis z turpissimus: tamē
yt fert eloquētissim'
sequit cū figuris.**

Marcolphus and his wife before King Solomon from the quarto printed
in Nuremberg, ca. 1500. Dresden (Lit. lat. rec B. 285,33) Incunabel
1351.

From the *Dialogo de Salomone e Marcolpho,* Venice: Augustino di Bedoni, 1541. Munich (L. eleg. m. 367 m.)

Jncipiūt collatiōes q̄s dicūtur feciſſe mutuo rex ſa
lomō ſapiētiſſimus ⁊ marcolpb̄ facie defoꝛmis et
turpiſſimus tamē vt fertur eloquētiſſimus feliciter.

From *Salomon et Marcolphus*, Magdeburg: Ravenstein and Westphal, ca. 1493. Dresden (Lit. lat. rec. B. 273) Incunabel 1060.

From *Dialogus Salomonis et Marcolfi*, Strassburg: Heinrich Knoblochtzer, ca. 1483. Munich, Incunabel s.a. 657.

From *Frag und antwort Künig Salomonis und Marcolphi*, Strassburg: Christian Müller, ca. 1550. In *XV Strassburger Holzschnitte*, Strassburg: J.H. Ed. Heitz, 1922.

1. How King Solomon went hunting, how one of his servants pointed out Marcolphus's house, and what the king asked Marcolphus.

2. Here Marcolphus brings to Solomon an earthen vessel of milk.

3. How Marcolphus accuses his sister.

4. How Marcolphus lets the mouse run from his sleeve onto the table.

5. Here came two women with a living and with a dead child.

6. Here Marcolphus releases a hare and the hounds run after it.

7. Here Solomon comes with his men to the aperture in which Marcolphus lay.

8. How Marcolphus was taken out to be hanged.

From *The dyalogus or communyng betwixt . . . Salomon and Marcolphus*, Antwerp: G. Leeu, 1492. Bodleian Library, Oxford.

THIS IS THE DIALOGUE OR COMMUNING

BETWIXT

THE WISE KING SOLOMON AND MARCOLPHUS

¶Here begynneth the dyalogus or compnicaci
on betwixt Salomon the kingof jherusalē· and
Marcolphus that right rude and great of body
was bnt right subtpll & wyse of wyt/and full
of vndrestådyng.as thereafter folowyng men
shall here.

Pon a season hertofore as king sa=
lomõ full of wisdome and richesse:
sate vpõ the kinges sete or stole that
was his fadres davyd :sawe co=
myng a mã out of theste that was
named marcolphus.of vysage greatly myssha=
pen and fowle/nevyrthelesse he was right tal=
katyf elloquend & wyse. His wif had he wyth
hym whiche was more ferefull and rude to be=
holde And as they were bothe comen before kīg
Salomõ/he behelde thaym well This marcolf
wa. of short stature and thykke Tf. hede had
he great:a brode for hede rede and f alf of wrin
kelys or frouncys:his erys hery ãd to the myd
dys of chekys hangyng.great yes and rēnyng.
his nether lyppe hãgyng lyke an horse. A berde
harde and fowle lyke vnto a goet. The handes
short ãd blocky ssh His fyngres great and thyc
ke Rownde feet.& the nose thycke and croked. a
face lyke an asse:ãd the here of hys heed lyke the
heer ef a goet:his shoes on his fete: were ovyr=
moche chorlysh and rude:and his clothys fowle
and dyrty.a shorte kote to the buttockys his ha/

The Dialogue of Solomon and Marcolphus

[Part I]

Here beginneth the dialogues or communication betwixt Solomon, the king of Jerusalem, and Marcolphus that right rude and great of body was, but right subtle and wise of wit and full of understanding, as thereafter following men shall hear.

Upon a season heretofore as King Solomon, full of wisdom and richesse,°¹ sat upon the king's seat or stool that was his father's, David,² saw coming a man out of the East³ that was named Marcolphus, of visage greatly misshapen and foul. Nevertheless he was right talkative, eloquent, and wise. His wife had he with him which was more fearful and rude to behold. And as they were both come before King Solomon, he beheld them well. This Marcolphus was of short stature and thick. The head had he great, a broad forehead red and full of wrinkles or frounces, his ears hairy and to the midst of [his] cheeks hanging, great eyes and running, his nether lip hanging like a horse, a beard hard and foul like unto a goat, the hands short and blockish, his fingers great and thick, round feet, and the nose thick and crooked, a face like an ass, and the hair of his head like the hair of a goat. His shoes on his feet were overmuch churlish° and rude, and his clothes foul and dirty, a short coat to the buttocks, his

---

richesse wealth, opulence.   **churlish** peasant-like.

lyn hynge.full of wrynkelys and alle his clothes
were of the moost fowle coloure. his wyf was
of shozt stature and she was ont of mesure thyc∕
ke wyth great bzestys: and the here of hyz hede
clustredz lyke thystelys. She had longe wynde∕
bzowes lyke bzostelys of a swyne.Longe erys
lyke an asse.Reyning yen:berdpdz lyke a goet hyz
vpsage and skyn blacke and full of wrynkelys ∕
and vpon hyz great bzestys she had of span bzo∕
de:a bzoche of leed: She had shozt fyngzes. full
of pzeurpngys.She had right great nosethzylles
Hyz leggys shozt.and hery lyke a bere∕ hyz clo∕
thes were rough and bzoken∕of suche a woman
oz of an othze lyke vnto hyze:a yongeman hath
made thies verses folowyng
Femina defozmis tenebzarū subdita formis
Cum turpi facie transit absqz die.
Est mala res multum turpi concedere cultum
Sed turpis nimitum turpe ferat vicium
That is to saye an evyll favourydz and a fowle
blacke wyf behovyth to shewe the dayes lyght.
It is to oure yes medycyne to se that fayze is ād
fyne
As kyng salomō thies two persones thus hadz
seen∕ε beholdē:he demaūdedz of thaym of whēs
they weryn ε of what lynage they were compn
Marcolph⁹ thereo āswerpd. Saye furste to vs
youre kynrede ε genleagie .ε of youze fadzes.ε
than shall J shewe ε declare pon of oures∕Salo∕

hose° hung full of wrinkles, and all his clothes were of the most foul color. His wife was of short stature and she was out of measure thick with great breasts, and the hair of her head clustered like thistles. She had long wynde° brows like bristles of a swine, long ears like an ass, running eyes, bearded like a goat her visage, and skin black and full of wrinkles, and upon her great breasts she had, of span broad, a brooch of lead. She had short fingers full of iron rings. She had right great nostrils. Her legs short and hairy like a bear, her clothes were rough and broken; of such a woman or of another like unto her, a young man hath made these verses following:

> Femina deformis tenebrarum subdita formis
> Cum turpi facie transit absque die.
> Est mala res multum turpi concedere cultum
> Sed turpis nimirum turpe ferat vicium.

That is to say, an evil-favored and foul black wife behooveth to show the day's light. It is to our eyes medicine to see that° fair is and fine.

[The Dialogue]

As King Solomon these two persons thus had seen and beheld, he demanded of them of whence they were and of what lineage they were come.[4] Marcolphus thereto answered: "Say first to us your kindred and genealogy, and of your fathers, and then shall I show and declare yon° of ours."

---

hose stockings or breeches.   **wynde** twisted.   **that** what.
yon afterwards.

mon. I am of the vij. kyndredes of patryarkes.
that is to wete·that iudas gate phares. phares
gat esron/ Esron gat aron/ Aron genderyd; aminadab Aminadab gat naazon/ Naazon gat salmō Salmō gat boos/ Boos gat obeth/ Obeth gat
ysay. ysay gat davyd king/ Dauid gat salomō the
king & that am I. Marcolf⁹ answeryd; I am of
the vij. kindred; of Chozlys. Rustic⁹ gat ruftam
Rusta gat rustum/ Rustus gat rusticellū/ Rusti-
cell⁹ gat tarcum/ Tarc⁹ gat tarcol/ Tarcol gat
pharsi/ Pharsi gat marcuel/ Marcuel gat mar-
quat/ Marquat gat marcolphū & that is I. And
my wyf is comen of the blood and .vij. kyndredes of vntydy wyues. That is to knowe/ of lupica tha gat lupicana. Lupicana gat ludibzac Lu
dibzac gat bonestrūg/ Bonestrung gat boledzut
Boledzut gat paldzut. Paldzut gat lozdan/ Loz
dan gat curta/ Curta gat Curtula. Curtula gat
Curtella. Curtella gat polica Polica gat polyca
na. & thys is my wyf Polycana. Salomon sayde I haue herd of the that thou kanst right wele clatre and speke/ and that thou art subtyle of
wyt·although that thou be mysshappn ād choz-
lysth: Lete vs haue betwene[vs altercacon. I
shal make questyons to the/ and thou shalt therto answere. Marcolphus answeryd; he that sin
gyth wozste begynne furste. Salo. If thou kāst
vnswere to alle my questyons I shall make the
ryche/ and be named; above alle othze withyn

Solomon: "I am of the twelve kindreds of patriarches, that is to wit° that Judas begat Phares, Phares begat Esron, Esron begat Aaron, Aaron gendered Aminadab, Aminadab begat Naazon, Naazon begat Salmon, Salmon begat Boaz, Boaz begat Obeth, Obeth begat Isaiah, Isaiah begat David king, David begat Solomon the king, and that am I."[5]

Marcolphus answered: "I am of the twelve kindred of churls. Rusticus begat Rustam, Rusta begat Rustum, Rustus begat Rusticellum, Rusticellus begat Tarcum, Tarcus begat Tarcol, Tarcol begat Pharsi, Pharsi begat Marcuel, Marcuel begat Marquat, Marquat begat Marcolphum and that is I. And my wife is come of the blood and twelve kindreds of untidy wives.[6] That is to know, of Lupica that [be]gat Lupicana, Lupicana begat Ludibrac, Ludibrac begat Bonestrung, Bonestrung begat Boledrut, Boledrut begat Paldrut, Paldrut begat Lordan, Lordan begat Curta, Curta begat Curtula, Curtula begat Curtella, Curtella begat Polica, Polica begat Polycana, and this is my wife Polycana."

Solomon said: "I have heard of thee that thou canst right well clatter° and speak, and that thou art subtle of wit although that thou be misshapen and churlish. Let us have between us altercation. I shall make questions to thee, and thou shalt thereto answer."

Marcolphus answered: "He that singeth worst begin first."[7] Solomon: "If thou canst answer to all my questions I shall make thee rich, and be named above all others within my realm."[8]

to wit to know.   **clatter** chatter, babble.

my reaume Marcol. The phisician promysyth
the seeke folke helthe whan he hath no power
Salo. J haue iuged betwixt two light women
whiche dwellyd in oon house and forlaye a chyl
de. Mar. Were erys are there'are causes.where
women be there are wordys Salo. God ya-
we wysdam in my mouth. for me lyke is none
in alle partys of the worlde Marcolf⁹. He
that hath evyll neighborys praysyth hym self
Sal. The wykkydman fleyth.noma folwyng
Marcol. Whan the kydde rennyth:men may'se
his ars Salomon A good wyf and a fayre.is
to hir husbonde a pleasure Mar. A potfull of
mylke muste be kept wele from the katte Sal.
A wyse woman byldeth an house:and she that
vnwyse and a fool is:distroyeth with hir handes that she fyndeth made Marc. A pot that
is wele baken may best endure/ and that clene
is browyn that may they fayre drinken Salo
mon A ferdefull woman shabbe praysed. Mar
colfus A Catte that hath a good skyn shalbe
flayne Salomon A shamefast wyf and a fayre
is mekyll to be belovyd Marcol. To pore men
whyte mete are to be kept Salo. A woman
stronge in doyng good who shall fynde. Mar.
Who shal fynde a catte trewe in kepyng mylke
Salo. Noon Mar. And a woman seldom/ Sa
lo. A fayre woman and an honest:is to be praysed above alle rychesse that a man fynde may

Marcolphus: "The physician promiseth the sick folk health when he hath no power."[9]

Solomon: "I have judged betwixt two light° women which dwelled in one house and forelay° a child."[10]

Marcolphus: Where ears are there are causes,° where women be there are words."[11]

Solomon: "God gave wisdom in my mouth, for me like is none° in all parts of the world."

Marcolphus: "He that hath evil neighbors praiseth himself."[12]

Solomon: "The wicked man fleeth, no man following."°[13]

Marcolphus: "When the kid runneth, men may see his arse."[14]

Solomon: "A good wife and a fair is to her husband a pleasure."[15]

Marcolphus: "A potful of milk must be kept well from the cat."[16]

Solomon: "A wise woman buildeth a house, and she that unwise and a fool is destroyeth with her hands that she findeth made."[17]

Marcolphus: "A pot that is well-baked may best endure, and that clean is brewed° that may they fair° drink."[18]

Solomon: "A fearful woman° shall be praised."[19]

Marcolphus: "A cat that hath a good skin shall be flayed."

Solomon: "A shamefast° wife and a fair is mickle° to be beloved."

Marcolphus: "To° poor men white meat[s] are to be kept."[20]

Solomon: "A woman strong in doing good, who shall find?"[21]

Marcolphus: "Who shall find a cat true in keeping milk?"

Solomon: "None."

Marcolphus: "And a woman seldom."

Solomon: "A fair woman and an honest is to be praised above all riches that a man find may."

---

light of ill repute.   **forelay** lay on top of and smothered.   **causes** law cases, points under discussion.   **like is none** I have no equal. **no man following** even when no one pursues.   **clean is brewed** properly mixed; prepared in a pure state.   **fair** safely.   **fearful woman** woman respectful (of God).   **shamefast** bashful, modest. **mickle** greatly.   **To** from.

Marcol. A fat woman and a great is larger in
yevyng than othre. Salo. A whyt kerchyf becomth wele a womās hede. Mar. It standyth
wryten:that the furre is not all lyke the slevys.
and vndre a whyte cloth often are hyd mothys
Sal'.He that sowyth wyckydnesse. shal repe e-
uyll. Mar .He that sowyth chaf shal porely
mowe .Salo. Out of the mouth of a holy man
shal come good lernyng & wysedom Mar. The
asse behovyth to be allweye where he fedyth
for ther it growyth:where he etyth oon gres:
there growe pl.ayen/where he dungyth: there
it fattyth:where he pyssyth there makyth he
wete/and where he wallowyth there brekyth
he the strawe. Sal.Iete an othre prey se the
Mar.yf I shulde my self dyspreyrse/nomā shall
I please .Sal.Thou shalt ete moche ony. Mar.
That beys dryve lykke faste theyre fyngres
Sal.In an evyll wylled herte the spyryt of wy
sedome shall not entre.Mar.As ye smyte wyth
au axe in an hard tre/beware that the chippes
falle not in youre ye. Sal'It it is hard to spurne
ayenst the sharp prykyl. Mar:The ox that drawyth bacwarde shalbe twyse prycked.Sal'Fe
de vp poure children & from thayre youthe ler-
ne thaym todo well. Mar.He that fedyth well
is cowe etyth often of the mylke.Salo.Allma-
ner kyndes turne ayen to theyre furste nature:
Mar.A worne tabyll cloth turnyth aȝe to his

Marcolphus: "A fat woman and a great is larger in giving than others."

Solomon: "A white kerchief becometh well a woman's head."

Marcolphus: "It standeth written that the fur is not all like the sleeves, and under a white cloth often are hid moths."[22]

Solomon: "He that soweth wickedness shall reap evil."[23]

Marcolphus: "He that soweth chaff shall poorly mow."

Solomon: "Out of the mouth of a holy man shall come good learning and wisdom.

Marcolphus: "The ass behooveth to be always where he feedeth for there it groweth; where he eateth one grass, there grow forty again; where he dungeth, there it fatteth;° where he pisseth there maketh he wet; and where he walloweth there breaketh he the straw."[24]

Solomon: "Let another praise thee."[25]

Marcolphus: "If I should myself dispraise, no man shall I please."

Solomon: "Thou shalt [not] eat much honey."[26]

Marcolphus: "That° bees drive,° lick fast their fingers."[27]

Solomon: "In an evil-willed heart the spirit of wisdom shall not enter."[28]

Marcolphus: "As ye smite with an axe in a hard tree beware that the chips fall not in your eye."

Solomon: "It is hard to spurn° against the sharp prickle."[29]

Marcolphus: "The ox that draweth backward shall be twice pricked."[30]

Solomon: "Feed up your children and from their youth learn them to do well."[31]

Marcolphus: "He that feedeth well his cow eateth often of the milk."

Solomon: "All manner [of] kinds turn again to their first nature.

Marcolphus: "A worn tablecloth turneth again to his first kind."[32] (on the proverb pair between this and the following)[33]

fatteth becomes fat, grows thickly.   **That** those who.   **drive** drive away, pursue.   **spurn** kick.

furste kynde Sal' What the iuge knowyth of
right & trouthe that spekyth he out. Mar. A bis∕
shop that spekyth not is made a porter of a yate
Salo. Honoure is to be yeuē to the maistre and
the rodde to be feryd (Mar. He that is wonte to
anoite the iuges hādes oftyn tymes he makyth
his asse lene Sal. A yenst a strōgr & myghty mā
thau shalt not fyghte/ne stryve ayēst the streme
Marc/ The vultier takyth the skyn of stronge
fowles & makyth thaym nekedz of theyr fethīs
/Salo Iete vs amēde vs in good that vnwy∕
thyngly we have mysdone/ Mar. As a mā wy∕
pyth his ars he doth nothing ellys/ Sal' Wyl∕
thon n ot disceyue any man wyth fayre wordz.
Mar/ By wyt he etyth that gretyth the ether:
Salo/ wyth brawlyng people holde no cōpanye
Marc/ It is reson that he of the swyne ete that
medlyth amonge te bren/ Sal' There be many
that kan have no shame /Mar/ They lyve vn∕
dre the mē that are lyke to howndes/ Sal' The∕
re are many that to theyr good.doers do evyl for
good Marcolphus He that yevyth bred to
an othre manys hownde shall have no thanke
Salomon It is no frende that dureyth not in
frendeshyp Mar The dung of a calf stynkyth
notlonge/ Sal' He sekyth many occasiōs that
wolk departe from his maist/ Mar/ A woman
that wolk not cōsente.seyth thath she hat a skab∕
bydz arse Salomon A kynges worde shul∕
de be vnchaungeable or stedfaste/ Marcolfus

Solomon: "What the judge knoweth of right and truth that speaketh he out."

Marcolphus: "A bishop that speaketh not is made a porter of a gate."

Solomon: "Honor is to be given to the master, and the rod to be feared."

Marcolphus: "He that is wont to anoint the judge's hands oftentimes he maketh his ass° lean."[34]

Solomon: "Against a strong and mighty man thou shalt not fight, nor strive against the stream."

Marcolphus: "The vulture taketh the skin of strong fowls and maketh them naked of their feathers."[35]

Solomon: "Let us amend us in good that unwittingly we have misdone."

Marcolphus: "As a man wipeth his arse he doth nothing else."[36]

Solomon: "Will thou not deceive any man with fair words."

Marcolphus: "By wit he eateth that greeteth the other."[37]

Solomon: "With brawling people hold no company."[38]

Marcolphus: "It is reason that he of the swine eat that meddleth among the bran."[39]

Solomon: "There be many that can have no shame."

Marcolphus: "They live under the men that are like to hounds."[40]

Solomon: "There are many that to their good-doers do evil for good."

Marcolphus: "He that giveth bread to another man's hound shall have no thanks."[41]

Solomon: "It is no friend that [en]dureth not in friendship."

Marcolphus: "The dung of a calf stinketh not long."[42]

Solomon: "He seeketh many occasions that will depart from his master."[43]

Marcolphus: "A woman that will not consent saith that she hath a scabbed arse."

Solomon: "A king's word should be unchangeable or steadfast."

ass donkey.

he is fone wery that plowyth wyth a wolf. Sa
lomō The radiſſh rotys are good mete but they
ſtynke in the Connſell. Mar. He that etyth Radyſſh rotys coughyth aboue and vndyr/ Sal. It
is loſt that is ſpokyn a fore people that vndreſtā
de not what they here. Mr. He leſyth his ſhafte
that ſhetyth in the ſande; Sal. He that ſtoppyth
his erys from the cryng of the pore people.oure
lord god ſhall not here hym Mar. He that wepyth afore a iuge leſyth his terys; Sal. Ryſe vp
thou northren wynde and come forth thou ſouthren wynde and blowe through my gardeyne
and the wele ſmellyng herbys ſhall growe and
multiplie; Marc. Whan the northren wyndes
blowe than ben the high howſes in great trouble and daunger; Salo. The deth nor poueryte
wyll not be hyd Mar; A man that is broſtyn
and hyde.it/they growe the moee/ Sal. As thou
ſyttyſt at a Richemans table beholde diligently
what comyth afore the; Mar. Alle metys that
is ordeyned for the body/ muſte through the bely:and it goth in the ſtomak; Salo. Whan thou
ſyttyſt at the tabyll beware that thou taſte not
furſt; Mar. He that ſyttyth in the hygheſt ſete /
he holdyth the vppermoſt place Sal. As the
ſtronge the weyke wynneth/ he takyth all that
he hath; Mar: The catte ſeeth wele whoos berde ſhe lycke ſhall; Salo: That he wycked feryth
that fallyth hym oftē; Mar: He that doth evyll
b

Marcolphus: "He is soon weary that ploweth with a wolf."[44]

Solomon: "The radish roots are good meat but they stink in the council."

Marcolphus: "He that eateth radish roots cougheth above and under."

Solomon: "It is lost that is spoken afore people that understand not what they hear."

Marcolphus: "He loseth his shaft° that shooteth in the sand."[45]

Solomon: "He that stoppeth his ears from the crying of the poor people, our Lord God shall not hear him."[46]

Marcolphus: "He that weepeth afore a judge loseth his tears."

Solomon: "Rise up thou northern wind and come forth thou southern wind and blow through my garden and the well-smelling herbs shall grow and multiply.

Marcolphus: "When the northern winds blow then be the high houses in great trouble and danger."

Solomon: "The death nor poverty will not be hid."

Marcolphus: "A man that is brostyn° and hide it they grow the more."

Solomon: "As thou sittest at a rich man's table behold diligently what cometh afore thee."

Marcolphus: "All meat that is ordained for the body must through the belly, and it goeth in the stomach."

Solomon: "When thou sittest at the table beware that thou taste not first."

Marcolphus: "He that sitteth in the highest seat, he holdeth the uppermost place."

Solomon: "As the strong the weak winneth, he taketh all that he hath."

Marcolphus: "The cat seeth well whose beard she lick shall."[47]

Solomon: "That [which] the wicked feareth that [be]falleth him often."

shaft arrow.   **brostyn** has a hernia, is ruptured.

and hoppth good/is difceyvyd in thaym bothe
Sal ffor the colde the flouthfull wolde not go to
plough/be heggyd his brede:and no man wolde
hym yeve Mar/A nakyd ars no man kan rob-
be or difpoyle Salo. Studye makyth a mayftre
wele wplledz Mar. Thandys that are vfyd in
the fyre/fere not the ketyll/ Sal. Brawlers and
janglers are to be kafte out of alle good companye
Mar.An angry howfe wyf/the fmoke/the ratte
and a broken plater/ are often tymes vnprofy-
table in an howfe Sal. For goddys love men
are bownden to love othre/ Marc/ If thou love
hym that lovyth not the thou lefyth thyn loue
Salo. Saye not to thy frende come to morowe
I fhal yeve the/that thou maifte forth wyth yeve
hym Mar.He fayth an othre tyme he fhall
doo it/that hath noth wherwyth redy for to do
it with alle Sal.He that is wyne dronke:hol-
dyth nothing that he fayth Marcolph° An
opyn arfe hath no lord Salo/ Many coveyte to
have rycheffe that with povertye are holdē vn/
dre/ Marcol.Ete that ye have/and fe what fhall
remaigne Salomō There are many that fuf-
teyne hungyr:and yet fede they theyre wyves
Mar. The pore hadz ne breedz ād yet he bought
an hownde/Sal The fole anfweryth aftyr hys
foliffhnes/for that he fhulde not be knowyn wy-
fe/ Mar/what the ftone heryth/that fhall te oke
anfwere Sal.wrathe hath no mercy /& trefore

Marcolphus: "He that doth evil and hopeth good is deceived in them both."[48]

Solomon: "For the cold the slothful would not go to plough: he begged his bread — and no man would him give."[49]

Marcolphus: "A naked arse no man can rob or despoil."

Solomon: "Study maketh a master well-willed."

Marcolphus: "The hands that are used in° the fire fear not the kettle."[50]

Solomon: "Brawlers and janglers are to be cast out of all good company."

Marcolphus: "An angry housewife, the smoke, the rat, and a broken platter are oftentimes unprofitable in a house."[51]

Solomon: "For God's love men are bound to love others."

Marcolphus: "If thou love him that loveth not thee thou loseth thine love."

Solomon: "Say not to thy friend, come tomorrow, I shall give thee that thou mayest forthwith give him."[52]

Marcolphus: "He saith another time he shall do it that hath not wherewith ready for to do it withal."

Solomon: "He that is wine-drunk holdeth° nothing that he saith."[53]

Marcolphus: "An open arse hath no lord."

Solomon: "Many covet to have riches that with poverty are held under."

Marcolphus: "Eat that ye have and see what shall remain."

Solomon: "There are many that sustain hunger, and yet feed they their wives.

Marcolphus: "The poor [man] had no bread and yet he bought a hound."[54]

Solomon: "The fool answereth after his foolishness for that he should not be known wise."[55]

Marcolphus: "What the stone heareth, that shall the oak answer."[56]

---

used in accustomed to.   **holdeth** believes; fulfils.

he that angrely spekyth/bepth evple or shrewd
ly/Mar/ Saye not in thyn angre to thy frende
no evpl/lest thou forthynke it aftreward Sal.
The mouthe of an ennemye kan saye no good.
ne hys lyppys shall sownde no trouthe:Mar.he
that lovyth me not/doth not diffame me/Salo.
Slepe as ye have nede/Ma/He that leyth hym
downe to slepe & kan not/is not at his hertys ea-
se/Sal We haue well fyllyd oure belys lete vs
thanke god/Mar/As the owsell whystelyth so
answeryth the thrusshe the hügery and the sulle
synge not oon songe/Sal.Lete vs ete ād drinke
we shall alle deye Marc. The hüngery dyeth
aswele as the full feddy:As a man playeth vpó
an harpe he kan not wele idicte Mar.So whã
the hownde shytyth he berkyth noth/Sal:The
wretchyd wombe is full go we now to bedde.
Marcol. He turnyth and walowyth & steppyth
evyl that hath not for to ete.Salo.Dyspyse thou
not a lytyll yifte that is yeven the of a trewe frē
de Mar.That aGeldyd man hath that yevyth
he to his neigborwes/Salo/Go thou not wyth
the evyll man or the brawelyng:lest thou suffre
evyll for hym or peryle Marcolph⁹ A dede bee
makyth no hony/Salo.If thou make frēdeship
with a false and evyl wylledy man.it shalhyndre
the more than proffyte: Marcolphus:
What the wolf doth/that pleasyth the wolfesse
    Salomon: He that answeryth afore

Solomon: "Wrath hath no mercy and therefore he that angrily speaketh buyeth evil or shrewdly."[57]

Marcolphus: "Say not in thine anger to thy friend no evil lest thou forthink° it afterward."

Solomon: "The mouth of an enemy can say no good, nor his lips shall sound no truth."

Marcolphus: "He that loveth me not doth not defame me."[58]

Solomon: "Sleep as ye have need."

Marcolphus: "He that layeth him down to sleep and cannot is not at his heart's ease."

Solomon: "We have well filled our bellies, let us thank God."

Marcolphus: "As the owsell° whistleth so answereth the thrush; the hungry and the full sing not one song."[59]

Solomon: "Let us eat and drink; we shall all die."

Marcolphus: "The hungry dieth as well as the full-fed."

[Solomon]: "As a man playeth upon a harp he cannot well indite."°

Marcolphus: "So when the hound shitteth he barketh not."

Solomon: "The wretched womb is full, go we now to bed."[60]

Marcolphus: "He turneth and walloweth and sleepeth evil that hath naught for to eat."

Solomon: "Despise thou not a little gift that is given thee of a true friend."[61]

Marcolphus: "That a gelded [dimwitted] man hath, that giveth he to his neighbors."[62]

Solomon: "Go thou not with the evil man or the brawling lest thou suffer evil for him° or peril."

Marcolphus: "A dead bee maketh no honey."[63]

Solomon: "If thou make friendship with a false and evil-willed man, it shall hinder thee more than profit."

Marcolphus: "What the wolf doth, that pleaseth the wolfess."

Solomon: "He that answereth afore he is demanded showeth himself a fool."

---

forthink regret.   **owsell** blackbird.   **indite** compose or speak (at the same time).   **for him** because of him.

he is demaundyd she wyth hym self a fole: Mar
Whan a man tredyth or a welto you/youre fete
Sal' Evry thing chesyth his lyke: Mar/ Where
a skabbyd horse is/he sekyth his lyke and eyther
of thaym gnappyth othre Salo. A mercyfull
mā doth wele to his sowle/ Mar: He dyspyseth
a great yifte that knowyth not hym self/ Sal'
He that skapyth te wolf/metyth the lyon/ Mar
colfus From evyll into worse/ as the Cooke to
a bakere: Sal' Ware that no man do the non
evyll/if he do/do it not ayen Mar/ The stylle stā-
dyng watyr/& the man that spekyth but lytyll/
beleve thaym not Salo. We may not alle be lyke Mar/ It standeth wryten in a boke/ he that
hath no horse muste go on fote. Salo. A Chylde
of an hundred yere is cursyd Mar. It is to late
an olde hounde in a bande to lede. Sal. He that
hath shalbe yeuen/& shall flowe. Mar. Woo to
that man that hath frendes & no breed/ Salom/
whoo to that man that hath a dowble herte/ād
in bothe weyes wyll wādre. Mar He that woll'
two weyes go muste epthre his ars or his breche tere/ Salom/ Of habundaunce of therte the
mouth spekyst/ Mar. Out of a full wōbe thars
trompyth/ Salo/ Two ope in one pocke drawē
lyke: Mar. Two veynes go lyke to oon ars.
Sal. A fayre woman is to belovyd of hire hus-
bande/ Mar/ In the necke is she whyte as a do-
ye. and in the ars blacke and derke lyke a molle.

Marcolphus: "When a man treadeth, draw to you° your feet."[64]

Solomon: "Everything chooseth his like."

Marcolphus: "Where a scabbed horse is, he seeketh his like and either of them gnappeth° [the] other.

Solomon: "A merciful man doth well to his soul."

Marcolphus: "He despiseth a great gift that knoweth not himself."

Solomon: "He that scapeth the wolf meeteth the lion."[65]

Marcolphus: "From evil into worse as the cook to a baker."

Solomon: "[Be]ware that no man do thee none evil; if he do, do it not again."[66]

Marcolphus: "The still-standing water and the man that speaketh but little, believe them not."[67]

Solomon: "We may not all be alike."[68]

Marcolphus: "It standeth written in a book, he that hath no horse must go on foot."[69]

Solomon: "A child of a hundred years is cursed."[70]

Marcolphus: "It is too late an old hound in a band° to lead."[71]

Solomon: "He that hath shall be given, and shall flow."[72]

Marcolphus: "Woe to that man that hath friends and no bread."[73]

Solomon: "Woe to that man that hath a double heart and in both ways will wander."

Marcolphus: "He that will two ways go must either his arse or his breeches tear."[74]

Solomon: "Of abundance of the heart the mouth speakest."

Marcolphus: "Out of a full womb the arse trompeth."[75]

Solomon: "Two oxen in one yoke draw alike."

Marcolphus: "Two veins go alike to one arse."

Solomon: "A fair woman is to be loved of her husband."[76]

Marcolphus: "In the neck is she white as a dove and in the arse black and dark like a mole."[77]

---

draw to you pull in.   **gnappeth** bites in snapping fashion.   **band** leash; collar.

Salo: Out of the generacið of inda is my moost
kyndrede/ñ the lord of my fadre hath made go=
uernoure ovyr his people: Mar. I knowe wele
a tabylcloth:and of what werke it is made. Sa
lomð Nede makyth a right wyse mã to do evyll
Mar. The wolf that is takyn ãd set fast/eythre
he byteth or shytyth/ Sal. Were it so that god al
le the world vndre my power had set/ it shulde
suffyse me/ Marc. Men kan not yeve the katte
somoche/ but that she woll hyr tayle wagge.
Sal. He that late comyth to dyner/his parte is
leest in the mete Mar. The glouton kan not se
or renne alaboute/ Salo . Though it be so that
thy wif be so wre fere hir not/ Mr The shepðde
that wakyth well : ther shall the wolf no wolle
shyte: Sal/ It becðth no foles to speke or to bryn
ge forth any wyse reason. Mar . It becomyth
not a dogge to bere a sadyli/ Salo/ whyles the
children are lytyll: reighte theyre lymmes: & ma
ners/ Marc: He that kyssyth the lambe/lovyth
the shepe: Salo. Alle reyght pathys goð to war=
des oon weye: Marc/ So done alle the veynes
renne towardes the ars: Salo. Of a good man
comth a good wyf: Marcolf Of a good mele co
myth a great torde that men wyth theyre fete
trede So muste mẽ also/alle the best pall wynes
trede vndre fote/ Salo: A fayre wyf becomyth
well by hir husbãd/ Marc. A pot full wyth wy=
ne becomth well by the thrusty/ Salo. wel beco

Solomon: "Out of the generation of Judah is my most kindred, and the lord of my father hath made [me] governor over his people."

Marcolphus: "I know well a tablecloth and of what work it is made."

Solomon: "Need maketh a right wise man to do evil."

Marcolphus: "The wolf that is taken and set fast either he biteth or shitteth."

Solomon: "Were it so that God all the world under my power had set, it should suffice me."

Marcolphus: "Men cannot give the cat so much but that she will her tail wag."[78]

Solomon: "He that late cometh to dinner, his part is least in the meat."[79]

Marcolphus: "The glutton cannot see or run all about."[80]

Solomon: "Though it be so that thy wife be sour, fear her not."

Marcolphus: "The shepherd that waketh well,° there shall the wolf no wool shit."[81]

Solomon: "It becometh no fools to speak or to bring forth any wise reason.

Marcolphus: "It becometh not a dog to bear a saddle."

Solomon: "While the children are little, right° their limbs and manners."[82]

Marcolphus: "He that kisseth the lamb loveth the sheep."[83]

Solomon: "All right paths go towards one way."[84]

Marcolphus: "So do all the veins run towards the arse."

Solomon: "Of a good man cometh a good wife."

Marcolphus: "Of a good meal cometh a great turd that men with their feet tread. So must men also all the bestial wines [wives] tread under foot."[85]

Solomon: "A fair wife becometh well by her husband."

Marcolphus: "A pot full with wine becometh well by the thirsty."

---

waketh well does not fall asleep.   **right** make straight; correct.

myth a fayre sworde by my syde. Mar/Wel be=
comth my hegge a great hepe of stonys Sal.
The gretter that ye be the more meke shulde ye
be in alle thyngys/ Mar/he rydyth well that ri=
dyth wyth his felawes/Sal The wyse chylde
gladyth the fadyr:& the folysshchilde is a sorwe
to the modyr/ Mar. They synge not al oon soge
the glad? & the sory: Salo.he that sowyth wyth
skaerstye/repyth skaersly: Mar:The more it fry
seth the more it byndeth: Sal.do alle thynges by
coüsell & thou shalt not astre forthinke it/ Mar/
he is seke y nough that the sekenesse drawyth or
folowyth: Sal. Alle thinges have theyre seasös
& tyme: Mar. Now daye to morwe daye. sayde
the oye:that the hare chacyd?.Sa.J am wery of
spekyng:lete vs therefore reste Mar:Therfore
shall not y leue my clapping: Sa:j may no more
Mar/yf ye maye no more yelde youre self ovyr
comë:& yeue me that ye have epromysed? Wyth
that spake to marcolf Hanany as the sone of jo=
iade:and zabus the kinges frende:and adonias
the sone of abde whiche hadden the charge and
gouernance ovyr the kyges tribute/and sayde:
Thou shalt not herefore be the thyrdde in the ki
gedome of oure soueraigne lord Më shall rather
put bothe thyn worst yen out of thy moost vyle
hede:for it becomyth the bettyr to lye amonge
berys:than tó be eßal ted? to any dignyte or ho=
nour/ Than marcolphus sayde wherfor hath

Solomon: "Well becometh a fair sword by my side."

Marcolphus: "Well becometh my hedge a great heap of stones."[86]

Solomon: "The greater that ye be, the more meek should ye be in all things."

Marcolphus: "He rideth well that rideth with his fellows."[87]

Solomon: "The wise child gladdens the father and the foolish child is a sorrow to the mother."

Marcolphus: "They sing not all one song, the glad and the sorry."[88]

Solomon: "He that soweth with scarcity reapeth scarcely."

Marcolphus: "The more it freezeth the more it bindeth."[89]

Solomon: "Do all things by counsel and thou shalt not after forthink° it."

Marcolphus: "He is sick enough that the sickness draweth or followeth."[90]

Solomon: "All things have their seasons and time."

Marcolphus: "Now day tomorrow day, said the ox that the hare chased."[91]

Solomon: "I am weary of speaking, let us therefore rest."

Marcolphus: "Therefore shall not I leave my clapping."°

Solomon: "I may no more."

Marcolphus: "If ye may no more, yield yourself overcome and give me that ye have promised."

With that spake to Marcolphus Hanany as the son of Joiade, and Zabus the king's friend, and Adonais[92] the son of Abde which had the charge and governance over the king's tribute, and said: "Thou shalt not herefore be the third in the kingdom of our sovereign lord. Men shall rather put both thine worst eyes out of they most vile head, for it becometh thee better to lie among bears than to be exalted to any dignity or honor."

Then Marcolphus said: "Wherefore hath the king then promised?"

forthink regret.   **clapping** chattering.

the king than pinpſed? Than ſayde thekinges
vij. prouoſtes/ that is to wyte Neuthur Bena=
dachar Beneſya Bena Benanides Banthabar
Athurady Bominia Joſephus Semes ad Sa=
mer/ Wherto comth this fole oure ſoveraign lor
de althus to trouble and mocke Why dryue ye
hym not out wyth ſtavys of his fyghte Tho ſay
de ſalomon/not ſo but yeue hym wele to ete and
drinke/and lete hym thau goo in peaſe To ſpak
marcolphus goyng his weye to the king/J ſuf=
fre y nough what that ye haue ſayde J ſhall al=
weyes ſaye There is no kipg were no lawe is

Onys vpon a tyme the king rode an huntyng
wyth his hunterys and howndes/aud fortuny
d? hym to come by the houſe of marcolf: And
turnyd? hym ſelf thidrewardes wyth his horſe
and demaunded? wyth his hede inclyned? vndre
the dorre bowe.who was wythin. Marcolf aſ=
weryd? to the king: wythin is an hool man & an
half.& an horſe hede/& the more that they aſcen
de the more they downe falle To that ſpak ſalo
mō what menyſt thou therwithall/ Tho aſwe
ryd? marcolphus The hole man is my ſelf ſyt=
tyng wythin/ ye are the half man ſyttyng wy=
thoute vpon youre horſe lokyng in wyth you=
re hede declyned?. And the horſe hede is the
hede of youre horſe that ye ſytte on: Than Salo
mon demaunded? of Marcolphus what they

Then said the king's twelve provosts, that is to wit, Neuthur, Benadachar, Benesya, Bena, Benanides, Banthabar, [Achinadai], Athurady, Bominia, Josephus, Semes, and Samer,[93] "Whereto cometh this fool our sovereign lord all thus to trouble and mock? Why drive ye him not out with staves of his sight?

Then said Solomon, "Not so, but give him well to eat and drink, and let him then go in peace."

Then spake Marcolphus going his way to the king, "I suffer enough what that ye have said. I shall always say, 'There is no king where no law is.' "

[Part II]

Once upon a time the king rode a-hunting with his hunters and hounds, and [it] fortuned him to come by the house of Marcolphus. And [he] turned himself thitherwards with his horse and demanded, with his head inclined under the door bow, who was within.

Marcolphus answered to the king, "Within is a whole man and a half, and a horse head, and the more that they ascend the more they down fall."

To that spake Solomon, "What meanest thou therewithal?"

Then answered Marcolphus, "The whole man is myself sitting within; ye are the half man sitting without upon your horse looking in with your head declined. And the horse head is the head of your horse that ye sit on."

Then Solomon demanded of Marcolphus what they

were that clymē vp and fallyn downe. Mar
col: Anſwerpd & ſapde: they are the benys boyl∕
lyng in the pott Salomō/ where is thy fadyr: thy
modyr/ thy Suſtyr/ and thy brothyr/ Mar/ My
fadyr is in the felde and makyth of oon harme
two. My modyr is goon and dooth to hir neigh∕
bor we that ſhe nevyr more ſhall do/ my brothyr
ſytting wythoute the houſe ſlepth alle that he
fyndeth My suſtyr ſyttypth in hire. Chambre &
be wepyth that a fore tyme ſhe laughyd. Salomō
What betokenth they Mar: My fadyr is ī the
felde and puttyth or ſettyth thornys in a foot
path/ & compyng men they make an othre path
therby/ & ſo he makyth of oon harme. two My
modyr is goon and cloſyth the yes of hir neygh∕
bor we deping/ the whiche ſhe ſhall nevyr more
do My brothyr ſytting wythoute the houſe ī the
ſonne & lo wſyth· & alle that he fyndeth he ſlepth
My suſtyr/ the laſte yere lovyd a yonge man ād
wyth kyſſyng/ laughig/ taſtyng: japyng & play
ing: ſhe was getyn wyth chylde: whereof ſhe
now travayllyth/ and that now ſſie be wepyth
ſore: Salomon   How compth to the alle this
wyſdome & ſubtyltye/ Marcolfus In the tyme
of king dauid youre fadyr there was a yongemā
his phiſiciā. & as he onys had takyn a vulture
for to occupye in his medicins/ and had takyn
therof that was to hym eppedyēt So toke you∕
re modyr Barſebea the herte & leyde it vpon a

were that climb up and fall down.

Marcolphus answered and said: "They are the beans boiling in the pot."

Solomon: Where is thy father, thy mother, thy sister, and thy brother?"

Marcolphus: "My father is in the field and maketh of one harm two. My mother is gone and doeth to her neighbor that she never more shall do. My brother sitting without the house slayeth all that he findeth. My sister sitteth in her chamber and beweepeth that aforetime she laughed."

Solomon: "What betokeneth they?"

Marcolphus: "My father is in the field and putteth or setteth thorns in a footpath and coming men° they make another path thereby and so he maketh of one harm two.⁹⁴ My mother is gone and closeth the eyes of her neighbor dying, the which she shall never more do.⁹⁵ My brother [is] sitting without the house in the sun and louseth,° and all that he findeth he slayeth.⁹⁶ My sister the last year loved a young man and with kissing, laughing, tasting, japing, and playing she was gotten with child whereof she now travailleth, and that now she beweepeth sore."

Solomon: "How cometh to thee all this wisdom and subtlety?"

Marcolphus: "In the time of King David your father there was a young man his physician, and as he once had taken a vulture for to occupy° in his medicines, and had taken thereof that was to him expedient, so took your mother Bathsheba the heart and laid it upon a

coming men when men come.   **louseth** looks for lice.   **occupy** make use of.

crufte of breed? and roftyd? it vpon the fayre/ad
yave you the herte to ete/ and J thãne beyng in
the kechi/fhe kaft at my hede the crufte through
moyfted wyth therte of the vulture: & that ete j
and therof J fuppofe is come to me my fubtiltie
lyke as to you is comen by etyng of therte wyfe
dom. Salomõ As verely god helpe the. jn gabaa
god appieryd? to me & fulfylled? me wyth fapiẽ
ce: Marcolph⁹ He isholdyn wyfe that reputyth
hym felf a fole: Sa. Hafte thou not herde what
rycheffe god hath yevyn me aboven that wyfe
dome Mar. J have herde it And j knowe well
that where god woll/there reynyth.it. To that
fayd falomõ all'laughyngly/my folkys wayte v
pon me withoute j may no leugyr wyth the tal-
ke/but faye to thy modyr that fhe fende me of his
befte cowe a pot full of mylke/and that the pot
of the fame cowe be coveryd? & bringe thou it to
me: Marcolph⁹ It fhalbe done· King falomon
wyth his companye rydyng towardys ierufalẽ
was honourably receyyd/as a riche and mooft
puyffãt king. And whan flofcemya marcolph⁹
modyr was comyn home to hir houfe/he dede
to hir the kiges meffage Thã fhe takig a pot full
wyth mylke of hir cowe/ and coveryd? it wyth
a flawne of the fame mylke made. and fent it fo
forth to the king by hirfone/as marcolph⁹ went
ovyr the felde the wethir was warme of the fõ-
ne fawe lying there a drye bakyn cowe torde: &

                                    &

crust of bread and roasted it upon the fire and gave you the heart
to eat, and then being in the kitchen, she cast at my head the
crust through-moisted with the heart of the vulture; and that ate
I and thereof I suppose is come to me my subtlety like as to you
is come — by eating of the heart — wisdom."[97]

Solomon: "As verily God help thee, in Gabaa[98] God appeared
to me and fulfilled me with sapience."

Marcolphus: "He is holden wise that reputeth himself a fool."

Solomon: "Hast thou not heard what riches God hath given
me above that wisdom?"

Marcolphus: "I have heard it and I know well that where God
wills, there raineth it.

To that said Solomon all laughingly: "My folks° wait upon
me without, I may not linger with thee [to] talk, but say to thy
mother that she send me of her best cow a potful of milk, and
that the pot of the same cow be covered,° and bring thou it to
me."

Marcolphus: "It shall be done."

King Solomon with his company riding towards Jerusalem
was honorably received as a rich and most puissant king. And
when Floscemia,[99] Marcolphus's mother, was come home to her
house, he did to her the king's message. Then she taking a pot
full with milk of her cow and covered it with a flawn° of the
same milk made, and sent it so forth to the king by her son. As
Marcolphus went over the field — the weather was warm of the
sun — saw lying there a dry-baked cow turd; and

---

folks company, followers.   **of the same cow be covered** be covered
by something made from the same cow.   **flawn** milk custard, flan.

for haſte he vnnethe cowde ſet downe the pot
to the erthe but that he hadȝ etyn the flawne/ ād
toke vp the cowe torde. and ther wyth copyrdȝ
the pot.And ſo copyrdȝ preſentyd it before the
king.and he aſkydȝ why is the pot thus copyrdȝ.
Marcolf My lord have not ye cōmaunded that
the milke ſhulde becopyrd of the ſame cowe/Sa
lo. J cōmaundedȝ not ſo to be done: Mar.Thus
J vndprſtode/Sal'.Jt hadȝ ben bettyr coverpd
wyth a flawne made wyth the mylke of the ſa
me Cowe.Mar.So was it furſte done/but hū
gyr chanigyd wpt/Sal'How: Marc. J wyſte
wele that ye had no nede of mete/and J havyng
great hūgyr ete the flawne wyth mylke anpon-
tedȝ and for that wyth wpt chungydȝ/the pot J
have thuscoverpd wyth a cowe torde.Sal'now
leve we all' this.and pf that thou thys nyght wa
ke not aſwele as J:thou mapſte haue no truſte
to morne of thy hede. Salomō & maccolph con-
ſentpd bothe.& wythin a lytyil whyle aftyr mar
colph began to rowte/Salo.ſayde/marcolf thou
ſlepyſt: Marcolph anſwerydȝ. Lord J do not J
thinke/Salomon/what thinkpſt thon/Marcolf
J thinke that there are as many jopntys in the
tayle of an hare/as I hire chyne: Salomō jf thou
pve not that to morne thou arte worthy to deye
Salomon beyng ſtylle/began marcolph to ſlepe:
ayen and ſayde to hym/thou ſlepyſt And he anſ
werydȝ J do not/for J thynke/Salomon what

for haste he unnethe° could set down the pot to the earth but that he had eaten the flawn, and took up the cow turd and therewith covered the pot, and so covered, presented it before the king.

And he asked, "Why is the pot thus covered?"

Marcolphus: "My lord, have not ye commanded that the milk should be covered of the same cow?"

Solomon: "I commanded not so to be done."

Marcolphus: "Thus I understood."

Solomon: "It had been better covered with a flawn made with the milk of the same cow."

Marcolphus: "So was it first done, but hunger changed wit."°[100]

Solomon: "How?"

Marcolphus: "I wist well that ye had no need of meat,° and I having great hunger ate the flawn with milk anointed, and for that with wit changed, the pot I have thus covered with a cow turd."

Solomon: "Now leave we all this; and if that thou this night wake not° as well as I, thou mayest have no trust to morn° of thy head."[101]

Solomon and Marcolphus consented both, and within a little while after Marcolphus began to rowt.° Solomon said, "Marcolphus, thou sleepest."

Marcolphus answered, "Lord I do not; I think."

Solomon: "What thinkest thou?"

Marcolphus: "I think that there are as many joints in the tail of a hare as in her chin."

Solomon: "If thou prove not that to morn, thou art worthy to die."

Solomon being still, began Marcolphus to sleep; again and said to him, "Thou sleepest."

And he answered, "I do not, for I think."

Solomon: "What

---

unnethe scarcely.	**wit** my mind.	**meat** food.	**wake not** do
not stay awake.	**to morn** tomorrow.	**rowt** snore.	

thynkeſt thou/ Marcolphus/ J thynke that the
pye hath as many whyte fethzys as blacke. Sa
lomõ But thou alſo pzove that trewe thou ſhalt
leſe thyn hede/ As ſalomon ayen began to be ſtyl
le Marcolph began ayen te rowte and to blowe
And Salomõ ſayd to hym thou ſlepyſt/ Marcol
phus Nay J thinke. Salomon/ What thinkeſt
thou/   Marcolph J thinke that vndze therhe
is no clerer thing than the daye   Salomõ Is the
daye clerer than mylke/ Marcolph Je/ Salomõ
That muſte thou pzove. Anone hervpon began
marcolphus to ſlepe · Salo. Thou ſlepyſt/ Mar/
J ſlepe not but I muſe/ Salomon What muſyſt
thou. Marcolph J muſe how that men may not
ſurely trnſte the women. Salomon/ And that
of the ſhalve pzovydz/ Anon aftyz as Salomon
was ſtylle began marcolf ayen to blowe and to
ſlepe. Salomo Thou ſlepyſt/ Marcolph J do not
but j thinke/ Salomõ What thinkeſt thou. Mar
coph J thinke how that nature goth afoze lernyng: Salomon: If thou pzove not that trewe
thou ſhalt leſe thyn hede/ Aftyz that the nyght
was ovyz paſſydz. and ſalomon wery of waking
put hym ſelf to reſte Than marcolf lefte the king
and ran haſtely to hys ſuſtyz Fudaſa: and fay-
nedz hym ſelf ſozwefull. and hevy. and ſayde to
hyze: The king Salomon is ayenſt me/ and
J may not bere hys thzeptys and ininries: and

thinkest thou?"

Marcolphus: "I think that the pie° hath as many white feathers as black."

Solomon: But thou also prove that true, thou shalt lose thine head."

As Solomon again began to be still, Marcolphus began again to rowt and to blow. And Solomon said to him, "Thou sleepest."

Marcolphus: "Nay, I think."

Solomon: "What thinkest thou?"

Marcolphus: "I think that under the earth is no clearer thing than the day."

Solomon: "Is the day clearer than milk?"

Marcolphus: "Yea."

Solomon: "That must thou prove."

Anon hereupon began Marcolphus to sleep. Solomon: "Thou sleepest."

Marcolphus: "I sleep not, but I muse."

Solomon: "What musest thou?"

Marcolphus: "I muse how that men may not surely trust the women."[102]

Solomon: "And that of thee shall be proved."

Anon after as Solomon was still, began Marcolphus again to blow and to sleep. Solomon: "Thou sleepest."

Marcolphus: "I do not, but I think."

Solomon: "What thinkest thou?"

Marcolphus: "I think how that nature goeth afore learning."

Solomon: "If thou prove not that true, thou shalt lose thine head."

After that the night was overpassed and Solomon, weary of waking, put himself to rest. Then Marcolphus left the king and ran hastily to his sister Fudasa,[103] and feigned himself sorrowful and heavy, and said to her, "The king Solomon is against me and I may not bear his threats and injuries; and

pie magpie.

but J shall take this knyf / & hyde it secretly vn∙
dyr my clothes / ād there wyth thys daye all pry
uely he not knowyng J shall smyte hym to ther∙
te and sle hym: now goodꝛ dere sustyr J praye
the accuse me not but iu any wyse kepe it secrete
ne shewe it not to myn owne brothyr Bufrydo /
Fudasa answerydꝛ my dere and leevest brothyr
Marcolf put no doubtes therin J had levyr dye
and be brent at a stake rather / thā J shulde disco
vre it oꝛ accuse the / Aftyr that retonrupdꝛ mar∙
colf all pryvely to wardys the kynges Courte
The sōne rysyng & spredyng hyr beamys ovyr
therthe jllumminedꝛ & fulfyllydꝛ the kigys palay∙
ce: and salamon rysyng from his bed / wente and
sat in the trone oꝛ sete of his palayce Than com
maundedꝛ he to bringe a foꝛe hym an hare. and
asmany joyntes iu his tayle as in hys chyne we
re fownden by marcolph and nombꝛedys   ❡
Thanne was there a pye bꝛought befoꝛe the
king / and asmaꝛy whyte fethꝛys as black we∙
re fownden by marcolph And thāne toke mar
colph a great panne wyth mylke ād set it in the
kinges bed chambꝛe all pryvely. aud closydꝛ to
alle the wyndowes that no lyght mpght in co∙
me Thanne kallydꝛ he the king into the chābꝛe /
And as he come in he stumblydꝛ at the panne &
was nygh fallyn therin Tho was the king an∙
gry and displeasydꝛ / & sayd thou fowle evyl bo∙
dy / what is it that thou doost Marcolph⁹ aswe

but° I shall take this knife and hide it secretly under my clothes, and therewith this day all privily, he not knowing, I shall smite him to the heart and slay him. Now good dear sister, I pray thee accuse me not but in any wise keep it secret, nor show it not to mine own brother Bufrydo."[104]

Fudasa answered, "My dear and liefest° brother Marcolphus, put no doubts therein. I had liefer die and be brent at a stake rather than I should discover it or accuse thee."

After that returned Marcolphus all privily towards the king's court. The sun rising and spreading her beams over the earth illumined and fulfilled° the king's palace, and Solomon rising from his bed went and sat in the throne or seat of his palace. Then commanded he to bring afore him a hare, and as many joints in his tail as in his chin were found by Marcolphus and numbered. Then was there a pie brought before the king, and as many white feathers as black were found by Marcolphus. And then took Marcolphus a great pan with milk and set it in the king's bedchamber all privily, and closed to all the windows that no light might in come. Then called he the king into the chamber. And as he came in he stumbled at the pan and was nigh fallen therein. Then was the king angry and displeased and said, "Thou foul evil body, what is it that thou doest?"

Marcolphus answered,

---

but therefore.   **liefest** most beloved.   **fulfilled** filled.

ryd? ye ought not herefore to be angry. For haue ye not sayd/that milke is clerer than the daye
How is it that ye se not aswele by the clerenesse
of the mylke as ye do bi the clerenesse of the daye
iuge egaly and ye shall fynde that I haue no-
thyng mysdone vnto you Salomon/God forye-
ue the.my clothys be all wyth mylke spzongyn
And nygh I had my necke bzokyn/and yet thou
haste me nothing trespasyd? Marcolphus āswe
ryd? ā othze tyme se bettyz to foze youlnevyzhte-
lesse fytte downe and do me iustyce vpon a ma-
ter that I shall shewe afoze you: Whan he was
set Marcolph complaynedz and shewpdz Lozd I
haue a fustyz that hath to name Fudasa and she
hath yeuen hyzself to hozedam and is wyth chil
de wherwyth she shamyth and dishonestyd alle
oure bloode and lynage: and yet wolde she parte wyth me in my fathzes good and herytage
Thanne sayde Salomon/ Lete hyz come a foze
vs: And we shall here hyz what she woll saye
herto. As Salomon sawe hyz come from ferre
sayde all laughyngly/ Thys may wele be Marcolphus fustyz This fudasa was shozt ād thyc-
ke/and therto was she great wyth chylde/and
thus was she thycker thā she was of lenghthe
She had thycke leggys and shozt. and went on
bote lame/wyth vysage/yen and stature lycke
to Marcolph. Salomon sayde to Marcolph/

c iij

"Ye ought not herefore to be angry. For have ye not said that milk is clearer than the day? How is it that ye see not as well by the clearness of the milk as ye do by the clearness of the day? Judge equally and ye shall find that I have nothing misdone unto you."

Solomon: "God forgive thee, my clothes be all with milk sprongen,° and nigh I had my neck broken and yet thou hast me nothing trespassed.

Marcolphus answered, "Another time see better to fore° you; nevertheless sit down and do me justice upon a matter that I shall show afore you." When he was set, Marcolphus complained and showed, "Lord I have a sister that hath to name Fudasa, and she hath given herself to whoredom and is with child, wherewith she shameth and dishonested all our blood and lineage, and yet would she part° with me in my father's good[s] and heritage."

Then said Solomon, "Let her come afore us and we shall hear her what she will say hereto." As Solomon saw her come from far, said all laughingly, "This may well be Marcolphus's sister."

This Fudasa was short and thick, and thereto was she great with child, and thus was she thicker than she was of length. She had thick legs and short, and went on both lame, with visage, eyes, and stature like Marcolphus.

Solomon said to Marcolphus,

sprongen sprinkled, spattered.   **to fore** in front of.   **part** share.

What complaynest oz askyst thou of thy susty.
Marcolph answeryd? My lozd J complayne ād
shewe oppnly afoze you of my systyz/that she is
a stronge harlot and a strumpet/ād is wyth chyl
de.as ye may se.and alle oure blood and kyntede
by hyz is shamyd?.that wythstandyng she wol‐
de dele and parte wyth me in my fathzes good
and herytage Whereoze J requyze you of iusty
ce.and that ye commaunde hire that she take no
parte ne make no clayme therto. This heryng
ffudasa replete wyth angze and woednesse czy‐
ed? on hygh and sayde: Thou fowle mysshappyn
harlot/wherefoze shulde not J have my parte in
oure fadzes good and herytage.and is not ffos‐
cempa moder to vs bote: Marcoph Thou shalt
not have any dele oz parte therin ffoz thin offēse
iugeth the clerely therfro/ffudasa Therfoze J
may not lese myn herytage.ffoz have j mysdone
j shall amende it / but oon thyng J pzomyse the/
and swere by god? and all hys myght.yf thou
wylt not lete me be in pease:and suffre me to ha‐
ue my parthe in the land.J shall shewe suche a
thyng of the.that the king oz it be nyght shall
do the to behangyd?: Marcolphus/Thou fowle
stynkyng hoze.what kanst thou saye of me J ha
ue no man mysdone/saye thy wozste J dyffye
the/thou haste moche misdone thou fowle facy‐
d? knave and rvbaulde that thou art.ffoz thou
gladly woldyst sse the king/and yf ye beleve not

"What complainest or askest thou of thy sister?"

Marcolphus answered, "My lord I complain and show openly afore you of my sister that she is a strong harlot and a strumpet and is with child, as ye may see, and all our blood and kindred by her is shamed. That withstanding, she would deal and part with me in my father's good[s] and heritage. Wherefore I require you of justice that ye command her that she take no part nor make no claim thereto."

This hearing, Fudasa, replete with anger and wodness,° cried on high and said, "Thou foul misshapen harlot, wherefore should not I have my part in our father's good[s] and heritage? And is not Floscemia mother to us both?"

Marcolphus: "Thou shalt not have any deal or part therein, for thine offence judgeth thee clearly therefrom.

Fudasa: "Therefore I may not lose mine heritage. For have I misdone I shall amend it, but one thing I promise thee, and swear by God and all his might: if thou wilt not let me be in peace and suffer me to have my part in the land, I shall show such a thing of thee that the king, or it be night, shall do thee to be hanged."

Marcolphus: "Thou foul stinking whore, what canst thou say of me? I have no man misdone. Say thy worst, I defy thee."

"Thou hast much misdone thou foul-faced knave and ribald° that thou art. For thou gladly wouldst slay the king and if ye believe not

wodness madness.   **ribald** rude jester; low-born.

me feke vndyr his cote & ye shall fynde the knyf
Tho was the knyf sought by the kinges seruaū
tys and it was not fownde Sayde marcolph to
the king and to the aboutestanders. And have J
not sayde trouthe: that men shulde not put ovyr
moche truste or cōfidēce in the womē, wyth that
they alle begā to laughē Tho sayd salomō. Mar
colph Thou doost alle thy thynges by crafte and
subtyltye/ Marcolph āsweryd? Iord it is no sub
tyltye. but that my sustyr had prompsed? me to
have kept it secrete/& she hath falsely discoverd?/
it as though it had ben of a trouthe. Salomon/
wherefore haste thou sayd that arte or nature.
goth before lernyng/ Marcolph Take pacyence
a lytyll/ and afore or ye go to bedde J shal shewe
you The daye passyd? ovyr and the tyme of sou
per cam on. The king sat to sowper and othre.
Wyth whom sat marcolph. and had alle pryve
ly put into hys sleve thre quyk myse There was
noryshyd? in the kinges house a Catte that eve
ry nyght as the king sat at sowper: was wont
to holde betwyxt hyre fore feet a brennyng kā
dell vpon the tabyll. Thanne lete marcolph oon
of the myse go out of his sleve. As the catte that
saugh/ she wolde have lept aftyr: but the king ya
ue hyr a wynke or countenaunce/ that she bode
stylle syttyng and removyd not. and in lyke wy
se dede she of the secunde mowse/ Thanne lete
marcolph the thyrdde mowse go: and as the kat

me, seek under his coat and ye shall find the knife."

Then was the knife sought by the king's servants and it was not found.

Said Marcolphus to the king and to the about-standers: "And have I not said truth, that men should not put over much trust or confidence in the women?"[105]

With that they all began to laugh. Then said Solomon, "Marcolphus, thou doest all thy things by craft and subtlety."

Marcolphus answered, "Lord it is no subtlety, but that my sister had promised me to have kept it secret, and she hath falsely discovered it as though it had been of a truth."

Solomon: "Wherefore hast thou said that art or nature goeth before learning?"

Marcolphus: "Take patience a little, and afore or◊ ye go to bed I shall show you."

The day passed over and the time of supper came on. The king sat to supper and other[s], with whom sat Marcolphus, and had all privily put into his sleeve three quick◊ mice. There was nourished in the king's house a cat that every night, as the king sat at supper, was wont to hold betwixt her forefeet a burning candle upon the table. Then let Marcolphus one of the mice go out of his sleeve. As the cat that saw, she would have leapt after, but the king gave her a wink or countenance that she bode still sitting and removed not. And in likewise did she of the second mouse. Then let Marcolphus the third mouse go, and as the cat

or ere.   **quick** live.

te sawe he cowde no lenger abyde.but kaste the
kãdell awaye and lept aftyr the mowse and toke it/ And as marcolph that sawe : sayde to the
king/ Here J have now provyd before you that
nature goth afore lernyng: Tho commaunded
Salomon his seruauntes.have thys man out of
my syghte:and if he come hythre any more / set
my howndes vpon hym. Marcolph⁹:now for
certayne J knowe and may saye that where as
the hede is seke and evyll at ease/there is no lawe
As marcolph was thus out dryven :he seyde to
hym self /neythre so nor so shall the wyse Salomon of marcolf be quyte. on the next mornyng
folowyng as he was out of his couche or kenel
rysen/he bethoughte hym in his mynde how he
myght beste gete hym ayen into the kinges cour
te wythout hurte or devouryng of the howndes
he wẽt & bought a quyk hare/& put it vndre his
clothis & yede ayen to the courte And whan the
kinges seruauntes had syghte of hym/they set v
pon hym alle the howndes & forthwyth he caste
the hare from hym:and the howndes aftre.& lef
te marcolph.and thus came he ayen be the king
And as he sawe hym he askyd who had letyn
hym in/ Marcolph ãsweryd wyth great sutyltie
am j in come. Sal Be ware that thys daye thou
spytte not but vpon the bare grow;nde/ The pa
layce was all coveryd wyth tapettys.& the wal
les hãgyd wyth riche clothys. Marcof wythin

saw, he could no longer abide, but cast the candle away and leapt after the mouse and took it.

And as Marcolphus that saw, said to the king, "Here I have now proved before you that nature goeth afore learning."[106]

Then commanded Solomon his servants, "Have this man out of my sight, and if he come hither any more, set my hounds upon him."

Marcolphus: "Now for certain I know and may say that where as the head is sick and evil at ease, there is no law." As Marcolphus was thus out driven, he said to himself, "Neither so nor so shall the wise Solomon of Marcolphus be quit."[107]

On the next morning following, as he was out of his couch or kennel risen, he bethought him in his mind how he might best get him again into the king's court without hurt or devouring of the hounds. He went and bought a quick hare and put it under his clothes and gede° again to the court. And when the king's servants had sight of him they set upon him all the hounds, and forthwith he cast the hare from him, and the hounds after° and left Marcolphus, and thus came he again by the king. And as he saw him he asked who had let him in.

Marcolphus answered with great subtlety, "Am I in comen?"[108]

Solomon: "Beware that this day thou spit not but upon the bare ground."

The palace was all covered with tapits,° and the walls hanged with rich cloths. Marcolphus within

gede went.   **after** ran after it.   **tapits** carpets.

short space aftyr/ wyth his talkyng & clateryng
wyth othre his mouth was full of spytyll began
to cough and reche vp/beholdyng alaboute hym
where he myght best spytte & cowd fynde no ba
re erthe: sawe a ballyd man stondyng by the kig
barehedyd?/and spatyld? evyn vpon his forehe
de. The ballyd? man was therwyth/ ashamyd?
made clene his forehede:and fyll on kneyes befo
re the kingys fete/and made a complaynt vpon
marcolph. Salomõ Wherefore haste thou ma
de fowle the forehede of this man. Mar. J have
not made it fowle but j have dungyd it /or made
it fat.for on a bareyne growwnde.it behovyth dũ
ge to be layde.that the corne that is therõ sowyn
may the bettyr growe and multiplye. Saolmon
What is that to this man. Mar. My lord have
ye not forbedyn me / that this daye J shulde not
spytte but vpon the bare erthe/ & J sawe his fo
rehede all bare of herys:and thynkyng it be ba
re erthe.and therefore J spyttyd? vpon it/ The
king shall not be angry for this thing/for j have
done it for the manys proffyte/for and if his fo
rehede were thus vsyd? to be made fat the herys
shulde ayen encrease & multiplye. Salo. God ye
ue the shame/for the ballyd men aught to be abo
uẽ othre men in honure.for balydnesse is no sha
me bnt a begynnyng of worship. Marcolphus/
Balydnesse is a flyes nest Beholde j not syre how
the flyes folowe more his forehede/thã alle the

[a] short space after, with his talking and clattering with other[s], his mouth was full of spittle, began to cough and retchup, beholding all about him where he might best spit, and could find no bare earth, saw a bald man standing by the king bareheaded, and spattled even upon his forehead. The bald man was therewith ashamed, made clean his forehead, and fell on [his] knees before the king's feet and made a complaint upon Marcolphus.

Solomon: "Wherefore hast thou made foul the forehead of this man?"

Marcolphus: "I have not made it foul but I have dunged° it, or made it fat,° for on a barren ground it behooveth dung to be laid that the corn that is thereon sown may the better grow and multiply."[109]

Solomon: "What is that to this man?"

Marcolphus: "My lord, have ye not forbidden me that this day I should not spit but upon the bare earth? And I saw his forehead all bare of hairs and thinking it be bare earth, and therefore I spitted upon it. The king shall not be angry for this thing for I have done it for the man's profit, for and if his forehead were thus used to be made fat, the hairs should again increase and multiply."

Solomon: "God give thee shame, for the bald men ought to be above other men in honor. For baldness is no shame but a beginning of worship."

Marcolphus: "Baldness is a fly's nest. Behold I not, sire, how the flies follow more his forehead than all the

dunged fertilized.   **fat** bountiful, fertile.

othre that ben wythin thys honse. for why they trowe that it be a veſſell turnyng full wyth ſom good dꝛike oꝛ ellys to be a ſtone anoynted₂ wyth any ſwete thyng. and therfoꝛe they haſte thaym to his bare foꝛehede. To this ſayd the bailyd man afoꝛe the kiᵹ: Wherto is this mooſt vyle rybaul de ſufferyd₂ in the kinges pꝛeſence vs to rebuke and ſhame. lete hym be kaſt out. Marcolph/and be it peaſe in thy vertn/and j ſhalbe ſtylle. here wythall come yn two women bꝛyngyng wyth thaym a lyving chylde/foꝛ the whyche they afoꝛe the king began to ſtryve: Foꝛ the oon ſayde it be/lōgyd to hyꝛe / but the od of thaym had foꝛlayne hyꝛe chylde ſlepyng So that they were in ſtryve foꝛ the levyng chylde/ Salomō ſayd to oon of his ſervauntis: take a ſwoꝛde ₢ departe thys chylde in two pecys: and yeve eyther of thaym the oon half/ That heryng the naturall bodyꝛ of the ly vyng chylde: ſayde to the king Loꝛd j beſeche y ou jeve it to that woman all hool lyvyng/foꝛ ſhe his the verraye modyꝛ therof. Than ſayde Salomō that ſhe was the modyꝛ of the chylde and yave it to hire/ Marcolph demaūded₂ of the king how he the modyꝛ knewe. Salomon By chaungyng of hir colure and affection/and by effuſyō of te rys/ Marcolphus ye myghthe ſo bediſceyved₂/ foꝛ beleue ye the wepyng of the womē/ and are ſo wyſe and knowe the crafte of thaym no bet tyꝛ/whyllys a woman wepyth ſhe laughyth

other[s] that be within this house? For why° they trowen° that it be a vessel turning full with some good drink or else to be a stone anointed with any sweet thing, and therefore they haste them to his bare forhead."

To this said the bald man afore the king, "Whereto is this most vile ribald suffered in the king's presence us to rebuke and shame? Let him be cast out."

Marcolphus: "And be it peace in thy virtue,° and I shall be still."

Herewithal came in two women bringing with them a living child for the which they afore the king began to strive. For the one said it belonged to her but the one of them had forlain her child sleeping,° so that they were in strife for the living child.

Solomon said to one of his servants: "Take a sword and depart this child in two pieces and give either of them the one half."

That hearing, the natural mother of the living child said to the king: "Lord I beseech you give it to that woman all whole living for she is the very mother thereof."

Then said Solomon that she was the mother of the child and gave it to her.[110] Marcolphus demanded of the king how he the mother knew.

Solomon: "By changing of her color and affection, and by effusion of tears."

Marcolphus: "Ye might so be deceived, for believe ye the weeping of the women and are so wise and know the craft of them no better? Whiles a woman weepeth she laugheth with

For why because.   **trowen** believe.   **virtue** soul.   **forlain her child sleeping** smothered her child while lying next to it.

wyth therte/ They kan wepe wyth oon pie /ād
lawgh wyth the othyr. They make contenaūce
wyth the vysage that they thinke not They speke wyth the tūge that they mene not wyth therte They promyse many tymes that they parfor
me not-bnt they chaunge theyre contenaunces
as theyre mynd es renne/The women have innumerable craftes/Salomon As many craftes
as they have/ so many good condicyons and pro-
pyrtyes they haue/ Marcolphꝰ Saye not good
condicyons or propyrtyes.but saye shrewdnes-
sys and decepcyons. Salomon Surely she was
an hore that bare suche a sone. Marcolph Wherefore saye ye so· Salomon For thou blamyst al
le women/and they are honest/chaste /meke/lo-
vyng and curtayse/ Marcolf To that myght ye
adde & saye that they are brotyll and mutable.
Salomō If they be brotyll: that have they of ma
nys condicyō /yf they be chaungeable that have
they by delectacioū. Womā is though made of
mānys rybbe/ and yeven vnto hym for his helpe
and comfort For womā is asmoche to saye as
a weyke erthe or a weyke thynge / Mar:jn like
wyse it is asmoche to saye as a softe erroure/
Sal There lyest thou false kaytyf Thou muste
nedys be evyll and onhappy .that sayst so moche
shame and harme of women For of womē we
are alle comen /and therfore he that seyth evyll
of the kynde of women/is greatly to be blamyd

the heart. They can weep with one eye and laugh with the other. They make countenance with the visage that they think not. They speak with the tongue that they mean not with the heart. They promise many times that they perform not, but they change their countenances as their minds run. The women have innumerable crafts."

Solomon: "As many crafts as they have, so many good conditions and properties they have."

Marcolphus: "Say not good conditions or properties, but say shrewdnesses and deceptions."

Solomon: "Surely she was a whore that bare such a son."

Marcolphus: "Wherefore say ye so?"

Solomon: "For thou blamest all women and they° are honest, chaste, meek, loving, and courteous."

Marcolphus: "To that might ye add and say that they are brittle° and mutable."

Solomon: "If they be brittle, that have they of man's condition; if they be changeable that have they by delectation.° Woman is though made of man's rib and given unto him for his help and comfort. For woman is as much to say as a weak earth or a weak thing."

Marcolphus: "In like wise it is as much to say as a soft error."

Solomon: "There liest thou, false caitiff.° Thou must needs be evil and unhappy that sayest so much shame and harm of women. For of women we are all come, and therefore he that saith evil of the kind° of women is greatly to be blamed,

they even when they.   **brittle** fragile, fickle.   **have they by delectation** they do for their own pleasure.   **false caitiff** base villain. **kind** nature.

foz what is rycheffe/ wat is kingdomes/ what
is poffeffiõs/what is goolð what is fylver what
is coftely clothyng oz pcioufe ftonys/what is cof
tely metys oz ozinkes.what is good cõpanye oz
folace/what is myztfje whitoute women On
trouthe they may kalle wele the wozld deed that
from women are exiled oz banyffhed? ffoz wo
men mufte bere the chyldzẽ they fede & nozpffhe
thaym vp/and love thaym well Sfje defyzyth
thayze helthys She gouernyth the houfehold?.
She fozwyth the helthe of hyz hufband & houfe
hold.women is the dilectacõn of alle thinges:fhe
is the fwetneffe of pouthe She is the folace of
joye of age. She is gladneffe of childze: Sfje is
joye of the daye She is folace of the nyght She
is the gladynd of laboure.of alle hevyneffes. fhe
is the fozgeter She fervyth whithoute grutc
hyng And fhe fhall watche my goyng out/ and
myn incomyng. Ther vpon anfweryð? marcol
phus.fje feyth trouthe.that thinkyth wyth his
herte.as he fpekyth wyth his mowth. ye haue
the women in great favoure/& therfoze ye pzay
fe thaym.Xycheffe/nobylneffe/fayzeneffe & wy
fedom be in you.and therfoze it behovyth you
to love women.but y affure you one thyng albe
it that ye now pzayfe thaym ovyz moche/ oz ye
ftepe ye fhal dyfpzayfe thaym as fafte . Salomõ
Therof thou fhalt lye/foz alle my lyve dayes J
have lovyð? women & fhall duryng my lyf.But

for what is riches, what is kingdoms, what is possessions, what is gold, what is silver, what is costly clothing or precious stones, what is costly meats or drinks, what is good company or solace, what is mirth without women?   In truth, they may call well the world dead that from women are exiled or banished.   For women must bear the children; they feed and nourish them up and love them well.   She desireth their health, she governeth the household.   She forewits° the health of her husband and household.   Woman is the delectation of all things.   She is the sweetness of youth.   She is the solace or joy of age.   She is gladness of children.   She is joy of the day.   She is solace of the night.   She is the glad end of labor.   Of all heavinesses she is the forgetter.   She serveth without grutching.   And she shall watch my going out and mine in coming."

Thereupon answered Marcolphus: "He saith truth that thinkest with his heart as he speaketh with his mouth.   Ye have the women in great favor and therefore ye praise them.   Riches, nobleness, fairness, and wisdom be in you and therefore it behooveth you to love women.   But I assure you one thing, albeit that ye now praise them overmuch, or ye sleep ye shall dispraise them as fast."

Solomon: "Thereof thou shalt lie, for all my live days I have loved women and shall during my life.   But

---

forewits anticipates what is needed for.

now go frō me/& se wele to.that before me thou
nevyr speke evyll of women Than marcolphus
goyng out of the kynges palayce.kallyd to hym
the womā that had hir childe to hyre yeven a yē
by the king and sayd to hyre knowyst thou not
what is done & concluded? in the kingps coūsell
to daye.She answeryd/my chylde is pevyn me
ayē a lyve/what ellys there is done. that knowe
not I.Tho sayd marcoph the king hath cōmaū-
ded? & is vttyrly detmyned that to morwe thou
and thy felawe shall come ayen afore hym: and
that thou shalt have the one half of thy chylde/&
thy felawe the other half Thā sayde the womā
O what evyll king/& what false & vntrewe sen
tēce pevyth he. Marcoph sayde yet shall j shewe
the grettyr matiers & more chargeable & of gret
tyr weyghte The kig & his coūseyle hath ordey
ned that evyr man shall have vij.wyves therfor
rem embre & thinke what therin is best to be do
ne.for as one man hath vij.wyves/so shall ther
nevyr more be reste or pease in thouse/one shalbe belovyd?/an othre shall displease hym/for hir
that he lovyth shalbe moost wyth hym: and the
othre nevyr or seldom She shalbe wele clothyd
& the othre shalbe forgetyn:hyr that he lovyth
best shall haue ryngys jowellys goold sylvyr fut
res & were sylkys She shal kepe the keyes of al
le the house She shalbe honouryd? of alle the ser
vauntys and be kallyd mastres Alle his goodes
                                            d

now go from me and see well to [it] that before me thou never speak evil of women."

Then Marcolphus, going out of the king's palace, called to him the woman that had her child to her given again by the king and said to her, "Knowest thou not what is done and concluded in the king's counsel today?"

She answered, "My child is given me again alive; what else there is done, that know not I."

Then said Marcolphus, "The king hath commanded and is utterly determined that tomorrow thou and thy fellow shall come again afore him, and that thou shalt have the one half of thy child and thy fellow the other half."

Then said the woman, "O what evil king and what false and untrue sentence giveth he."

Marcolphus said, "Yet shall I show thee greater matters and more chargeable,◇ and of greater weight. The king and his counsel hath ordained that every man shall have seven wives; therefore remember and think what therein is best to be done.[111] For as one man hath seven wives, so shall there never more be rest or peace in the house. One shall be beloved, another shall displease him, for her that he loveth shall be most with him, and the others never or seldom. She shall be well-clothed and the others shall be forgotten. Her that he loveth best shall have rings, jewels, gold, silver, furs, and wear silks. She shall keep the keys of all the house. She shall be honored of all the servants and be called mistress. All his goods

---

chargeable blameworthy.

ſhall falle to hire: what ſhall thau ſaye the othꝛe
vj. And yf he love tweyne: what ſhall the othꝛe
v. ſaye/ꝫ yf he love thꝛe what ſhal ſaye the othꝛe
iiij. ꝫ yf he love iiij: what ſhall the othꝛe iij. do ꝯꝫ.
That he lovyth beſt he ſhall alwayes have by
hym ꝫ kyſſe hire and halſe hyꝛe The othyꝛ ſhall
mowe ſaye that they are neythꝛe wydowes noꝛ
weddyd/noꝛ yit vnweddyd. noꝛ wythoute huſ-
bande They ſhal mowe well foꝛthynke that
they have theyꝛe mayndehede loſte There ſhall
evyꝛ ſtryff angre envye and bꝛawelyng reigne ꝫ
if there be not fownde a remedy herefoꝛe many
great inconvenyencys ſhall growe there of And
by cauſe that thou arte a woman/ and well ac-
quepnted ꝫ wyth the condicyons of womē: haſte
the and ſhewe thys to alle the ladyes and womē
wythin this citie/ād advyſe thaym/that they ꝫ-
ſente not to it in any wyſe. but wythſtande it/ ād
ſaye ayenſt the king and his counſeyll/ Marcolf
retourned ꝫ ād went ayen to the courte ꝫ pꝛyvely
hyd hym in a coꝛner And the womā trowyd his
woꝛdys to be trewe. rāne trough the citie ꝫ clap
pyd ꝫ hire handys to gydꝛe and cryed ꝫ wyth oppn
mowthe ꝫ ſhe wyd ꝫ all that ſhe had herd ꝫ ād more And eche neyghboꝛwe oꝛ goſſyp ſaide it foꝛth
to another/ So that in ſhoꝛt tyme there was a
great aſſemble oꝛ gaderyng of women wel nigh
that alle the women that weren wythin the

shall fall to her. What shall then say the other six? And if he love twain, what shall the other five say? And if he love three what shall say the other four? And if he love four what shall the other three do, etc? That he loveth best he shall always have by him and kiss her and halse° her. The others shall mowe° say that they are neither widows nor wedded, nor yet unwedded, nor without husband. They shall mowe well forthink° that they have their maidenheads lost. There shall ever strife, anger, envy and brawling reign, and if there be not found a remedy herefore, many great inconveniences shall grow thereof. And by cause that thou art a woman and well-acquainted with the conditions of women, haste thee and show this to all the ladies and women within this city and advise them that they consent not to it in any wise, but withstand it and say against the king and his counsel."

Marcolphus returned and went again to the court and privily hid him in a corner. And the woman trowed° his words to be true, ran through the city and clapped her hands together and cried with open mouth and showed all that she had heard and more. And each neighbor or gossip° said it forth to another, so that in short time there was a great assembly or gathering of women well-nigh that all the women that were within the

halse embrace.   **mowe** (may) rather.   **forthink** regret.   **trowed** believing.   **gossip** friend.

Citie.and se gadredy/went to the kynges palayse
well by the nombre of. vj. Mi. women/and brak
vp dorys and ovyr wēt the kyng and his coun¬
sell wyth great malyce and lowde crying: The
kiug as he this herde/ayyd what the canse was
of thayre gaderyng/To that oon woman that
wyser and more eloquent than the othre: sayde
vnto the king. Moost myghty prynce to whom
goold/sylver/precioufe stones and alle rychesse of
the world tho you are brought/ye do alle thyng
as ye woll.and non ayensayth youre pleasure:
ye have a Quene and many Quenys. and ovyr
that ye have cōcubynes or paramours wythou
te nombre or as asmany as you pleasyth/for ye
have all that ye wol: So may not every man do/
Salomon answerydy God hath anoyntedy and
made me king in ftrahei·may I not than do and
accomplyssh all my wylle Do youre wylle wyth
youre owne.and medle not wyth vs. we are of
the noble blood of Abraham and holde moyses
lawe/Wherefor woll ye thaue that chaunge and
altre·ye are bownden to do right and iustyce.
wherefore do ye vnryght/ Tho sayde Salomō
wyih great vnpacyence.Thou sham full wyf
what vnright or wronge do y She ās̄werȳd:as
great vnright do ye as kā be thought or ymagi¬
ned For ye haue ordeyned that every mā shal ha
ue mowe lawefully vij.wyues/& certaynlt that
shall not be: For there is not that prynce/duke/

city, and so gathered, went to the king's palace well by the number of six thousand women and broke up doors and overwent° the king and his counsel with great malice and loud crying. The king, as he this heard, asked what the cause was of their gathering.

To that, one woman that wiser and more eloquent than the others said unto the king, "Most mighty prince to whom gold, silver, precious stones, and all riches of the world though you are brought, ye do all things as ye will, and none againsaith° your pleasure. Ye have a queen and many queens, and over that ye have concubines or paramours without number, or as many as you pleaseth, for ye have all that ye will. So may not every man do?"

Solomon answered, "God hath anointed and made me king in Israel; may I not then do and accomplish all my will?"

"Do your will with your own and meddle not with us. We are of the noble blood of Abraham and hold Moses's law. Wherefore will ye have that change[d] and alter[ed]? Ye are bound to do right and justice, and wherefore do ye unright?"

Then said Solomon with great impatience, "Thou shameful wife, what unright or wrong do I?"

She answered, "As great unright do ye as can be thought or imagined, for ye have ordained that every man shall have mowe lawfully seven wives, and certainly that shall not be. For there is not that prince, duke,

---

overwent overpowered, overran.   **againsaith** contradicts.

oz erle/that fo riche and puyffaunt is/but that oõ
woiñã alone ſhall mow fullfylle.alle ſjis defyzes
and wylle.what thanne ſjulde ſje do wyth.vij
wyves:it is aboveu any mannys myght oz po⸗
wer:Jt were bettyz ozdeyned⸗ that oon woiñã
ſhulde have vij.huſbondes Than ſayd Salomõ
all laughyngly J had not trowed⸗ that of men
had ben fewer in nombze than of women Tho
krped⸗ alle tſje women as mad people wyth ou⸗
te any reaſou/ye are an evyle king ⸗ poure ſenten
ces ben falſe aud vnrightfull Now may we wel
here ⸗ ſe that it is trouthe that we have herd of
you:and that ye have of vs ſayde evyll:and ther⸗
to ye ſkozue ⸗ mocke vs befoze oure vyſages
that we ſe it☉ lozd god who was fo evyle as ſau
le that regnyd⸗ ovyz vs furſte yet davyd was
wozſe/and now this Salomõ werſt of alle than
the king beyng full of wzathe ſayde There is no
hede moze worſe than the ſerpent/and there is
no malyce to tſje malyce of a woman:foz it we⸗
re bettyz to d velle wyth ſerpentys and lyõs/thã
wyth a wyckyd woman Alle evyll are but lytyl
tho the curſydneſſe:of a ſhzewd woman Alle
wyckydneſſe falle vpon women/as the ſande
fallyth in the ſhoes of the oolde people goyng vp
an hylle So a talkatyf woman and diſhobedyēt
is a great confuſyon That wyf that is hlr huſ⸗
bondes maiſter is evyz cõtrarye to hym An evyl
wyf makyth a pacient herte. and a ſozy vyſage

or earl that so rich and puissant is but that one woman alone shall mowe fulfill all his desires and will. What then should he do with seven wives? It is above any man's might or power. It were better ordained that one woman should have seven husbands."

Then said Solomon all laughingly, "I had not trowed that of men had been fewer in number than of women."

Then cried all the women as mad people without any reason, "Ye are an evil king and your sentences be false and unrightful. Now may we well hear and see that it is truth that we have heard of you, and that ye have of us said evil, and thereto ye scorn and mock us before our visages that we see it. O Lord God. Who was so evil as Saul that reigned over us first, yet David was worse, and now this Solomon worst of all?"

Then the king being full of wrath said, "There is no hede° more worse than the serpent, and there is no malice to° the malice of a woman, for it were better to dwell with serpents and lions than with a wicked woman. All evils are but little to the cursedness of a shrewd° woman. All wickedness fall upon women as the sand falleth in the shoes of the old people going up a hill. So a talkative woman and disobedient is a great confusion." That wife that is her husband's master is ever contrary to him. An evil wife maketh a patient heart and a sorry visage,

hede head; quality.   **to** like that of.   **shrewd** malicious.

& it as plage of the deth A woman was the be=
gynnyng of fynne/and through hire we dye alle
The woman that is luxuriouse may men kno=
wen in the vppermeft of hire yes.ād by hir bro=
wes ffor hire yes are wythoute revyzēce & ther
nede nomā wondze although fhe forgete hir huf
bonde As the king althus had fayd? fo fpak na=
than the prophete and fayde My lozd why rebu
ke ye & fhame ye thus alle thies women of iheru
falē.Salomō have ye not herd what diffhonoure
they have fayd of me wythoute defer vyng / Na
than anfwerpd? he that woll wyth hys fubgiet=
tys lyve in refte & peafe/he mufte fom tyme be
blynde dūme.& deef.Salomō.jt is to be āfwerpd
to a fole aftyr his folyffhnes. Tho fpzāge Mar=
colph out of the cozner that he fat in/ ād fayde to
t he king/now have ye fpokyn aftyr myn intent.
foz ones thys daye ye prapfed? womē out of alle
mefure/and now have ye difprapfed? thaym as
moche.that is it that J fought: alwayes ye ma=
ke my faying trewe:Salo.Thou fowle evyle bo
dy /knowpft thou of this cōmocion: Marcolph/
nay.nevprtheleffe ye fhulde not peue credence to
alle thing that ye here Tho fayd the king falomō
go from hens out of my fyghte: & J charge the
that j fe the nomere betwixt the yes/forth with
was marcolph kaft out of the kinges palapfe/
Than they that ftode by the king faydē:my lozd
fpeke to thiefe womē fumwhat that may pleafe

and it as plague of the death.° A woman was the beginning of sin, and through her we die all. The woman that is luxurious may men know in the uppermost of her eyes and by her brows. For her eyes are without reverence and there need no man wonder although° she forget her husband."

As the king all thus had said, so spake Nathan the prophet and said, "My lord, why rebuke ye and shame ye thus all these women of Jerusalem?"

Solomon: "Have ye not heard what dishonor they have said of me without deserving?"

Nathan answered, "He that will with his subjects live in rest and peace, he must sometime[s] be blind, dumb, and deaf."

Solomon: "It is to be answered to a fool after his foolishness."

Then sprang Marcolphus out of the corner that he sat in and said to the king: "Now have ye spoken aften mine intent. For once this day ye praised women out of all measure, and now have ye dispraised them as much. That is it that I sought. Always ye make my saying true."

Solomon: "Thou foul evil body, knowest thou of this commotion?"

Marcolphus: "Nay. Nevertheless ye should not give credence to all thing[s] that ye hear."

Then said the King Solomon, "Go from hence out of my sight, and I charge thee that I see thee no more betwixt the eyes."

Forthwith was Marcolphus cast out of the king's palace. Then they that stood by the king said, "My lord speak to these women somewhat that may please

---

it as plague of the death she is like the deadly plague.   **although** that.

thaym to here. to thentēt that they may departe
Than turnyd the king towardes thaym & sayd
youre goodnesse shal vndrestande. that J am not
to be blampd/ in that: that ye laye to my charge/
That evyl sayer marcolf/ that ye here late sawe.
hath out of hym self alle this matier surmysed &
fayned/: ād every man shall have hys owne wyf
& hyr wyth faythe & honestie love and chery sshe
That J have spokyn ayenst the wyves J haue
not sayde it but ayenst the froward wyves who
shulde of the good wyves speke any evyll ff oz a
good wyf makyth hyr husbande glad ād blythe
wyth hyre goodnesse She is a parte the lyvyng
of hyre husbond vpon erthe. and hyr lernyng ad
vauntagyth oz fozthzyth hys body She is a yifs
te of god/ A wyse wyf and a stylle is a grace abo-
uen graces/ A good shame fast and an honeste
wyf is lyke the sonne clymmyng vp to god. A
wyf of good condicyons is the oznament oz ap-
parayle of the house · She is a lyght shynyng
bzyghther/ than the lyght of cādellys: She is lyke the goolden pyller standyng vpon hir feet and
an ovyr faste fundament grwnded/ vpon a sure
stone wythonte mutacions and the commande-
mantys of god evyr in hyr mynde/ The hooly
god of Israhel blesse you and multiplye youre se
de and kyndzebede/ vnto the ende of the wozlde
Tho sayde they alle/ amē: And toke leve of the

them to hear, to the intent that they may depart."

Then turned the king towards them and said, "Your goodness shall understand that I am not to be blamed in that that ye lay to my charge. That evil sayer, Marcolphus, that ye here late saw hath out of himself all this matter surmised and feigned, and every man shall have his own wife, and her with faith and honesty love and cherish. That I have spoken against the wives I have not said it but against the froward wives who should of the good wives speak any evil. For a good wife maketh her husband glad and blithe with her goodness. She is a part the living of her husband upon earth, and her learning advantageth or furthereth his body. She is a gift of God. A wise wife and a still° is a grace above graces. A good shamefast and an honest wife is like the sun climbing up to God. A wife of good conditions is the ornament or apparel of the house. She is a light shining brighter than the light of candles. She is like the golden pillar standing upon her feet and an overfast fundament° grounded upon a sure stone without mutations,° and the commandments of God ever in her mind. The holy God of Israel bless you and multiply your seed and kinderbed° unto the end of the world."

Then said they all, "Amen," and took leave of the

still quiet one.   **fundament** foundation.   **mutations** changes.
kinderbed kindred? childbed?.

king and went theyre weyes. Marcoph beryng
in his mynde of the vnkynonesse that the king
had commanded hym that he shulde no more
se hym betwixt the yes Thought in hym self.
what was best to do. It happenyd that the next
nyght folowyng fyll a great snowe Marcolph
toke a lytyll Cyve or Temse in his oon hande &
a foot of a bere in the othre hande: ād he turnyd
hys shoes tyat stode forwardes vpon his feet
bakward/and vpon the mornyng erly he began
to go lyke a beste vpon alle fowre feet through
the strete. and whan he was comen a lytyll wy-
thouthe the towne: he fownde an olde ovyn / ād
crept into it. And as the lyght of the daye was
on comen. oon of the kingys seruauntys founde
the footstappys of marcolph/and thougt that it
was the trace or stappys of & merveyous beste
& in alle haste wēt & shewyd it to the king Thāne incontynent wyth huntres and howndes he
wente to hunte and seke the sayd wondrefull
beeste and folowed it vnto they comen before
the oven where they had loste and fownde no
more of the steppys. The king Salomon discen
ded from hys hors and began to loke into the
oven. Marcolpus laye all crokyd hys vysage
from hym wardes. had put dowme hys breche
into hys hammes that be myght se hys ars ho -
le and alle hys othre fowle gere. As the kyng

king and went their ways.

Marcolophus, bearing in his mind of the unkindness that the king had commanded him that he should no more see him betwixt the eyes, thought in himself what was best to do. It happened that the next night following fell a great snow. Marcolphus took a little sieve or temse° in his one hand and a foot of a bear in the other hand, and he turned his shoes that stood forwards upon his feet backward. And upon the morning early he began to go like a beast upon all four feet through the street, and when he was come a little without the town he found an old oven and crept into it.

And as the light of the day was oncome, one of the king's servants found the footsteps of Marcolphus and thought that is was the trace of steps of a marvelous beast and in all haste went and showed it to the king. Then incontinent° with hunters and hounds he went to hunt and seek the said wonderful beast and followed it until they came before the oven where they had lost and found no more of the steps. Then King Solomon descended from his horse and began to look into the oven. Marcolphus lay all crooked, and his visage from him wards,° had put down his breeches into his hams that he might see his arsehole and all his other foul gear. As the King

---

temse a strainer.   **incontinent** immediately.   **from him wards** out of the king's sight.

Salomō that ſeyng demawnded whatlaye the=
re Mar.aſweryd? j am here:Sal' whereforelye=
eſt thou thus/ Marcolf.for ye haue commann=
ded? me that ye ſhulde nomoreſe me betwyxt
myn yes Now and ye woll notſe me betwyxt
myn yes:ye may ſe me betwene my buttockys
in the myddes of myn arſehole: Than was the
king ſore meovyd cōmaunded? his ſeruauntys
to take hym & hange hym vpona tre/ Mar.So
takyn.ſayde to the kyng: My lord well it pleaſe
you to yeve me leue to choſe the tre wherypon
that j ſhall hāge Sal' ſayde be it as thou haſte de
ſyred?/for it forcyth not on what tre that thou be
hangyd/ Than the kinges ſeruautes toke & led=
dyn marcolph wythoute the citie/& through the
vale of ioſaphath & ovyr the hyghte of the hylle
of olyuete from theus to ierirho & cowde fynde
no tre that marcolf wolde cheſe to be hanged on
ffrom thens went they ovyr the flome iordane
and alle arabye through And ſo forth all the gre
at wylderneſſe vnto the rede ſee:And nevyr mo
re cowde marcolph fynde a tre that he wolde che
ſe to hange on And thus he aſkappyd out of the
dawnger & handes of king ſalomō/ and turnyd
ayen vnto hys howſe/and levyd in peaſe & ioye
And ſo mote we alle do aboven wyth the fadre
of heven Amen

　　　　　(Empzentyd at ande werpe by
　　　me M.Gerard leeu

Solomon that seeing, demanded what lay there.

Marcolphus answered, "I am here."

Solomon: "Wherefore liest thou thus?"

Marcolphus: "For ye have commanded me that ye should no more see me betwixt mine eyes; now and ye will not see me betwixt mine eyes, ye may see me between my buttocks in the midst of mine arsehole."

Then was the king sore moved [and] commanded his servants to take him and hang him upon a tree.

Marcolphus, so taken, said to the king, "My lord, will it please you to give me leave to choose the tree whereupon that I shall hang?"

Solomon said, "Be it as thou hast desired, for it forceth not° on what tree that thou be hanged."

Then the king's servants took and led Marcolphus without the city and through the vale of Jehosaphat and over the height of the hill of Olivete, from there to Jericho, and could find no tree that Marcolphus would choose to be hanged on. From thence went they over the flume° Jordan and all Arabia through, and so forth all the great wilderness unto the Red Sea. And nevermore could Marcolphus find a tree that he would choose to hang on. And thus he escaped out of the danger and hands of King Solomon, and turned again unto his house and lived in peace and joy. And so may we all do above with the Father of Heaven. Amen.

Printed at Antwerp
by me, M. Gerard Leeu

---

it forceth not doesn't matter.   **flume** river.

Textual Notes and Commentary

1 I Kings 10:23.

2 I Kings 2:12; I Kings 2:24.

3 This reference to the East is undoubtedly a vestige of a former tradition in which the Solomonic challenger comes from the orient, with all its connotations of magic, demons, and arcane wisdom. In the two ninth-century Anglo-Saxon poems, the learned and riddling Saturn has arrived at Solomon's court explicitly from points east, including India and Chaldea. For lack of further texts from the period, however, we can only surmise that it was a general feature of the genre.

4 In earlier versions of the text the dialogue begins at this point, and thus this speech, though no longer in direct discourse, was numbered by Benary as the first of Solomon's questions.

5 The lineage of Solomon is drawn from Matthew 1:1–6, and is not much changed here from what one finds in the Vulgate. Variants are Esron for Esrom, Aaron for Aram, Naazon for Naasson, Boaz for Booz, but curiously Isaiah for Jesse. This sets up the following parody in which Marcolphus plays on Latin grammar in rehearsing his family history.

6 This continuation of play with family names in the form of school exercises—here Lupicana setting up the order of untidy wives—is further confirmation of the origin of our textual tradition in the ecclesiastical schools.

7 Singer, p. 53, found only a few early references to this proverb, but they include citations by Bebel and Luther in his *Sprichwörter*, p. 157.

8 The Latin source used by Leeu reads, "ditabo magnis operibus et nominatissimus eris in regno meo" (I will enrich you with great works and you shall be the most famous of all in my realm). This promise is in apparent anticipation of the far more specific promise following the match, namely that he should be made "third in the kingdom of our sovereign lord," which is in turn an allusion to the promise made by Belshazzar to Daniel that he "shalt be the third ruler in the kingdom" if he interpreted the famous handwriting on the wall. Daniel 5:16.

9 Bebel, No. 267.

10 I Kings 3:16. Solomon here refers to his famous judgment as an event
   of the past, even though it is enacted in the present in the second
   part. "Forelay" is the translation of "opprimo" meaning to smother;
   the word is used because the death occurred while mother and child
   were asleep side by side. In I Kings 3:16 these "light" women are
   called harlots; they are also light because they have just given birth.
11 This is Marcolphus's first denigration of Solomon's putatively remarkable decision. He implies that if Solomon is ready to listen to
   such matters, there will be plenty of cases, and that women — who
   love to talk — will impose these situations frequently. This is implicit
   in his citation of a proverbial formula that had many Latin parallels,
   and that appeared in a number of vernacular analogues including one
   which Singer cites, p. 50, from the *Oxford English Dictionary*, "There
   ben women, ther ben wordes; There ben gese, there ben tordys."
12 Singer, p. 50, believes this proverb is German in origin. He cites
   Freidank among others, "Der mus zisch zelbir loben, her hot boze
   nogber" (One must then praise himself who has evil neighbors).
13 Proverbs 28:1
14 The vernacular version in the ninth-century St. Gall MS. III has been
   cited in the Introduction. (See Müllenhoff and W. Scherer, *Denkmäler
   deutscher Poesie und Prosa aus dem VIII.–XII. Jahrhundert*, II, p. 135.) The
   Latin source reads "Fugit impius nemine subsequente. Quando fugit
   capreolus, albescit eius culus." Here, Marcolphus's reply, "when the
   kid runs away, his arse becomes white" is almost a riddle, for in
   running the tail is lifted and the white markings become visible.
   Marcolphus does not seem to be making any comment on the behavior of the guilty. The humor of his response comes from the
   imitation of Solomon's sententiousness with the parallel structure
   and the repetition (in the Latin) of "fugit," coupled with the dig at
   Biblical wisdom in the doggerel rhyme and the scatological content.
15 Proverbs 12:4. Here "pleasure" is the translation of "ornamentum"
   meaning more appropriately "an asset" or "honor."
16 There are several variants on this proverb pair, but none provides
   hints regarding the parodic relationship, whether for content or for
   style, between the pleasure of an attractive and virtuous wife and
   keeping milk from a cat.
17 Proverbs 14:1. The translation is awkward in having the foolish
   woman destroy what "she findeth made," insofar as the Latin follows
   the literal biblical opposition: a wise woman builds her house; a
   foolish one tears down that which she has built ("constructam") with
   her hands.

18 Here is an instance of a radical departure from the earlier Latin manuscripts; our translator read in his source, "et qui mundam distempat mundam bibit," which is to say, "whoever brews well drinks well." But Benary's 1434 version, 10b, clearly states, "Olla bene cocta melius dirat, et qui merdam distemperat merdam bibit," that is, "a well-baked pot lasts better, and he who stirs in shit drinks shit," indicating that "merdam" has been turned to "mundam." Neither reading explains the parallel with wise and foolish women, although there is a contrasting action of making good pots, or perhaps stew, given this alternate reading of "olla," and making bad stew, or brew, through uncleanliness or the addition of excrement. The sequence is typical in its lowering of the contents from women to pots and excrement on Marcolphus's part. Samuel Singer, pp. 35–36, cites at least twenty parallel versions and variations, and places the origins of this saying in France.

19 Proverbs 31:30. In the Book of Proverbs this quality stands in opposition to deceitful favor and vain beauty. Again the relationship of the two proverbs is not especially clear. But in this pairing the humor seems to be in the stylistic paralleling:

> Mulier timens deum ipsa laudabitur.
> Cattus cum bona pelle ipse excoriabitur.

> The woman who fears God, she is to be praised.
> The cat with a good skin, he is to be flayed.

20 Benary's version, 12b, says, "vacca lactiva est pauperi retinenda." The Latin source give "Lacticinia sunt pauperi retinenda." One sees right away the course taken by our translator. With a bit of changing we could also imagine "A milk cow will be kept by the poor." In the parallel phrasing the cherished object falls from a fair woman to a milk cow. Here the oppositional pattern is maintained, but Marcolphus does not appear to have any particular point in mind.

21 Proverbs 31:10.

22 *Fecunda ratis*, No. 45.

23 Proverbs 22:8.

24 This proverb about the ass as the farmer's beast of burden is of interest. Our version obscures the sense of the main tradition in which the donkey is seen as an agent of fertility and fecundity, for even in the harvest his every bodily function contributes to new life. In earlier Latin versions, including the source, his wallowing breaks up the dirt clods ("glebas"), whereas in the translation, he breaks the straw, thus diluting the meaning somewhat.

25 Proverbs 27:2.

26 The Latin source is negative and stated in the subjunctive: "Multum mel ne comedas" (You should not eat a lot of honey). The probable source is Proverbs 25:16, "Hast thou found honey? Eat so much as is sufficient for thee lest thou be filled therewith, and vomit it." See also the *Fecunda ratis*, No. 450.

27 The Latin source states, "Qui apes castrat digitum suum lingit." (He who castrates bees, licks his own finger.) One castrates bees, presumably, by taking their honey?

28 *Wisdom* 1:40.

29 Acts 9:5.

30 The pairing is based on word echoes that link them to a common figure of kicking backward where there is a driver with a goad. Hence the biblical kicking against the prick is answered by another that says nearly the same thing. The first is figuratively intended, however, whereas Marcolphus speaks literally. This phrase with its biblical associations enjoyed wide medieval popularity and was frequently cited by early French authors. See Singer, pp. 36–37. It appears in the *Fecunda ratis*, No. 570. See also Adolf Tobler, *Altfranzösiche Sprichwörter*, No. 251 (p. 114): "Qui contre aguilon enchauce, dous fet se poit."

31 Proverbs 22:6.

32 The source reads, "Nappa digesta revertitur ad stupam" (A worn out tablecloth turns back into hemp or flax). The translator wanted to create word play on the word "nature," or else simply wished to avoid the word for flax. This Latin source, however, is a corruption of earlier versions, such as Benary's 37b, which reads, "Planta de genista revertitur ad scopam" (The broom plant reverts back to a broom). One would have thought it should be the other way around. Perhaps that fact accounts for the variations in search of a meaning. One cannot imagine what the intermediary forms would have been. In effect, Solomon gives a generic statement and Marcolphus follows with an example. The two are linked by the word "revertitur." Singer, p. 37, mentions French parallels.

33 This pair, passed over at some point by the copyists whose work provided the source for our text, is one of the more strikingly literal minded of Marcolphus's replies. Solomon states that, "The four evangelists support the world." Marcolphus replies that "Four supports hold the toilet, so that anyone sitting on it will not fall."

34 The source reads, "qui suo iudici solet ungere buccam solet macerare suam asellam." (He who anoints the cheek of his judge makes his own ass lean), which is to say, presumably, whoever spends money in bribing judges gets nothing for it.

35 For this proverb, the source, "vultur excoriat duram volucrem, de-
plumatque pellem" was derived from "qui vulturem scoriat durum
volucrem plumat," found, for example, in Benary 43b. The shift in
meaning is as follows: "The vulture that skins rough birds, removes
feathers and skin," as opposed to "Who skins a vulture, [de]feathers
a tough bird." Early French sources are known, including Marcabru's poem No. XXIV. See Singer, p. 37; A. Tobler, *Altfranzösiche
Sprichwörter*, No. 78, "Dur oisel peile qui escorce votur," and the
Florileg of St. Omer, No. 62.

36 This proverb is related to a version in the MS. tradition that reads,
"Postquam pedem et culum stringis, nihil est quod agis" (After you
tie your foot to your buttock you won't go anywhere). Benary, 44b.

37 Benary 45b gives, "Per ingenium manducat qui manducantem salu-
tat" (By wit he eats who greets him who is eating). Our translator
left out the fact that the one greeted is dining and hence is likely to
share the food with the opportunist who greets him. In this way
Marcolphus indeed shows how a man may be deceived with fair
words.

38 Proverbs 22:24.

39 "Merito hunc manducant sues qui se miscet inter furfures" is a
corruption of "Merito manducant illum canes, qui se mittet inter
furfures." Benary, 47b. See the *Fecunda ratis*, No. 9, and J. Werner,
Lateinische Sprichwörter und Sinnspruche des Mittelalters, Nos. 37.37,
34.80, 44.148: "Hos porci comedent qui se sub furfure miscent."

40 "Vivunt cum hominibus, qui similis sunt canibus" (They live with
men who are similar to dogs). Benary, 49b.

41 Singer, p. 54, finds Greek and French parallels for this proverb, although they are somewhat remote in their details. In Benary 50b,
Marcolphus offers only the first part, "Qui alieno cani panem suum
dederit, malum mecedem habebit," the second part being the more
familiar, "talem graciam habet qui dormientem suscitat," preserved
in the familiar "let sleeping dogs lie." Concerning this latter phrase,
Singer states that it had some form in nearly all major Western languages from the twelfth century onward.

42 If this is a chosen parallel to the advantage of long-lasting friendship,
we must interpret the intended contrast in terms of the youth of the
calf and the stinking dung, which, for not stinking long, would seem
to be an advantage. Does it mean that youths are not loyal in friendship any more than calves' dung is long in lasting? This is Singer's
reading, pp. 37–38. There are a number of early French versions, and
the saying was popular among the *Fastnachtspiele* writers. We are
even less sure of the popular application of such early versions of

the French "Calf turds don't last all winter." Perhaps, it signifies that certain disagreeable things don't last and are hence tolerable?

43 Benary 52a gives, "Occasiones querit qui vult ab amico recedere" (He who wishes to depart from his friend searches out the right moment).

44 Earlier MSS. read "vulpe" (fox), perhaps relating to an ancient proverb concerning the yoking of foxes as an impossible task; "vulpes iungere" was quoted by Horace as a proverb. Plowing with a wolf may derive from classical sources, but many medieval analogues are known, including those of the *Fastnachtspiele* writers. See Singer, p. 38. For the classical origins, see Erasmus's *Adagia*, I,3,50.

45 The word translated as "sand" is "tripum," in the source, meaning a three legged-stool, which is a corruption of "scirpum," Benary 56b, meaning "bullrushes." The word also appears in several other forms, none of them meaning "sand." This is the solution of our translator, baffled by a corruption in the source.

46 The sense of earlier versions is that "The hard-hearted person, when he cries out in turn will not be heard."

47 The Latin source reads: "Bene videt cattus cui barbam lingit voluntariam" (The cat knows well whose beard she is licking). The earliest versions are encountered in French and English sources. One finds it in Hendyng. See Singer, pp. 38–40, and the *Fecunda ratis*, No. 7. The proverb carried various meanings. One sense marks a situation in which something can be done with impunity. Another is that the individual knows just how far he can go in annoying or coercing someone. Yet another is that a person knows what risks must be taken in order to achieve certain ends. It may be, too, that the proverb signifies a high degree of egoism, for as Gaston Paris points out, the cat usually licks only its own whiskers and seldom anyone else's. But the sense here, in answer to Solomon's observation concerning the strong who strip the weak, is that the weak then realize what must be suffered and endured. Or perhaps Marcolphus refers to someone like himself, an underdog who is poor but cunning and able to get away with all sorts of scullduggery. "Li chaz set bien cui barbe il leche." *Li Proverbe au vilain*, No. 4; Serlo of Wilton, "Proverbia magistri Serlonis," Poèmes Latins, No. 11f., p. 149.

48 A number of alleged parallels to this proverb have been cited by Benary and Tobler, but according to Singer, p. 40, none of these is related to Marcolphus's proverb about the dual deception of evil doers. Compare, "Qui bien set et le mal prent, fous est tres naivement" (He who sees the good and takes the bad, he is completely foolish). Tobler, No. 168.

49 In the MS. version of 1534, Benary 68a, this proverb reads, "mendi-cabit autem estate et non dabitur ei" (On the other hand, he will beg passionately, and nobody will give him anything).

50 The source gives, "Assuete manus currunt ad caldarium" (Accus-tomed hands run to the kettle).

51 Earlier MSS. mention nothing of rats. "An angry mistress and a broken plate are a curse to a house." By some process Leeu's Latin text reads "ratta" and a word taken for smoke that probably meant "woman." I suspect we are dealing with errors in transmission. Müllenhoff and Scherer in *Denkmäler deutscher Poesie* cite "sunt tria dampna domus: imber, mala femina, fumus" (There are three do-mestic curses: a rain storm, a bad woman, and smoke).

52 Proverbs 3:28. That is, "Do not tell your friend to come back to-morrow for what you can give him immediately." A widely current proverb, sometimes attributed to Seneca. It appears, for example, in the *Consaus d'Amours* (Advice on Love) of Richard de Fournival in *The Comedy of Eros*, p. 118. See also *Diz et proverbes des sages*, p. 11, st. 32.

53 The translator gives a literal reading of his source (Culus confractus non habet dominum), but earlier versions include "dominium," and thus "an enfeebled arse has no power," though what is meant thereby is still unclear.

54 The source has "Miser homo panem non hebat (sic) et tanem cane sibi comparabat."

55 Both Leeu's Latin edition and the MS. of 1434 are corrupt, and hence the curious reading of a passage otherwise straightforward. The Vulgate reads, "Responde stulto juxta stultitiam suam, ne sibi sapiens esse videatur" (Respond to a fool according to his foolishness, lest he seem to himself to be wise).

56 The MS. of 1434, Benary 85b, has, "Petra quod audit, illi respondet echo" (What the stone hears, echo will reply to it).

57 That is, "Anger has no mercy, and therefore he who speaks in anger, buys or achieves evil."

58 The source gives, "Qui te non amat, ipse te non diffamat" (The person who doesn't love you, does not himself defame you). The MS. of 1434 does not have the second "non," giving, "he who loves you does not defame you." Benary discusses other examples that say, in essence, the same thing.

59 The word "whistleth" is a translation of "jubilate." "Birds of different feathers sing the same joyful song, but people of different conditions do not sing the same song."

60 The source gives, "Saciatas est iniquitas ventris; nunc eamus dormitus" (Fulness is the bane of the stomach; now let's go to bed), signifying either that one should eat moderately before retiring, or that if one can eat no more one may as well go to bed.

61 The source gives, "Exiguus munus (sic) dat tibi pauper amicus, noli despicere" (The gift is given by a poor friend; such little gifts should not be despised).

62 The "gelded man" derives from "castratus," which is no doubt a corruption of "crassatus" meaning a dense person: hence, "what a dim wit owns he gives away."

63 The source has, "Apis mortuus non caccat mel" (A dead bee shits no honey).

64 The sense here is that when someone is pestering you, leave.

65 See the *Fecunda ratis*, No. 244.

66 The second part should read, "if he does try it, don't allow him to do it."

67 This proverb may be traced back to the *Distiches of Cato*, IV, 31 (see Marcus Boas, ed.), "Demissos animo et tacitos vitare memento: quod flumen placidum est, forsan latet altius unda" (p. 232), from which all the later versions are derived. See the *Fecunda ratis*, No. 28.

68 The source has, "Non amnes amnia possunt" (All things are not able to be everything), which would appear to be a version of the adage about a man not being able to be all things to all people.

69 Singer, pp. 44–45, believes that the *Fecunda ratis*, No. 599, which offers a more elaborate version of this saying, must go back to our text for its source: "Hoc canit indiculus: vector dum desit equinus, / Ire pedes, si sic placeat, viator." As he points out in two pages of commentary, the saying was known in several languages and in sources going back to the Carolingian period. The literal meaning is clear, but bears an oblique relationship to Solomon's observation that all men are not alike.

70 See the *Fecunda ratis*, No. 256.

71 See the *Fecunda ratis*, No. 21. The proverb was widely current and is known in many German and French sources. See Singer, pp. 521–52. Benary thinks it is French in origin, Singer that it is German. Putting an old dog in a collar is related to the inability of old dogs to learn new tricks. Singer's list of early variants covers almost two pages. A. Tobler, No. 33, "Tart est viel chi[e]n mettre au lien."

72 Matthew 13:12. The MS. of 1434, Benary 111a, reads, "Omni habenti dabitur et habundabit" (It shall be given to all those who have, and he shall flourish).

73 The immediate Latin source says not "friends," but "relatives." The
    1434 MS. says, "Woe to the man who has teeth but no bread." Benary
    111b. Other variants say, "He who hath bread will have relatives."
    Here two separate ideas have been conflated.
74 A number of variants are known of the consequences to a man for
    attempting to go two ways at once. Solomon offers a moral abstrac-
    tion, Marcolphus a figurative hyperbole. One deals with duplicities
    of the heart, the other with more practical dilemmas. Singer, p. 52,
    offers a sampling, including those in the *Fecunda ratis*, No. 147, and
    Freidank, 129,7 23: "Swer zwêne wege welle gân, Der muoz lange
    schenkel han" (He who wants to follow two ways at once must have
    long shanks).
75 The source has, "Ex saturitate ventris triumphat culus" (When the
    stomach is full, the arse triumphs), "triumphat" suggesting trumpet-
    ing to the translator.
76 The MS. of 1434, Benary 118a, says, "Mulier pulchra ornamentum
    est viro suo" (A beautiful woman is an asset [or ornament] to her
    husband).
77 The word "irsuta" means "hairy," thus, "dark and hairy like a mole."
78 In essence, "It doesn't matter how much you give a kitten, it will
    never wag its tail." Marcolphus mocks Solomon's grandiose ideas.
    J. Werner, No. 57,136 offers, "Non catulo detur quociens sua cauda
    movetur."
79 The second half reads, "suspensus est a cibo," that is, "he gets nothing
    to eat" or, "he is excluded from the banquet."
80 The Latin source reads, "currit," meaning "to run," but the 1434 MS.
    has "comedit," which is "to eat up all in sight." A glutton not being
    able to gobble up all in sight does not follow, and thus the search for
    new meanings: "a glutton can't run around very much."
81 Our translator repairs a corrupted source. The 1434 MS. reads,
    "Where the shepherd is weak, the wolf shits wool," that is, eats
    the sheep. In the immediate source "Where the shepherd is weak,
    the wolf does not shit wool." There are many earlier versions that
    confirm the MS. reading. Our translator states much the same thing:
    "Where the shepherd is attentive, the wolf does not have an occasion
    to eat the sheep." Singer, p. 48, has a generous sampling. Most of the
    early sources appear to be French. One of the more interesting ana-
    logues for English readers appears in Langland's *Piers the Plowman*
    C text, Bk. IX, ll. 264–65, Ed. Pearsall, p. 172. "Thy shep ben ner al
    shabbede, the wolf shyt the wolle, Sub molli pastore lupus lanam ca-
    cat." Chaucer also alludes to the proverb of the negligent shepherd

and the torn sheep in the "Physician's Tale," ll. 101–02. The common French proverb, "La mauvaise garde paist souvent le loup" (Ill watching often feeds the hungry wolf), is in Cotgrave, *A Dictionary of the French and English Tongues*, p. Mmmiii[r]. See the *Fecunda ratis*, No. 174, Tobler, No. 26, and Werner, No. 95,179: "Sub molli pastore cacat lanam lupus agni."

82 The source gives, "Tunde latera filij tui, dum tenera sint" (Beat your children on the flanks while they are tender).

83 Marcolphus says, "Qui osculatur agnum, amat et arietem" (He who kisses a lamb loves the ram).

84 Marcolphus offers here a version of one of the best known of all proverbs. However, no mention was made of Rome until the twelfth century; the reference first appears in the *Parabolae* No. 5 of Alanus de Insulis, whose point of departure was Flanders. Further to the north the converging point of many roads was traditionally the forest, in Italy, the piazza, in Spain, the bridge, and in Provence, the village.

85 Literally, "From a good meal comes a good crap, which one may cover with one's feet; thus should vulgar women be trodden underfoot." In this instance, Leeu's compositor misread the translator's "wives" for "wines."

Earlier versions read simply, "After a good meal, a good crap," but along the way this nasty turn has been added to the end.

86 The source has, "Bene decet strues iuxta sepem meam" (Well becometh a heap next to my hedge). "Stones" is merely intuited by the translator. Several equally nonsensical parallels have been collected. My guess is that Marcolphus had something more scatological in mind.

87 The source gives, "Bene equitat qui cum paribus equitat" (He rides well who rides with his equals or suitable companion).

88 See the *Fecunda ratis*, No. 211.

89 The proverb is widely known, but its meaning is subject to interpretation. Does it mean the more difficult the circumstances, the more people are greedy? Another is that long repeated misfortune is particularly hard to endure. Or, the greater the misery, the more one is compelled to do what one would avoid. "Cum plus gelat, plus stringit," Benary 137b, could also signify "The colder it gets, the more people huddle together." See Singer, p. 49, and Tobler, No. 76, "Con plus giele, plus estraint." In *Le chastoiement des Dames* (Advice to Ladies) of Robert de Blois (mid-thirteenth century), this proverb closes the poem, "car quant plus giele, plus estroint," and appears to mean the more a man is fixed or frozen in his pains of love, the more he is firm or frozen in his loyalty. See *The Comedy of Eros*, p. 84.

90 See the *Fecunda ratis*, No. 568.

91 The complex tradition behind this proverb is based upon the figurative notion of the slow ox who chases the rapid hare, and repeats
to himself in his failure that tomorrow is another day like today,
and presumably that it provides another opportunity to continue the
chase, or that it allows for some progress in an ostensibly hopeless
situation: plodding hope or plodding resignation. It stands in relation to Solomon's statement that all things have their own times
and seasons. Singer, pp. 49–50, says that the proverb was not widely
known in the Middle Ages, but that it had wide circulation in subsequent years, especially in Scandinavia, Germany, and England. Sam
Weller recites it in Dicken's *Pickwick Papers*. Erasmus in his *Adagia* IV,
4, 44 traces it back to Plutarch, and it is cited by Arnaut Daniel, the
troubadour poet. In France it carried the sense of slow determination
as in the story of the hare and the turtle, "step by step the ox catches
up with the hare." This is presumably the interpretation intended by
Marcolphus.

92 I Kings 4:5–6. Zabud the son of Nathan was the king's friend and
principal officer; Adonais is the biblical Adoniram, and was in charge
of the tribute. The corruption of these names and of those to follow
is difficult to explain. In earlier Latin versions they were much closer
to the Old Testament versions.

93 I Kings 4:8–19. The names of the fathers of the twelve officers who
provided the king with provisions from each of the twelve tribes of
Israel.

94 Earlier sources suggest that the father is motivated by a desire to
repossess the land under the footpath and in doing so in this manner
he creates two areas of thorns. In the early German translation (the
Spruchgedicht Salomo und Morolf), the meaning is clearer: "My father
sowed his seed in the field, and then people made a footpath through
it; now the fool is blocking the path so that instead of one he'll have
two." That is to say, he should realize that people will simply make
a second path and thereby destroy even more of his crop. There are
many analogues. Cosquin found one in J.F. Bladé, *Contes populaires
da la Gascoigne*, III, pp. 6–9 which, rendered into English, reads, "My
father is working in the vineyard and he does well and he does
badly," which means that in pruning the vines he does well when
he prunes well and vice-versa. The story is Eastern in its origins. In
the *Kanjur*, Mahaushada goes in search of a wife; he encounters a
beautiful girl in a field; he asks her questions to which she replies in
riddles. Concerning her father she says, "he has gone to make two
roads from one. After collecting brambles he makes the road and

thus people will have two." Through her wit the country girl attracts a rich husband.   The grouping that follows involving the activities of father, mother, sister, brother occurs as a sequence in many sources and in many countries from Morocco and Tangiers to Bengal and Kashmir according to Biagioni, pp. 50–51.

95   Gregor Hayden, in his verse translation of the Latin *Solomon and Marcolphus*, substitutes this riddle and its explanation for another. There the mother is baking bread that is "already eaten" ("eegessen prot"). The explanation is that the mother is making bread to replace a borrowed loaf "already eaten." This is a version of a generic Indo-European motif.   It can be a field that is eaten, as in the Kashmir tale of the old peasant and his daughter in which the riddle appears as a test of wisdom.   The young girl improves her social station by answering aptly that a field is already eaten when the proceeds of the sale of the crop are needed to pay off creditors.   Joseph Zabara offers a version in *The Book of Delights* written in Spain around 1300.

96   The riddle concerning lousing has many versions.   Here the brother rather factually slays what he finds, but the question is not posed as something paradoxical as in the version, "whatever he kills, he leaves, and whatever he does not kill, he takes with him."   The motif is mentioned by Suidas in his *Lexicon*, compiled in the late tenth century, where its origins are credited to the ancient Greeks.

97   The origins of this episode can be traced only in a general way.   There are several identifying features.   During the Middle Ages meat was traditionally served on large loaves of bread functioning as plates. After the nobles had taken their fill, the bread soaked with the drippings was distributed to the poor about the gates.   The vulture in this story was first taken for medical purposes.   The heart was left over and given to Solomon's mother who in turn prepared it for her son to eat on the assumption that eating the heart would make him wise.   The principle is related to ritual magic whereby it was understood that in consuming an animal, or part of that animal, one takes on its qualities.   There are many tales of eating animal hearts in order to gain the virtues of the animal.   J.M. Kemble reports that "the hearts of all birds, serpents and of many animals were supposed capable of communicating this wisdom.   In the North, it particularly consisted in understanding the language of birds," p. 115.   He offers many examples.   It was a major motif in the Norse sagas.   There were also traditions regarding the intelligence of the vulture.   Angelo de Gubernatis in *Zoological Mythology* II, p. 185, tells of the Indian vulture Gâtâyus, who, because he had passed from one end of the earth

to the other, thus knew all things past and future. He is the "all-seeing one," and is associated with the Vedic sun, just as in Egyptian mythology the vulture is associated with the sun god Re. Concerning the version involving Solomon and Marcolphus, we must conclude that at some point this lore was incorporated into the Solomonic myth, and that the formulators of our text knew of the tradition and burlesqued it by making Marcolphus the ironic co-beneficiary of the ritual repast. Early readers may have known this story as part of a serious Solomonic myth.

98 This is the city of Gibeon, about eight kilometers north of Jerusalem. It was there that Solomon made his offerings, and there that God came to him in a dream and gave to him his wisdom (I Kings 3:4–15). Through this allusion Solomon rejects Marcolphus's theory that his wisdom came through eating a vulture's heart.

99 In the MS. of 1434 she was called Flocenna.

100 Such is the translation of "sed fames mutavit ingenium." Our translator reasoned that by "ingenium" wit was intended, in the sense of "to change his mind." A few lines later the same word appears, "ingenio mutato," translated as "and for that with wit changed." The word "mutato" does not occur in the 1434 MS., however, and appears to have been included in order to explain the second "ingenio." The German version explains the difficulty: "ich war hungrig und hab den fladen gessen und dem hafen mit dem andern fladen zugedeckt." The joke is based on the double use of the word "fladen" to mean both flan and cow pie. Here is an instance suggesting that the vernacular nourished the Latin, for if the Latin scribe wished to duplicate the pun, he would have had to find a Latin word that might serve double duty. The word "ingenium" could also mean "whatsit" or "whatchacallit" which would account for the awkward parallels that persisted in the Latin, expressing a pun that our translator missed because of the addition of "mutato." See Cosquin, p. 531. The story of the flan and the cow dung may be Western, rather than Eastern, in origin. There is a version of it in the *Florileg of St. Omer*, ca. 1200.

101 The waking contest is of ancient origins and has survived in numerous versions, each with its own circumstances and details. The accused poses riddles to prove that he is not sleeping but thinking — riddles that are strange facts and anomalies concerning animals which in turn must be proven true as a condition for avoiding punishment. In effect, the riddles serve to deflect the threat of punishment for sleeping on the job to a threat of punishment for offering ostensibly untrue statements that the defendant can, in fact, prove true. Marcolphus is under threat of decapitation by Solomon should he

fail to give satisfactory answers. We wonder, first, why the risks are so high just for falling asleep. The answer is that in earlier versions keeping awake was part of a man's military duty. The episode again raises the question of whether this sequence travelled from East to West with the name of Solomon in a collection of riddles. Given the many early analogues, the borrowing could also have been local. There is a version in *El Libro de exemplos por A.B.C.* by Climente Sanchez de Valderas, active in the early fifteenth century. This book follows in a line of Latin grammars going back to the thirteenth century. This detail is a reminder that the Latin *Solomon and Marcolphus* may have begun as a compilation of lore taken from pedagogical materials. In the version by Sanchez de Valderas, Theodoric the Goth, after the capture of Rome, makes his rounds at night to ensure that all his guards are awake. One Cariolo was found sleeping. Theodoric challenged him and received the answer that he was not sleeping but thinking. "Of what?" asked the king, and among the replies we find that magpies have as many white feathers as black, and that foxes have as many joints in their tails as in their back bones. In order to escape death, Cariolo had to prove these assertions true. These clever responses lure the king away from the death penalty for sleeping. Cariolo adds one further observation that caps the others, namely that Theodoric was possessed by the devil and that his master would fetch him that very night — which also turned out to be true. Neglect of duty explains the rigor of the penalty, although certain of the early riddle contests also carried the death penalty for failure. The story was known in Spain as early as the end of the twelfth century in a version by Joseph ben Zabara of Barcelona. It can be traced to the *Kanjur*, Pt. II, Sect. 2, No. 2, where King Pradyota interrogates the man from Gandhara who stands guard. This man, in the middle of the night, poses and proves riddles, including the assertion that the monkey has a tail as long as its body, and that the partridge has an equal number of contrasting feathers. In a Tarantchi version the famous question-and-answer formula appears: "Are you sleeping? No, I am thinking." No doubt it was the wisdom contest features of this story that caused it to be attached to the Solomonic tradition; it may have been a part of a collection of the kind suggested in the Introduction in which both Solomon and Marcolphus played roles as serious opponents.

102 Marcolphus adds this anti-feminist statement to the list of riddles in order to set up a trick on his sister that Solomon asks to have demonstrated in his presence. Thus, the waking contest provides the circumstances for the demonstration of five riddle sequences.

103 In the MS. of 1434 his sister is called Fusadam.
104 In the MS. of 1434 his brother is called Busardi.
105 In most contemporary versions this trick is played, not on a sister, but on a wife, as in the *Gesta Romanorum*. The working formula involves telling a woman a dark secret and then insulting her in a way that provokes her to betray this confidence. The trickster feature is in setting up evidence that, in fact, does not exist, and thereby escaping incrimination. Stories involving secrets told to women are of many kinds; for classical, biblical, and rabbinical sources, see Biagioni, pp. 59ff.
106 This is a brief relation of the famous story of the cat and the candle, researched late in the nineteenth century by Cosquin. The version in the *Apologia* of Guido de Bazoches has already been brought to attention; it can also be found in the *Lai d'Aristote* of Henri d'Andeli, and in a fourteenth-century MS. in the Bibliothèque Nationale, Fr. 14971, Sup. Fr. 632.28. There is also a version in *Pluemen der Tugent* (Flowers of Virtue) by Hans Vintler, ll. 6754ff. One of the more interesting versions for comparison occurs in a Bodleian Library MS. from the end of the thirteenth century published in Tobler's edition of *Li proverbe au vilain*.

> L'en puet bien par usage
> Faire le chat si sage
> Qu'il tient chandoile ardant;
> Ja n'iert si bien apris,
> Se il voit la souris,
> Qu'il ni aut maintenant.
> Mieux vaut nature que nourreture
>   Ce dit li vilains.

> One can, by training, quite easily
> Make a cat sufficiently obedient
> That it will hold a burning candle;
> But no matter how well it is trained,
> If it sees a mouse
> It can now think of nothing else.
> Instinct is stronger than training,
>   This the peasant said. [my translation]

Cosquin, pp. 394–95, also gives an account of the story in Russian, where Solomon disguises himself as a stranger, goes to the court of his father David and there plays out the same routine, to the annoyance of his father. The motif does not solve an enigma, but it does illustrate the principle of nature's dominance over nurture.

This story was undoubtedly associated with Solomonic lore before its inclusion in our textual tradition. It was known to Luther and Agricola, and seems to have enjoyed a vogue in medieval England, for which see the article by Braekman and Macaulay.

107 In Leeu's Latin edition appears the phrase "Marcolpho britone pacem habebit." The word would have meant "Breton." No doubt baffled by it, our translator simply leaves it out. The word is a corruption of "bricone," meaning "rogue," and would originally have formed a parallel with "wise Solomon."

108 These words offer a brief and cryptic conclusion to the episode. Marcolphus seems to make light of the trick and to play the innocent. Earlier versions are more pointed. In the MS. of 1434 Solomon asks how he got in, and Marcolphus replies, "by wit, not pity."

109 Spittle is an ambiguous substance associated both with miraculous healing powers, as in the biblical healing of the blind man through the application of a mixture of spittle and dust, and with a display of contempt. Marcolphus relies on this ambiguity in order to spit on a man's head and then claim that it was to heal his baldness. The story comes from Diogenes Laertius, II, 75. Simus, showing Aristippus his costly house with its fine tessellated floors, the later "coughed up phlegm and spat in his face. And on resenting this he replied, 'I could not find any place more suitable.'" Bertoldo makes use of the episode in order to spit on his rival. He asks the king's permission to spit, which is granted, provided he spit in the least important place in the palace. Bertoldo became a stock figure of the Comedia dell'Arte. See Duchartre, *The Italian Comedy*, pp. 257ff.

110 I Kings 3:16–28. For the origins of this story see Moncure Daniel Conway, *Solomon and Solomonic Literature*, pp. 14–15. In the biblical account a more complex tale has been simplified; in earlier, non-Hebraic versions, the women were at odds because one was a man's widow, the other his concubine, and they were arguing over the heritage that belonged to the child. The child belonged to the concubine and the property to her offspring. The barren wife sought the property by provoking the death of the child; she wished to keep what was already in her possession. Marcolphus is interested in how Solomon could have been duped by women playing their respective roles with feigned emotions and reactions. He sees more deeply into the legal and logistical nature of the situation insofar as the women lacked clear motives in their struggle over the child. Solomon as judge became a focal point for many similar cases in which the offending party could be tricked into self-exposure. An old French *fabliau*, cited by Guerrini, p. 222, tells of two brothers fighting over

their inheritance. Solomon had the corpse of the father fastened to a post. He then commanded both sons to throw their lances at him, promising that the son with the surest aim would receive the inheritance. The oldest son was cruel enough to pierce the body, while the younger could not bring himself to strike his dead father. To the younger the inheritance was given. This story circulated widely in the East as well as in the West, and can be traced to the *Talmud*, in which account several sons strike their father's grave, as commanded by the Rabbi, while only one refrains out of respect. This story, like that of the two women and the dead child, predates the time of the historical Solomon.

111 There are many medieval versions of the story of the seven wives. A parallel in the *Gesta Romanorum*, the story of Papirius, No. 126, has been discussed in the Introduction, and the editor, Osterley, has located dozens of analogues. The story's origins are in the *Saturnalia* of Macrobius, Bk. I, ch. 6, relying in turn on the *Attic Nights* of Aulus Gellius, I, 23. Johann Enenkel (Jansen Enikel) retells the story in the thirteenth century in his *World* Chronicle as an event that took place during the reign of Domitian. Biagioni, pp. 78–82, discusses versions of Solomon's judgment in Arabic literature, in the Benfrey Panchatantra (2, 544), in the Tibetan *Kanjur*, the Tamul *Kathacintamani* (12), the *Vikramacarita*, and the Tibetan *Dsanglun*.

Hans Folz

Appendix

Hans Folz

KING SOLOMON AND MARKOLF

(Ein Spiel von Konig Solomon und Markolfo)

(1497)

Introduction and Notes by

Donald Beecher

Translation by
Randall W. Listerman

Solomon and Marcolphus
and the German *Fastnachtspiel*

One of the most innovative and successful adaptations of the *Solomon and Marcolphus* textual tradition appeared in the form of a German Shrovetide play or *Fastnachtspiel*. The transformation from text to dramatic performance gave new impetus to the carnival functions inherent in the work. Through this new medium the old argument between king and peasant could enter the dual world of satire and festive topsy-turveydom that characterized these plays and the milieux of their performance. Complaint against the abuses of official power could be underscored all the more through the license granted to this art form, and in the context of special holiday seasons. This relationship between dramatic form and traditional substance was a potentially fertile one for the development of the Shrovetide play, for just as the plays promoted the carnivalization of themes latent in the textual tradition, so the dramatic potential within the jest narratives and riddle-in-action helped the playwrights turn their static recitations into a theater of conflict and action.

The experiment was first carried out by Hans Folz in his *Ein spil von Konig Salomon und Markolfo* (variant spellings). The work was derived from the Latin text through a German translation in the *Volksbuch* tradition called *Frag und Antwort Salomonis und Marcolfi*, published circa 1482. A long detour could be taken here to explain the complicated relationship between the surviving fragment of this text, the Latin *Solomon and Marcolphus*, and the vernacular *Spruchgedicht Salomo und Morolf*, but these questions have little bearing on our reading of the play.[1] The changes that

---

[1]The two earliest editions of this work are: *Von dem Kunig Salomon und Marckolffo un einem Narrn*, printed, without date, in Nürnberg by Johannem Stuechs, and *Von dem König Salomon und Marckolffo und einem*

THE MODERN LANGUAGE REVIEW
(English and American Literature)

THE YEARBOOK OF ENGLISH STUDIES

With the compliments of the Editor

Professor Andrew Gurr
English Department, University of Reading, Box 218
Reading RG6 2AA
England

arise with the transition from narrative to theatrical dialogue are striking, and the play is a little *chef-d'oeuvre* in its own right. Folz was a barber by trade, born in 1450 in Worms, and died in Nuremberg in 1513. This was a leading center for the performance of these plays and boasted such other playwrights from the period as Hans Rosenplüt, Hans Sachs, and Jakob Ayrer. Folz wrote at least eight such plays, and in so doing contributed to the development of the genre. During carnival time all the tradesmen got involved, not only the barbers, but the carpenters, smiths, butchers, and bakers. It was a time of drinking, dancing, riddles, jokes, and stories. The plays were performed without stages and with few properties. Taverns and inns were favored locations. Typically these plays dealt with family scenes, village knavery, tricks on priests, the taming of shrews, or at least complaints against them. The gullible farmer made frequent appearances, along with rogues, vagabonds, students, quack doctors, servants, and cheating clergymen. It was to this climate of performance and socializing that the materials of the *Solomon and Marcolphus* tradition were adapted.

Narren, Nürnberg: Johann Nuhs (Stüchs), 1521. The work was first edited by Adalbert von Keller from the manuscript version, circa 1494, in *Fastnachtspiele aus dem fünfzehnten Jahrhundert*, Stuttgart, 1853, Pt. II, No. 60, pp. 521–40. On the question of sources see Eckehard Catholy, *Das Fastnachtspiel des Spätmittelalters: Gestalt und Funktion*, and Dieter Wuttke, "Die Druckfassung des Fastnachtspiels Von König Salomon und Markolf," pp. 140–70. The manuscript version edited by von Keller, written sometime before 1494, has generally been looked upon as the earliest and hence the most authoritative text. This edition has circulated widely over the past 140 years, and for that reason has been selected as the base text for the translation presented here. But it should be stated for the records that the changes appearing in the early sixteenth-century printed version may be authoritative. In the 1521 edition the text differs from the MS in the number of the cast, which has been reduced from fourteen to eleven roles, and in the overall length, which has been extended by 163 verses, not to mention a number of improved readings scattered throughout. The question of the authority of these changes is still under discussion, for which see the article by Wuttke cited above in the *Zeitschrift für deutsches Altertum und deutsche Literatur*, XCIV, Vol. 2 (July, 1965): 140–70.

Just as the *Jests of Scoggin*, in a sense, revealed the court jester latent in Marcolphus, so Folz's play revealed the order of carnival latent in his pranks. At the same time, the drama inherent in the premeditated trick contributed to the technical development of the *Fastnachtspiel*. The genre began in the *Reihenspiel*, which consisted largely of comic recitations offered in a nondialogic process that featured characters undifferentiated from one another in terms of their personal identities or their specific roles in a plot. Often they were but subdivisions of a class or type; such is the presentation of farmers I, II, III, and IV at the end of Folz's play. There were no dramatic entries or exits, no real, causally determined plots. Not until the rise of the *Handlungspiel* do we see dramatic encounters, genuine comic conflicts, individualized characters, and specifically prescribed domestic or commercial settings. In dramatizing the conflict between Salomon and Markolfo, Folz, at an early moment in the emergence of the Shrovetide play, creates an authentic little episodic drama by drawing upon the codified identities of the antagonists and the motivational qualities of the individual episodes. In this material the playwright found ways to develop situational conflict, contrasting character types, and bits of dialogue. In the antifeminist episodes he found further pretext for the representation of an attitude omnipresent in the Shrovetide play. The potential for progress represented by these elements is difficult for us to appreciate from a perspective in which such things are taken entirely for granted. But Eckehard Catholy, in his close study of the play and its source, concludes that Folz was a near genius in terms of the advancements this play represented for the genre.

In terms of the play's relationship to our textual tradition, we note that the exchange of proverbs has been scaled down to a more manageable duration for the theater. The pranks begin with the spitting episode and conclude with the business of the seven wives. It is for this reason that Markolfo is sentenced to hang — after which, without any ado whatsoever, he joyfully disappears in search of a suitable tree. His fellow farmers then appear, thinking he has been removed from their company by an outrageous miscarriage of justice and an abusive use of power. Thus they begin their complaint. At the appropriate dramatic moment, however, Markolfo makes a triumphal entry, declaring his conversion to the new religion of St. Sow, St. Merde, and St. Open-Mouth, thereby initiating the transition from histrionics to festive eating and drinking. Only moments earlier the women in the audience had been called to join in a dance. The play writes in its own transition to forgiveness, forgetfulness, and frivolity. Folz's work is marked by an economy of expression, by a fast pace of action, and by an almost cryptic citation of several of the now familiar episodes. One even wonders if the dramatist counted on a general familiarity with the textual traditions of Solomon and Marcolphus as a precondition for enjoying his play to the fullest.

Markolfo, as a German peasant, also fully represents his class. He is the egalitarian-minded farmer who fights for his own whenever he thinks he has been injured or insulted. In this play, all traces of the oriental Marcolphus have been eliminated. He is a spirited and boastful champion of the common folk, although it may be argued that in his baiting of authority and his maligning of women, he never creates gulfs that cannot be bridged through laughter and good will. If there is a degree of subtlety in this play, it is not in its representationalism or in its so-called realism, but in the variety of functions it performs for its audience as a combination of satire, horseplay, and carnival escapism. There may be a measure of realism sufficient to encourage a suspension of disbelief of sorts, but the more interesting ties with the audience are established by the play's continual recognition of its own artifice. In this way, moods of innocence, attack, and conciliation can appear in rapid sequence — because conventions allow for such transformations. That this play qualifies Folz for the category of near genius in absolute terms, one could doubt, but as a play among Shrovetide plays it has considerable merits.

The matter of Solomon and Marcolphus attracted further playwrights toward the middle of the sixteenth century. Zacharias Bletz wrote a work entitled *Marcolfus: Ein Fahsnacht spil zu Lucern gespillt Aa. 1546* — a Shrovetide play about Marcolfus performed in Lucerne in 1546. The play is just over 1800 lines long and is hence the lengthiest dramatic development of the story.[2] Around 1550 Hans Sachs composed a *Lustspiel* called *Ein comedi, mit acht personen zu recidirn, juditium Salomonis,* and a *Fastnachtspiel* on the subject calling for four actors. On October 23, 1685, the *Comoedie von König Salomo* by Christian Weise was performed in the Zittauischen Theatro, in which Marcolf and the black fool Knass do a parody of a riddle match between Solomon and the Queen of Sheba, a bizarre amalgamation of formal and historical elements alluded to in the Introduction.

---

[2] Ed. Renward Brandstetter, "Marcolfus: Ein Fahsnacht spil zu Lucern gespillt Aa. 1546," *Zeitschrift für Deutsche Philologie* 17, Halle (1885): 421–24.

Hans Folz

King Solomon and Markolf

(1497)

King Solomon and Markolf

Herald

King Solomon

Markolf, farmer

Knight

Good Woman

Fusita, Markolf's sister

Executioner

Dancer

First Woman

Second Woman

First Farmer

Second Farmer

Third Farmer

Fourth Farmer

King Solomon and Markolf

(The herald enters addressing the audience)

Herald: Greetings to you one and all. Bartender, Innkeeper, guests, and rabble-rousers. Pay attention! Whoever among you seeks redress or repayment, let him come before the rich and wise King Solomon for justice and reparation. Whoever needs help or is in need, don't hesitate. Here all your complaints will find quick remedy. Here! Here!

(King Solomon, Markolf, and the knight enter.
Markolf addresses the King)

Markolf: Greetings and God be with you dear sir! I come bringing all sorts of good things to you. Let's see, here is parsley, turnips, and even onions. And look here, tied to my boot is a wild quail—all gifts for His Majesty. And gentlemen, do you remember the King even sent me a horse which I never expected and much less demanded?

Knight: Listen my good farmer! Who let you in here?

Markolf: My cunning slyness got me in and justice and decency will let me stay.

Knight: Farmer, you're about as clean as a manure hoe. Will you foul the whole earth with your ranting and raving? Spare us any more of your vomitings and just leave the hall.

(Markolf spits on the knight's bald head)

Knight: Pfui on you! You're sent by the devil! Why the hell did you hit me on the head?

Markolf: So that you will follow your own advice! Now listen up! I don't vomit after decorations and money here at court. I don't foul the bare earth any more than your bare, bald head. Why you don't have one finger's worth of growth. I hit you for your own good. To fertilize you some growth. Come over here and let me fertilize a real stand.

Solomon: Farmer, farmer. We are well-advised of your brawling and slanderous intentions. Would you care to formally introduce yourself?

Markolf: Dear sir, I am not called the veal-man as some suspect. If you'll listen for a moment you'll recognize me as part of your family.

Solomon: Very well. But go over there and stand awhile. For in truth we are all descended from the twelve tribes of Judah. Abraham begat Jacob who begat Joseph who begat Ephraim who begat Aaron who begat Gibeah who begat Benjamin who begat Nathan who begat Solomon who begat Boaz who begat Obed who begat Jesse who begat David. And I am Solomon son of David.

Markolf: Well, so am I descended from twelve tribes of farmers. Knotty gave birth to Farmer Troll who gat the Rag-family who gat the Threshers who gat the Apple- pokers who gat the Sautits who gat the Big-spoons who gat the Cider-taps who gat the good ol' Cauliflowerus. Me, my name is Marcolphus. I am descended from twelve families of farmers, as you can see, King. I don't feel above you in any way. In fact, I'm a person just like you.

Solomon: Listen Marcolphus, and listen well. We want to ask you something. Are you trying to insult us?

Markolf: Well, King, nobody gets away with insulting me. Whoever scorns me can expect the same right back.

Solomon: Marcolphus, if you would speak to all of us in a civil manner, we would certainly treat you in an honorable way.

Markolf: Dear King, even the tanner praises the honor which he doesn't possess.

Solomon: God give us wise counsel and good behavior so that nobody will be our equal. Then each of us will be rich as kings.

Markolf: Whoever has evil neighbors can certainly be better and worthy of praise, that's my thinking.

Solomon: Whoever stops, looks, and listens — learns.

Markolf: When the goose flies, her ass whistles.

Solomon: God has chosen us for wisdom.

Markolf: Whoever thinks himself a fool is wise.

Solomon: Marcolphus, nobody should praise himself!

Markolf: So if I scold myself — then what?

Solomon: Concealed injury is more praiseworthy than open shame.

Markolf: The longer you keep your legs crossed, the more you gotta go.

Solomon: There are four seasons for every year.

Markolf: There are four sides to every out-house.

Solomon: The bickering person isn't believed when he is sincere.

Markolf: If we mix you in small pieces with the pig-slop, the sow will eat you.

Solomon: A friend in need is a friend indeed.

Markolf: Friends are light as feathers.

Solomon: The sayings of a king should be sufficient.

Markolf: He who plows with a fox pulling has a rough row to hoe.

Solomon: One does not win by tricks alone.

Markolf: One who stirs the shit raises the stink.

Solomon: The more miserly one is the more one becomes entangled in oneself.

Markolf: What more is needed than a fat pig with a greased ass?

Solomon: The angry can't restrain themselves from foolishness.

Markolf: A punctured jug holds no water.

Solomon: A sick person can't hide his illness.

Markolf: A shitting dog can't bark at the same time.

Solomon: He who has worldly goods is always suspected.

Markolf: Woe to the one who has bread but no teeth!

Solomon: Woe to the one who has great aptitude but no curiosity or love of inquiry.

Markolf: Whoever wants to go in two directions must rip his asshole in two.

Solomon: Why do we want to be bigger than we are when God already has made everything to be our subjects?

Markolf: The dog is only partially rewarded, whatever it demands by its tail.

Solomon: Whenever clouds form, rain follows.

Markolf: Whenever the dog squats, it wants to shit.

Solomon: A sword in our flesh always sticks.

Markolf: Just like manure in my hair.

Solomon: Teachings, temperance, and virtue come from the wise man's mouth. Wherever there is strife and war therein will man waste away. But the wise man turns away from evil and increases goodness so that evil then fades away.

Markolf: The jackass doesn't do anything useful. Wherever it eats, the grass grows back fuller, and where it shits it grows back all the more.

Solomon: I am going to keep silent, and I hope you'll go away.

(Markolf moves to the background. Two women
enter. The good woman speaks first and the
evil woman is carrying a baby)

Good Woman: King, give us your judgment. This woman came to my peaceful room by night. She stole my living child as I slept and left her dead baby by my side.

Solomon: Woman, how do you answer the accusation?

Fusita, Evil Woman: King, she is lying. It is my baby here that you see. Let her keep her own dead child.

Solomon: Bring me my sword! I'll cut the child in two and that will end this strife.

Good Woman: Oh, King, give her the baby! Gladly will I give the child away. Please, I beg you in the name of all your honor. I'll never ask to see the child again.

Fusita, Evil Woman: King, let your judgment be held firm and fixed in spite of all her whining and whimpering.

Solomon: You — give the good woman her child, for she is truly the real mother.

Good Woman: Oh, King, most worthy of praise! You are the wisest and fairest of all times. I shall praise your name eternally.

(Markolf comes to the foreground with his head down)

Solomon: Markolf, tell me, why is your head down to your chest?

Markolf: I'm not sleeping, I assure you, I'm just thinking how one should never trust a woman.

Solomon: So you have learned something. One should recognize your observation even though you will probably disgrace the women now.

(Markolf speaks to his sister)

Markolf: Listen to me sister, Fusita. The King wants me to leave immediately. Nothing I say pleases him. Give me your advice, sister. What should I do? Why are you quiet? You are not your chatterbox self. I should be so obstinate as you and go hang around his neck. I figured we'd have it out between us, and I brought my knife. Now, sister, just keep your mouth closed.

Fusita: Go on. By my word nobody will hear me say anything. Nobody young or old even pays me heed. We're not good enough for him so why should I butt in?

Solomon: Where in the world does this Markolf come from?

Markolf: From around here, both of us — sister and me. She's a whore and wants the same inheritance that I have. Too bad she has squandered hers in whoring and unprofitable tricks.

Fusita: You scab, just mind your own business. I was born a Cauliflowerus too, you know.

Markolf: Yeah, just like me. But all your sins will damn you forever.

Fusita: Go on. I don't even want to bother cussing you out anymore. King, just look in his boot. This morning I saw him stick a knife in there. I heard him swear by your unsuspecting goodness and trust to come here and kill you. Look and see. If you don't find it, let me have my inheritance anyway. If you find it, lock him up before he hurts Your Majesty.

(The Knight steps in between Solomon and Markolf)

Knight: Markolf, hand over the knife! Do you want to be a murderer? If I find the knife in your boot, you'll be a dead man.

Markolf: Go ahead, search me all you want! Take your time, too. The whore is just trying to set me up.

Knight: Your Majesty, I can't find any knife.

Markolf: King, didn't I just tell you that you can't trust any woman? For that same reason I was amazed that you recognized which woman was the true mother of the baby.

Solomon: That was clearly proclaimed in the face and behavior of the true mother. She couldn't have deceived us.

Markolf: Any king who blindly believes any woman will be duped by her. She'll cry and whine on the outside and laugh like hell on the inside. She'll show on her face something totally different from her heart. Women have the skill, the targets, and the aim.

Solomon: Well, it's true they have plenty of tricks. But, on the other hand, they are full of piety. A woman gives man comfort and courage, and she is truly a flexible creature.

Markolf: Yes, sir. You speak convincingly.

Solomon: Whoever shames a woman for whatever reason is not worthy of any woman or wife. What good is gold, silver, or precious stones if we can't share them with women? I say the whole world is dead to the man who doesn't enjoy the friendship of woman. Don't you see, women can manage the house, take care of their husbands. When they have children and nourish them it is the pride and joy of the husband. She's a friend and pleasure to her man. She's a jewel to him by day and a joy at night.

Markolf: Well, King, I used to think just like that too. Your nobility, your kingdom, your wisdom — all stand alongside a woman's happiness. Maybe I won't spit out what I've had in my mouth for a long time. But you would be wise not to overlook something that will profit you. As quickly as you are now praising women, just as fast and firmly you will rail at them — today.

Solomon: Leave my presence! Go to the devil! Don't appear before my eyes ever again, you impudent liar!

(Markolf addresses the women)

Markolf: Ladies, why are you still here?

Good Woman: Dear Markolf, tell us, why not?

Markolf: Don't you know that King Solomon has issued a command — one that applies and fits you all — that gives every man the right to seven wives? You women know very well what to do. No house will have peace. One wife will be loved, the other not. Love will be with the man; the others will suffer. The beloved will be dressed as she wishes, the others will have precious little. The beloved will do and command; the others will be right useless. While the beloved gets all the kisses and cuddles, who knows what the others will get. They won't be widows, yet they won't have a man. It would be better to be banished, or ask the King to revoke the commandment before its declared throughout the land.

(The women gather in a group. One speaks to the others)

Woman: All you women, listen to me. Come with me to beg the King to lift his commandment.

(All the women raise their voices.
All begin speaking at once)

Solomon: What is the meaning of all this hub-bub? Can't anyone be quiet?

(One woman steps forward)

Woman: Oh, King, you wear your gold, silver, and precious stones alone if you do merely as you please. Leave women in peace. We appeal to the law of Moses. Give us rights and justice.

Solomon: Impudent lady! Tell me, what injustice I have done to you.

Woman: What justice is there when a man takes seven wives for himself? Isn't one wife enough for one man? Would you ever give seven husbands to one wife? You are doing a great evil.

Solomon: You speak and represent the women very well — not that there should be fewer wives but more men.

Woman: Whoever heard such a ridiculous thing? Your judgment is unjust. That's why people say best seldom comes after good. Saul treated his people with open and heavy vengeance. Your father was fond of dainty morsels too. You're the third and you pile even more on your plate than anyone ever before.

Solomon: Ah-hah! We are now seeing the head of the snake. And there is no head in the whole world fuller with bad, deceitful tricks than the head of an evil woman. With backbiting and with caresses her evil puffs up and spreads. One knows all too well that her rebellious nature is the cause of all sin. Anger, curses, quarreling, objections, challenges — nothing is worse than an evil woman. Blows, tricks, disputes should not come from a woman.

Knight: Who knows what His Majesty is saying when he speaks so disparagingly and in this fashion? It's no way to treat a woman!

Markolf: Dear King, that is what I've been waiting to hear from you. I am delighted you agree with me and stick to the truth.

Knight: Markolf, you scoundrel! You are shame incarnate.

Markolf: So, King, is this what you call praising the women? You vilify them even as you are raging. But I like you much better this way than before.

Solomon: Vice is your middle name.

Markolf: Not mine. But yours is stupidity.

Woman: Pfui on you, Markolf! Shameless! You've brought us all to discord. You don't overlook a thing. Not a trick.

(Solomon addresses the women)

Solomon: Women, please, withdraw in peace. All this talk I made in anger. This rogue Markolf is to blame. After all this controversy, let's have some peace and quiet.

Woman: Oh King, praise and honor to you that you have so favorably considered our silliness and simplicity! It will never happen again henceforth. It's all Markolf's fault. He tricked us. Therefore, let us retire in peace.

Solomon: Since I've brought you to your senses, so be it. But now that troublemaker will pay the price. Guards, take him out and hang him from the nearest tree. He deserves it a thousand times over.

Markolf: Oh King, grant me at least one last wish and favor. Let me pick a tree where it will please me to be hung from.

Solomon: Wish granted! Now just get him out of here. Hurry!

(Markolf is quickly led out. Four farmers appear)

First Farmer: I say, the devil's behind all this! Should my friend be hung just for this? What a fate! Although I thought that he might end up on the gallows someday. My, how he carried on! Why the hell didn't he keep quiet?

Second Farmer: Look here, my friend! He asked for it! He was hollering and bellowing like a cow. Now you are the one whining. You ought to be ashamed of yourself in front of all these people! Why, you blubber like an old fool. Shut up now or I'll give you one on top of the head! You know doggone well you're blubbering 'cause that's what you do best.

Third Farmer: Any mouse that fights with the cat knows how it ends . . . with his bellows torn out. He who wants to be around later doesn't try to silence a king. Whoever wants to cut cherries with nobles better lie low so the stems don't poke out the eye. The owl makes the flopping fish pay the price. Many dogs get the rabbit. If you insult the king with words that all can hear . . . . The raven who wants to be an eagle will not escape the fox. And just like the owl that seizes what it wants — so will arrogance be snatched and shook.

Fourth Farmer: Now listen up, dear friends! Whoever heard or saw such wild nonsense and childishness? One of you groans, the other moans, and the third one clucks like a hen. Has the devil got you all? You're all a bunch of fools, jackasses, and rubbish. Are you crazy or just plain mad? Why are you screaming? Shut up or I'll really give you something to howl about. You're giving me a headache with all your crying. Try singing instead. Maybe you'll succeed. Whatever you do — complain or sing — do it softly. You sound like cows, tarts, or apes! Don't you have anything better to do? Quit whining and hold your peace or you'll wake the dead.

(Executioner runs on stage)

Executioner: King, Markolf has escaped. He just disappeared — hopped right out of our hands. Nobody knows where he is. Maybe the devil came and got him.

(A Dancer enters)

Dancer: Ladies and gentlemen! Enough bickering, fighting, and nonsense! Come on, farmers form a new line! Come on gals, you too! You've waited for long enough. Come on, let's really strut our stuff!

(All come together when Markolf enters
dressed in a pilgrim's outfit)

Markolf: God be with you one and all — pious and honorable folk! Whereas before I cursed, swore, and praised myself, let me tell you now the Holy Trinity has changed me. The first saint is called Saint Sow and is found in a pigsty. I gave him a 12 pence offering which he grabbed before I let it go. He's quicker than you eating sausage. The other holy saint is called Saint Merde who was sitting there eating as fast as he could cram. The third saint is called Saint Open-Mouth who was stirring a tub full of shit so that he can spread it around among all the people. He was downing — or should I say drowning — a hefty muscatel wine at the same time. Ladies and gentlemen, can't you see how my vow of alms help, bless, and succor? Oh yes, the bans and the bulls were not lacking anywhere either. Help me truly, and may God pay them back!

Herald: Ladies and gentlemen, the King blesses you all and wants to know if you enjoyed the play? He knows that bickering and brouhaha are favorite tunes at carnival time. If you liked the play, he hopes there'll be more yet to come. Spend some time, forget your troubles, and learn a little something. Let's drink to carnival time and peace and joy!

Bibliography

Balzer, Bernd. *Bürgerliche Reformationspropaganda: Die Schriften des Hans Sachs im den Jahren 1523–1525*. Bern, 1974.

Beecher, Donald A., and Massimo Ciavolella, eds. *Comparative Critical Approaches to Renaissance Comedy*. Ottawa, 1986.

Brandstetter, Renward, ed. "Marcolfus: Ein Fahsnacht spil zu Lucern gespillt Aa. 1546." *Zeitschrift für Deutsche Philologie* 17, Halle (1885): 421–24.

Brunner, Wurzburg. *Meistergesang und Reformation*. Stuttgart, 1984.

Catholy, Eckehard. *Das Fastnachtspiel des Spätmittelalters: Gestalt und Funktion*. Tübingen, 1961.

——. *Fastnachtspiele*. Stuttgart, 1966.

Endres, Rudolph. *Zur Lage der Nürnberger Handwerkerschaft zur Zeit von Hans Sachs*. Erlangen, 1977.

Folz, Hans. *Ein Spiel von König Solomon und Markolfo*. Ed. Adalbert von Keller. *Fastnachtspiele aus dem fünfzehnten Jahrhundert*. Stuttgart, 1853: Pt. II, No. 60, 521–40.

——. *Von dem Kunig Salomon und Marckolffo und einem Narrn*. Nürnberg: Johannem Stuechs, n.d.

——. *Von dem König Salomon und Marckolffo und einem Narren*. Nürnberg: Johann Nuhs (Stüchs), 1521.

Freitag-Stadler, Renate. *Die Welt des Folzes und Sachs: Eine Ausstellung der Stadt Nürnberg Stadtgeschichtliche Museen*. Nuremberg, 1976.

Georg, Larry. *The Cessation of Meisterlieder Production*. Ann Arbor, 1971.

Kartschoke, Erika. *Studien zur frühburgerlichen Literatur im 16. Jahrhundert*. Bern, 1978.

Keller, Adalbert von. *Fastnachtspiele aus dem fünfzehnten Jahrhundert II*. Stuttgart, vol. I, 1853, vol. II, 1858; rpt. Darmstadt, 1965.

Kinser, Samuel. *Presentation and Representation: Carnival at Nuremberg, 1450–1550.* Berkeley, 1986.

Köster, Albert. *Die Meistersingerbühne des sechzehnten Jahrhunderts.* Halle, 1921.

Knudsen, Hans. *Deutsche Theatergeschichte.* Stuttgart, 1970.

Krause, Helmut. *Die Dramen des Hans Folz und Hans Sachs: Untersuchungen zur Lehre und Technik.* Berlin, 1979.

Listerman, Randall. *Miguel de Cervantes' Interludes/Entremeses.* Lewiston, 1991.

——. *Nine Carnival Plays by Hans Sachs.* Ottawa, 1990.

——. "The Boccaccian Influence in the Dramatic Craftsmanship of Hans Sachs." *University of Dayton Review* 10 (1983): 99–105.

Martini, Fritz. *Das Bauerntum im deutschen Schrifttum bis zum 16. Jahrhundert.* Halle a.S, 1944.

Paquet, Alfons. *Marcolph der Bauer und der König Solomo.* Frankfurt a.M, 1921.

Sobel, Eli. "Martin Luther and Hans Sachs." *Michigan Germanic Studies* (1984): 129–41.

Rudwin, Maximilian. *The Origin of the German Carnival Comedy.* New York, 1920.

Theiss, Winfried. *Exemplarische Allegorik: Untersuchung zu einem literarhistorischen Phänomen bei Hans Folz und Hans Sachs.* Munich, 1968.

Wimmer, Albert. *Individualizing Characterization of Occupational Figures in the Shrovetide Plays.* Ann Arbor, 1975.

Wuttke, Dieter. "Die Druckfassung des Fastnachtspiels *König Salomon und Markolf.*" *Zeitschrift für deutsches Altertum und deutsche Literatur* XCIV, Vol. 2 (July, 1965): 140–70.

The Barnabe Riche Series

This volume of the Barnabe Riche Series was produced using the TEX typesetting system, with Adobe Palatino POSTSCRIPT fonts and in-house critical edition macros.